FOREIGN POLICY IN THE SIXTIES:

THE ISSUES AND THE INSTRUMENTS

IN HONOR OF ARNOLD WOLFERS

FOREIGN POLICY IN THE SIXTIES:

The Issues and the Instruments

ESSAYS IN HONOR OF ARNOLD WOLFERS

EDITED BY ROGER HILSMAN AND ROBERT C. GOOD

THE JOHNS HOPKINS PRESS
Baltimore and London

ACKNOWLEDGMENTS

The editors wish to thank Deirdre Henderson, who performed much of the executive work involved in getting this book started, and Robert McGeehan, who compiled the index. For typing help, our thanks go to Dorothy Jones, Karen Rich, Carol Tyler, Lorraine S. McCottry, and Virginia Battle.

The editors also wish to note that those authors who are officials of the United States government wrote in their individual capacities and their views do not necessarily represent those of the United States.

CONTENTS

INTRODUCTION

The nineteen-forties were years of war. In the forties, international politics were the politics of coalitions and alliances directed toward the single object of bringing the enemy to surrender, and the painful attempt to organize the world once victory was accomplished.

The nineteen-fifties were years of cold war. In the fifties, international politics were more diverse in their forms of competition but still simple and straightforward in their harsh antagonisms—the politics of limited warfare, as in Korea; of threat, as in Berlin; and of attempting to contain the unrelenting, brutish pressure of Stalinist expansionism.

The nineteen-sixties have brought us a world which, though the legatee of the forties and fifties, is also new in fundamental ways. It is not simply that the structure of world politics and the resulting system of international relationships have shifted; it is that structure and system have in so many respects disappeared altogether and we are now largely dealing with an inchoate world, postdating the old structures and predating new and as yet not clearly discernible relationships. Accordingly, the degree of unpredictability in world politics has vastly increased.

Stalin is dead, and so is Stalinism. Khrushchev has been removed from power in the Kremlin in the closest parallel to a constitutional change in leadership that the Communist world has known. Whatever the ultimate significance of these and other events, it is obvious that change is percolating throughout Soviet society, effecting a transformation, if not from night to day, at least from total dark to twilight.

Not only is the Soviet Union changing, but the Communist Bloc as a whole has increasingly shown cracks in its formerly monolithic structure. The European satellites have more and more asserted their own national interests and pursued policies, domestic and foreign, that diverge from Soviet orthodoxy. Most important, there is the fundamental schism between Moscow and Peking—a dispute that future historians may well perceive to be as important in changing the character of our world as was the Reformation in ending the world of European feudalism.

In the nineteen-fifties a bipolar world achieved nuclear parity, changing fundamentally the relationship of military force to political objectives in competition between the super powers. France and Communist China have now exploded nuclear devices and the problem of the sixties is nuclear proliferation in a world no longer exclusively bipolar in character. Meanwhile, in the early sixties, the world went through its first nuclear crisis, when both the United States and the Soviet Union, on the issue of Russian missiles in Cuba, looked down the gunbarrel of nuclear war and drew back. As a result, history's first nuclear arms control agreement was signed—the Test Ban Treaty—and the United States and the Soviet Union took the first tentative step toward détente.

The implications of these developments for both the "third world" and the Atlantic community are potentially very great. "I realize," Nehru is once supposed to have said, "that it takes three to make a neutral." When the super powers begin to bridge their differences, what happens to neutralism? Indeed, when the enemy is no longer so monolithic or so crudely hostile and when the unifying threat to national survival begins to recede and separate national interests begin to express themselves, what happens to the Grand Coalition that was formed to meet the threat? Thus two more promontories on the cold war landscape are subject to erosion.

Equally disequilibrating has been the emergence of the postcolonial world. First in a trickle, then a rush, former colonies have gained their independence, the process culminating in the advent of Africa in the first half of the present decade. Fifty-one nations formed the United Nations in 1945; it now numbers one hundred and fifteen. Not only is the character of the United Nations thereby affected, but also the configuration of world politics. The sources of independent decision-making have burgeoned and so too have the sources of potential international disorder.

The world of the nineteen-sixties, in sum, is profoundly different from the war world of the forties and the cold war world of the fifties. It is extraordinarily more subtle and complex, though surely no less dangerous.

But both the war years and the cold war years have left us with a much larger kit-bag of instrumentalities for dealing with international politics. Foreign aid has an established place among the tools of foreign policy; we have means for gathering more information on what is happening in the world and for interpreting it more meaningfully; we are learning more about the dynamics of political as well as economic development; and we have experimented, however painfully, with new forms of diplomacy and multilateral techniques for monitoring and abating conflict. The real trick, of course, is to adapt both the new and old instrumentalities of foreign policy to the new environment, which is a continuous process since both the instruments and the environment change in interaction with one another.

In this book, the authors have attempted to analyze the environment and instrumentalities of foreign policy in the nineteen-sixties. Part I includes several essays on the contemporary arena, examining in some depth selected dynamics and issues of international politics today. Part II discusses selected instrumentalities, not in the abstract but in the context of problem areas and approaches for dealing with them. Many of the essays approach the subject through a case study and attempt to throw light, not only on the instrumentality itself but on a specific policy problem and, again, on the nature of the foreign policy environment.

In Part III the reader is reminded that the new dynamics and the novel instrumentalities of contemporary world politics have in no way annulled the perennial issues and basic factors of international relations. We have selected several of these—the balance of power, the role of personal style, *raison d'état,* and the unending debate between moral theory and political necessity.

This volume, then, is an inquiry into contemporary policy, but hopefully at a level that illumines the environment within which policy is determined and the underlying nature of some of the problems, both contemporary and perennial, to which policy must respond.

In proportion as we have done this, we have been faithful to the deepest interests of the man, Arnold Wolfers, whom we, his former students, seek to honor in writing this book. For Arnold Wolfers has excelled in making theory relevant to policy and in making the analysis of policy yield insights that further refine theory. His writings are a marvelous blend of political philosophy and history on the one hand, and, on the other, discerning analyses of policy situations and problems. His excellence in the one field is accounted for in large measure by his excellence in the other. For in Wolfers' work, the conceptual and the concrete constantly engage one another. In this, he brilliantly combines the theoretical genius of Europe with the pragmatic genius of America without succumbing to the banalities and excesses of either.

Thus, for example, Wolfers was an early realist, a colleague of Nicolas J. Spykman, and the discomfiter of those well-intentioned but idealistic writers who did so much to shape (and distort) the study of international relations in the years following World War I. But Wolfers—always too close to the real world of statecraft to become a dogmatist—was never a *Realpolitiker.* He could never have fully endorsed Spykman's assertion that the "statesman can concern himself with values of justice, fairness and tolerance only to the extent that they contribute to or do not interfere with the power objective." For Wolfers, while acutely aware of the statesman's responsibility to the nation's interest, has rightly been impressed with how ambiguous are the definitions of the content of interest and has correctly discerned that the policies of states in fact run the spectrum from the pole of power acquisition to the pole of relative power indifference.

And far from drawing a hard line between the presumed amorality of *raison d'état* and the principled morality of individual ethics, Wolfers has learned from careful inquiry that the nature of man's moral response to critical problems is determined more by the context of amity or enmity in which the problem presents itself than whether the individual acts as individual or as custodian for the welfare of his state.

Arnold Wolfers' career spans four critical decades and two continents. In each time and place his contribution has been notable. In 1930, already a recognized international economist, he became the director of Berlin's famed Hochschule fuer Politik. In 1933, he moved to Yale University, where he was to become one of the prime architects of that university's outstanding program of international studies. He is presently Sterling Professor Emeritus of International Relations at Yale University and, since 1957, director of the Washington Center of Foreign Policy Research at The Johns Hopkins School of Advanced International Studies.

The reader wishing to examine Wolfers' thought would be well-advised to begin with a collection of some of his landmark essays, titled *Discord and Collaboration: Essays on International Politics* (Johns Hopkins Press, 1962). It should come as no surprise that the themes explored there are not unlike the several categories of the present volume, for these concerns—the nature of the world political arena, the analysis of policy issues and instruments, and the perennial problems of morality and statecraft—are necessarily the central concerns of the author who seeks to combine in the analysis of world affairs the skills and insights of the scholar and the statesman.

If this volume succeeds in reflecting something of Arnold Wolfers' richly varied interests and approaches, we hope it may also be useful in its own right. The last thing he would want is a purely decorative tribute. Our hope, then, is that the volume will be of some use in furthering the teaching of international relations—to which Arnold Wolfers has given so many years so brilliantly, to the lasting profit of so many.

Winter, 1965

ROGER HILSMAN
ROBERT C. GOOD

PART I

The Contemporary Arena

CHAPTER 1

THE COLD WAR AND THE
CHANGING COMMUNIST WORLD

RAYMOND L. GARTHOFF

I

The cold war is the conflict between the Communist powers and the rest of the world that is waged by means short of overt major war. It comprises both the whole complex of political, psychological, economic, subversive, and indirect military measures used by the Communist powers to extend their power in the world and to weaken ours and the efforts of other countries to preserve and extend freedom from Communist domination. Conflict was present in the world long before communism and will doubtless continue after it. But in the period since World War II the extent of power and the nature of the ambitions of the U.S.S.R., and increasingly of Communist China, have posed a transcending challenge.

For this reason, we often tend to look at the globe simply as divided into the Communist world and the free world. From the standpoint of Communist aspirations, this may be justifiable. Thus it appears that the Communists gradually chip off countries or parts of countries, in one or another area, by one or another means. This perspective sometimes gives rise to discouragement or, in the extreme, to the belief—with the Communists—that they are riding on the wave of history.

Yet there is a basic fallacy in this view of the world. The aspirations, or even the concrete objectives, of an adversary are not the whole of international politics. To look upon the political globe as divided in two systems accepts too much of the Communist supposition. In the first

RAYMOND L. GARTHOFF is special assistant for Soviet Bloc Politico-Military Affairs, Department of State, and lecturer in the School of Advanced International Studies of The Johns Hopkins University. He is the author of *Soviet Military Doctrine* and *Soviet Strategy in the Nuclear Age*.

place, it is not a conflict between two politico-economic systems, but between imperialist communism and states with various systems which oppose Communist aggrandizement. Moreover, much of the world lies between and aside from the two camps headed (at least symbolically) by Moscow and Washington. Many of the countries of Asia, Africa, and the Middle East do not regard themselves as part of an anti-Communist free world of which the United States is the leader. And these areas are the major battlegrounds of the cold war. Often people in these areas are obstinately unaware of their involvement or are unwilling to recognize it and concern themselves exclusively with their own local issues. But we should not conclude from this fact that the cold war is being waged only in *our* backyard—because these countries, in fact, are not "ours." Instead of regarding Communist successes in Indochina, or even Cuba, or elsewhere as taking something from us, we should recognize that these are, in effect, only the consolation prizes in a game where freedom is winning the main stakes in the vast "third world."

Ever since consolidating the advantages in Eastern Europe and East Asia to which they fell heir in the wake of World War II, the Communists have placed their main expectations on the disintegration of the colonial system and the rise of several score new nations eager to modernize, often with a proclivity to "socialism," and usually with grievances toward the West. Yet the initial and probably most vulnerable period of transition from colonialism has already passed, and has passed the Communists by. The underdeveloped and often unaligned "middle billion" are, with a few exceptions, and with many difficulties, *becoming* ever a more mature part of a free world.

Paradoxically, as the Communists have probed more deeply and more widely in large areas of the non-Communist world, they have not only acquired opportunities to press various lines of cold warfare, but also have often become tangled in these lines. In many cases, contact with the virus of communism has produced immunization rather than illness. Communist performance has lagged and deviated from Communist promise. Countries and peoples which originally were willing to buy the Communists' protestations that they were the disinterested champions of peace, disarmament, anti-colonialism, and social progress have now in many cases had enough direct exposure and experience to learn better. History may well show that the decisive phase of the cold war was this first decade and a half. I do not mean to suggest that the cold war is over and the victory is already ours, but we may sometimes be insufficiently aware how far the non-Communist world has come, and how little the Communists have gained.

Let us simply take note of some of the major Soviet failures of the past five years. Basking in the confidence which they derived from the first Sputnik, the Soviet leaders have sought to force us into gradual concessions on our position in Berlin. This policy met "defensive" aims in shoring up Communist hegemony in Eastern Europe, and the "offensive" objective of dividing the Western alliance. They failed in 1958–59. By 1961, when their second major push on Berlin was proving unsuccessful, they did, to be sure, build "the wall." But this was a fallback position on their part to deal with some of the more desperate problems of East Germany, and not part of a preferred strategy of evicting us from West Berlin. They have continued intermittently to keep the Berlin issue alive. Nonetheless, it has been six years since the Soviets, in November, 1958, gave us six months to agree to a changed status of West Berlin, and in this time they have been unable to force us to do so.

The so-called missile gap is another case in point. Soviet advantage in the missile field was grossly exaggerated from 1958 to 1961, and the Soviets drew such support as they could from it. The inflated image of a missile gap was punctured, however, and it is now quite clear to all that, in fact, the real missile gap of the mid-1960's is the other way around— in our favor.

In 1960 the Soviets had considerable influence in Guinea and a strong foothold in the Congo. But two years later their Ambassador had been thrown out of Guinea and their influence in the Congo was virtually nil. To be sure, the Soviets have acquired a "volunteer" in the person of Castro, who subverted his own successful revolution from within. Other "volunteers" may emerge here and there. But even in the case of Cuba the ambitious Soviet attempt to establish a missile base not only failed, but led to a serious setback for Soviet prestige.

In Western Europe, the rate of economic growth has consistently surpassed that of the U.S.S.R. and Eastern Europe. The Common Market has prospered beyond all expectation, notwithstanding the differences over admitting Great Britain. NATO, though under internal stress, remains intact and stronger than ever before. Indeed, the West is so strong it can afford the luxury of such disagreements as De Gaulle's challenge. Communist strength in the Western capitalist countries continues to be very small. To be sure, the Communist parties of Italy and France are considerable in numbers and poll respectively about 25 and 20 per cent of the vote. But even these exceptions are no index of real potential for Communist power. The Left in the West is more gauche than sinister. And, of course, Communist membership and influence in the West has greatly receded from its high-water mark in the immediate aftermath of World War II, and it shows no sign of reversing its march toward oblivion.

Meanwhile, a deep and debilitating division has developed within the Communist camp. "Polycentric" tendencies have cut deep inroads into the former discipline of Moscow's leadership. The Sino-Soviet rift has developed into sharp internecine conflict, a fact which has profound implications. But it is not the only rift among Communist states. Not only has the monolithic image been shattered, but also the actuality of Moscow's former iron control over world communism has been damaged. To be sure, the majority of Communist parties and Communist states continues to give allegiance to Moscow and remains generally subject to its direction. But now Moscow's own relation even to them has changed. Indeed, there is a growing number of states now beyond the point of no return. Even tiny Albania can defy the U.S.S.R. and do so with full impunity. And Rumania, an ally of the Soviet Union which shares its position on the substantive policy issues with Peking, nonetheless adamantly—and successfully—refuses to follow Moscow's lead. Tito's Yugoslavia is both in the Communist world and yet not quite in the Communist camp; he has surrendered none of his independence, and in terms of military alliance Yugoslavia is unaligned. Yet Moscow acknowledges it as a socialist country (while Peking does not). But if Yugoslavia is a good socialist country, why can't Rumania or Hungary or Czechoslovakia have "workers' councils," or non-collectivized agriculture—or even nonalignment? Dissident radical and revisionist Communists can and do exploit the weakened discipline in the movement for their own ends. The Soviet Union wants the world to be Communist, but it wants—perhaps even more—for the Communist world to be centered in Moscow. A remarkable variety of cold war techniques is being used by Communists against one another. But before we look further into this aspect of the subject, let us examine the Soviet position.

II

Soviet political strategy, as it has evolved over the post-Stalin decade, has come to place primary emphasis on the avoidance of nuclear war. This means that Soviet policies to expand Soviet influence and to extend communism have been channeled into courses of action which do not include serious risk of war. Soviet policy has become neither pacifist nor passive, but it is grounded in an avoidance of courses that are recognized to hold a risk of war.

The Cuban missile crisis of October, 1962, was undoubtedly the most dramatic confrontation risking nuclear war. Whether it was in fact the most dangerous, I personally would question. The Soviet leaders obviously miscalculated the reaction of the United States (and of the Latin American and Western alliances, though this was less crucial). But they did not, in my judgment, ever seriously consider a military response to whatever American action might have been undertaken. In any case, they did choose a humiliating withdrawal of their missiles rather than risk nuclear war. And, if they needed the lesson on the dangers of brinkmanship, they also learned that lesson. The Cuban missile crisis confirmed the general rule of avoiding confrontation risking war, as well as making the Soviet leaders more cautious in judging when they could take initiative without such risk. Moreover, it also appears to have led Khrushchev to be more ready to reach some arms control agreements. At the same time, emphasis shifted to other political strategies.

One of the key elements of over-all Soviet strategy remains the effort to fragment the non-Communist world, and especially the Western alliances. It has always been a Soviet objective to aggravate and capitalize on differences among the Western powers, which in Marxist-Leninist eyes are inevitable contradictions in the world capitalist system. But before they could effectively begin to make inroads, it was necessary to modify the more crude over-simplifications in the Marxian image. Not until about the time of Stalin's death did they begin to show signs of recognizing that the world was not all Red or White, but that there were various neutral and pink shadings in-between. And not until well after Stalin's death did they actually begin to do anything about it.

This more correct and useful differentiation between the various shades of leftist neutralist, neutral, pro-Western neutral, allied, and "hard-core" NATO countries—and the belief that on some issues even the unity of the principal Western powers might be affected—has become part of the foundation for their political strategy. This new orientation permits the Soviets to drive wedges more effectively into the Western alliances. Nevertheless, the Soviet campaign to weaken the Western alliance system has proved relatively ineffective, and the Soviets are aware of this. It remains, however, a premise of Soviet political strategy that ultimately the West can be compelled to draw the necessary conclusions from the objective relation of forces in the world—which they believe to be gradually shifting in their favor. This means, for example, that if the relation of power seems to them to be such that the West must accept the status quo of a divided Germany and Soviet hegemony in Eastern Europe, then it is incumbent upon them to prod us into eventual reluctant recognition of the fact (and of its logical consequences, such as a new status for West Berlin).

Without abandoning their hopes and their efforts to fragment the capitalist world, the Soviet leaders have evidently come to conclude that there would be mutual advantages in a limited détente with the Western powers. Yet they are hobbled, and in some cases tripped up, by trying to pursue both objectives at the same time. Moreover, as we shall see, even if they are fully satisfied with the wisdom of a policy including some détente with the West, there are political costs and hazards within the Communist movement from the opposition of others who can no longer be ignored.

The Soviet leaders are pushing a rapid development of their economy as a foundation for national power. The Soviet economic aid and trade program in the economically underdeveloped and politically uncommitted countries is important especially for its political effect, as well as for the opportunities it affords for imposing economic dependence and for indirect infiltration. However, they have found that these programs in many cases do not give them the political leverage they expected—as in Guinea, Egypt, and Iraq. Even so, the general economic growth and scientific advance of the U.S.S.R. is considered to be one of the most significant weapons in the Soviet arsenal, and indeed it is the main external effect of Soviet internal development. Many people, and even some governments, are willing to overlook—and in some cases secretly to envy—much of the regimentation of life in Communist states, while concentrating their focus on the rapid achievement of industrialization, modernization, and power status in the world. The Soviets constantly refer to the power of the example of Soviet economic advances as a major factor or even the major factor in bringing other peoples to communism. This is true despite the increasingly evident signs of economic slowdown in the U.S.S.R. and other Communist countries, and it helps to explain the seriousness of this adverse economic development to the Soviet leadership.

Another major facet of Soviet cold war policy is the effort to propagandize Communist support for disarmament. Clearly, to the extent they are able, the Soviet leaders would prefer to disarm the United States—in all senses of the word. But it is also clear to them that while they may sometimes embarrass us or even somewhat inhibit our freedom of action, they cannot seriously get us to disarm unless they take comparable action themselves. In much of Soviet policy in this area—especially concerning a nuclear test ban and limitations on nuclear weapons deployment—the Soviets seek to neutralize some of the political effect of United States military power and to place restrictions on our use of nuclear weapons for any limited war. They have already helped to place a stigma on nuclear weapons in the eyes of many people throughout the world. If they reduce our confidence in our ability to resort to the use of such weapons, they gain; and if in some local case we should feel compelled to use them, we would then, at the least, suffer substantial onus for doing so. We now have a "hot line" between Washington and Moscow, a partial nuclear test ban, and a ban on weapons of mass destruction in outer space. But on the major disarmament issues, owing to the Soviet unwillingness to allow effective inspection controls, and despite a probably genuine Soviet interest in reducing arms outlays, the prospect for any comprehensive agreement is very dim.

Akin to the Soviet efforts to identify themselves with, and to capitalize on, widespread yearnings for peace and against atomic weapons, are their efforts to get a free ride on the wave of nationalism in the former colonial areas. The Soviets seek to appear as the champions of disinterested and noble anti-imperialism. The Soviets have, of course, always seen support for the national liberation movement as only an initial stage, the stage of removal of Western influence in the areas involved. The second stage, that of movement toward the Communist camp, is expected to follow. And it is precisely this move which, not unnaturally, displeases the first-stage nationalists who in turn become the target for displacement. Meanwhile, the Soviets have equipped as many anti-Communist armies in the Middle East and South Asia as the United States has.

Three aspects of the internal political situation in the U.S.S.R., as it affects the Soviet challenge to us, also deserve attention. First, major changes have been occurring in the Soviet Union over the past decade. The situation of the people as a whole has generally improved both materially and in some other ways. The regime now relies much less on terror to coerce and much more on persuasion to attain cooperation. *1984* was nearer in 1948 than it is today. The Soviet regime is today probably more "accepted" at home than at any time since its inception. Moreover, there is genuine national pride in Sputnik, the exploits of Soviet cosmonauts, and other achievements.

Second, and notwithstanding these changes, the system essentially is unaltered. It remains a totalitarian dictatorship, ruled through a monopoly party, with an expansionist doctrine. It is not moving toward representative government. And while it has broadened the base of its popular acceptance, it is supported not because it is Communist, and certainly not because it harbors aggressive aims, but despite these things and mostly because it is simply the Russian government. In addition, many in an articulate if small minority are learning enough about the rest of the world to realize how little they have in so many important respects. Finally, in order to build its rapport with the people, the regime in effect has had to move nearer to them, and thus—even though not "forced" to do so—it has consented to place some limitations on its own freedom of action.

The third relevant aspect of the internal scene is that while we may welcome a moderation of internal repression and the growth of the welfare of the people, such developments are no assurance that the Soviet Union will necessarily become easier to get along with. Indeed, the opposite could be argued, since if the giant no longer has feet of clay he is the more dangerous an opponent. In short, the internal situation —despite significant changes—cannot be counted on to cause a fundamental modification in Soviet external policy in the foreseeable future.

III

For Soviet policy, probably the most important long run development has been the splitting off of the Chinese Communists and the more radical element in the world Communist movement, and the related diffusion of discipline in the entire Communist movement. The Chinese do not accept the Soviet premise that the avoidance of nuclear war must be given highest priority. They do not, as the Soviets polemically allege, wish to see a nuclear war, but they are quite willing to run the risks and accept the costs involved in an aggressive Soviet-led challenge to the West. Basically, the Chinese are quite right in saying that the Soviets place considerations of their own security above supporting advances of the Communist revolution elsewhere in the world, although the Chinese also go further in their polemical criticisms of Soviet "treason" to communism than is warranted.

As the Chinese point out, their estrangement from the Soviets began with the Twentieth Party Congress in 1956. This Congress not only saw Khrushchev's secret speech attacking the cult of Stalin, it also was the occasion for the revised doctrine on the non-inevitability of war. In the fall of 1954, Khrushchev and other Soviet leaders had visited Peking to try to improve relations. The year 1955 was almost certainly the high water mark of good relations. By 1956 and 1957 doubts and differences were growing on both sides. For example, the new Soviet line of economic assistance to bourgeois neutrals (like India) developed in the years 1955–58; so did Chinese resentment of it. Similarly, the Chinese distrusted and disliked the implications of the new Soviet interest in disarmament during this period. Moreover, such events as the tepid Soviet support in the Quemoy crisis of 1958 sowed suspicions. Active, though secret, Sino-Soviet disagreements sharpened in 1959 at the time of the limited U.S.–Soviet détente, Vice President Nixon's trip to the U.S.S.R., and Khrushchev's visit to the U.S. Also at that time the Chinese Minister of Defense, Marshal Peng Teh-huai, made an unsuccessful attempt to challenge Mao's line, with at least tacit Soviet support. He was purged.

In the spring and summer of 1960 the growing differences erupted into the open, and active lobbying among the Communist parties began. Behind-the-scenes compromises in the November, 1957, Declaration of Communist Parties gave way to negotiation of the compromise Moscow Declaration of November, 1960. But the Moscow Declaration did not even calm the surface of the turbulent disagreement for long. Border troubles between the U.S.S.R. and the Chinese People's Republic started to get serious in that same year. The sudden and virtually complete withdrawal of Soviet technical and military assistance in the summer of 1960 had seriously adverse effects on Chinese capabilities, but its political significance was even greater. In 1961–62 Soviet rapprochement with Tito, the attack on the Albanians (already closely tied to China), and open divergence with China over India all marked the rapid deterioration of relations. Meanwhile, the period of 1960 to 1962 also saw failure of the "Great Leap Forward" and an internal Chinese economic crisis.

Without attempting to review in greater detail the many sources and expressions of deep Sino-Soviet discord, it is useful to note a few which bear directly on the Communist challenge to the rest of the world. The question of the strategy which the Communist powers should pursue in support of the "national liberation movement" has become a bone of contention between the Soviets and the Chinese. The Chinese not only have been more ready to assume risks in active Communist Bloc support of revolutionary activity, but also less ready to believe there are serious risks in such support. They have also been concerned over the ineffectiveness (or perhaps the effectiveness) of Soviet efforts to establish rapport with the new non-Communist regimes. Parenthetically, we might note that the Sino-Soviet controversy has stimulated some *doctrinal* support for the national liberation struggle in the U.S.S.R. It was only in the course of polemics with the Chinese that the Soviets were led to formulate the doctrine expressed in Khrushchev's speech of January, 1961, distinguishing national liberation wars (which were supported in theory) from both general and local wars between states (which were not).

In the deepening rift within the "bloc" of Communist states and the whole international Communist movement, the Chinese have sought to outflank the Soviets on the "Left." They therefore encourage and support Castroist emphasis on subversive activity in other Latin American states, Vietcong and Pathet Lao revolutionary guerrilla warfare in Indochina, and direct violence in Africa. A number of local Communist parties, and many elements of other Communist parties, have reciprocated by supporting Peking against Moscow in the conflict within the Communist movement. The Chinese, however, have very little more than encouragement to give (except in Southeast Asia). The Korean and Vietnamese Communists, like the Chinese, are champions of maximum pressure against the "imperialists," perhaps above all because they see this as the only means through which they might hope to unify under their control their divided countries. But the Chinese also have a general confidence and belief in a revolutionary stage of world development which the Soviet and Western Communists do not share. In other words, apart from such questions as to whether it is *tactically* wise for the Communists to attempt seizure of power in the Latin American Afro-Asian world, there is a real gulf in *strategic* evaluation between Moscow and Peking.

In practical terms these differences may occasionally be blurred. Thus the Soviets, in certain cases, presumably favor revolutionary action. The Chinese, in practice, are less ready to assume risks of direct confrontation with the United States than the tone of their discourse would suggest. Nonetheless, differences in the two orientations are highly significant, and they will be especially so in the future.

One should also note that, while it is less pertinent to current policy differences, there is a similar discrepancy in Soviet and Chinese views on the prospect for revolution in the West. The Soviets take a much longer view of the kind of changes in the world which, they believe, will lead to the eventual victory of communism in the capitalist countries. The Chinese believe, or purport to believe, that more activist revolutionary activity should be undertaken even in the prosperous, advanced countries.

The Chinese are not interested only in revolutions and the purity of revolutionary doctrine and strategy. As the Soviets now point out, the Chinese pose of devotion to pristine revolutionary principle has not prevented their trading with South Africa, tolerating Portuguese Macao, cultivating relations with De Gaulle and West Germany, and giving token economic assistance to several bourgeois and even pre-bourgeois regimes. At the same time, and probably related, we see Chinese concern not only at Soviet influence in the politically unaligned areas, but also, and perhaps above all, we see deep oriental suspicion of any improvement of Soviet relations with the West. The Soviet détentes with the United States in 1959–60 and again since late 1962 have probably antagonized the Chinese as much as anything else. Clearly, one of the reasons that the Chinese have tried to push the Soviets into a more belligerent posture vis-à-vis the West, quite apart from considerations of expanding Communist gains, is to prevent a Soviet-Western détente.

Finally, as noted earlier, the Chinese have specific grievances of their own which stem from Soviet unwillingness to support Chinese pursuit of their objectives in the Taiwan Straits, Indochina, and India. And, significantly, the Soviets have made very clear that while their nuclear umbrella is intended to protect the whole socialist camp, it would *not* extend to support of China in difficulties which the Chinese might provoke in pursuing policies not in the common interest of the socialist camp. The Soviets, of course, reserve to themselves the right to determine what they consider to be the legitimate common interests of the socialist camp.

The Chinese have gained the full support of Albania and North Korea, general support of North Vietnam, and considerable sympathy from Cuba, within the one-time "bloc" of Communist states. In the Communist movement, party leaders responsive to the Peking line have control over all the Asian Communist parties except India and Australia. Moreover, pro-Peking factions or elements have appeared in a large number of other Communist parties. For example, Brazil, Australia, Ceylon, and Belgium each has two Communist parties now: one pro-Muscovite and one pro-Chinese. (Burma, which had always had two Communist parties, now has four, of which two are pro-Chinese.) The Indian Communist Party is badly split. Also in Italy, Great Britain, the United States, and indeed most other Western Communist parties pro-Peking elements have arisen.

One should also note that the weakening of discipline in the Communist movement also permits greater freedom in directions other than Chinese militancy. The Rumanians and Italians in particular, and also the Poles and Hungarians, have sought to take advantage of lessened discipline to promote independent or revisionist lines. It should be noted that there is no simple or over-all trend. Czechoslovakia and especially Hungary have become more "liberal" in internal affairs, without attempting to become more independent of Moscow; Rumania has become much more independent, but remains less liberal than most of the East European states; Poland has become less liberal than it was a few years ago; East Germany is much less liberal than the U.S.S.R. itself but the most dependent puppet of Moscow. As noted above, many parties not in power have moved both ways—that is, have split into more liberal and more revolutionary factions or even separate parties.

IV

I should like to close by noting four conclusions, particularly significant for the United States, based on implications of the changing Communist world.

First, while there is no occasion for complacency in the West, it is not possible to conclude that the nature of the Communist threat is unchanged and undiminished by the serious division and disarray in the Communist camp. The lack of coordination, consistency, and common operative policy objectives between the U.S.S.R. and Communist China to some extent *does* weaken them both. The case of divergence over the Chinese invasion of India is one kind of example. The divergence over the nuclear test ban is another. The constraints on freedom of action, which are provoked by the need to look over one's own shoulder at what a hostile critic on one's own side of the street is saying or doing, is yet a third. Finally, the devotion of considerable energy and attention to fighting on a second front is a real consideration that should not be overlooked. The Soviets may, in some cases, be more assertive in order to reduce vulnerability to Chinese charges of being "soft on capitalism," but they will not let themselves be pushed backward into the risks they have refused to face frontally. It is often said that both the Soviets and the Chinese Communists are "out to bury us," and that we can take little comfort about who our undertaker is. But that analogy is not quite accurate—there is a big difference whether people are out to bury us by sticking voodoo pins in ideological images, or by direct attempts at assassination, and this difference affects both the real threat and our counter-measures.

A second conclusion concerns the significance of the Sino-Soviet conflict and other polycentric developments for the future of communism. It may mean that, with two or more brands of Communist doctrine and action to choose from, the gross appeal of various Communist groups added together will be larger. Against this, of course, a judgment on net influence would have to take account of in-fighting among them and the lesser influence of the separate parts. There have even been reported incidents of one Communist faction covertly helping a bourgeois government to kill off its rival. More basically, we may see a transformation into "legal-reform" Communists on the one hand, and revolutionary Communists on the other. There is also the question of internal developments within the Communist states. A cynical anecdote I heard in 1963 in Moscow concerns the entry in the *Great Soviet Encyclopedia* edition of 1999 on Khrushchev: "A minor deviationist literary and art critic in the era of Mao Tse-tung"! The Sino-Soviet conflict must, however, be viewed in the context of the broader centrifugal tendencies which have been unloosed by the actual and symbolic deaths of Stalin. China has been able, and ready, to assert its independence more belligerently than most other Communist states could do, but so has Albania. Rumania, while preserving its alliance with the U.S.S.R., has not only declared but established a substantial degree of independence. Tito has returned to the "camp" without giving up any of his independence. And a Communist world which embraces both Tito's Yugoslavia and Xoxa's Albania is a very loose grouping indeed. Similarly the growth of diverging and even bitter rival "Communist" parties bears witness to the advanced stage of erosion of the one overriding distinction and strength of the Stalinist Communist world—its unwavering discipline and monolithic unity.

Third are the implications for the military strength of the U.S.S.R. and Communist China. On the Soviet side, attention must now be given to the absence of a reliable associate on its long southeastern frontiers, and even the need to protect these borders. Also, the Soviets have lost their only Mediterranean foothold—the submarine base at Vlone, Albania. On the Chinese side, the impact has been much greater. While lack of Soviet willingness to assist China to acquire an independent nuclear capability was one of the factors causing the rift, the break in technical and military assistance and a sharp decline in trade has had additional adverse military as well as economic consequences. Communist China today is perceptibly weaker in military capabilities than it was four years ago. Its aging air force, with substandard training, is becoming obsolete and is also declining in numbers and proficiency. The same is largely true of the small Chinese navy. The army has been less directly affected, but it too feels the pinch to some extent. Even more importantly, uncertainties about Soviet support must inhibit the Chinese. Thus, the dissolution of the Communist Bloc into separate Soviet and Chinese "blocs" has directly weakened the Soviets slightly, but the Chinese considerably. Moreover, the long-run military implications of the weakening ties of the Eastern European Warsaw Pact members to Moscow cannot yet be forecast.

Finally, while some of our long-term problems are eased, it is probably true to say the *number* of policy problems and their subtlety has increased. We must now face separate Soviet-inspired, Chinese-inspired, and local Communist initiatives, and deal in some cases with simultaneous "soft" and "hard" pressures. There are problems of affixing responsibility, for example, for direction of the policy of the Pathet Lao. In general, greater autonomy for separate Communist regimes and parties reduces the threat to the rest of the world, but not always; for example, Castro's Cuba retains a potentially dangerous autonomy. Thus the deep changes in the Communist world make the Communist challenge to the rest of the world more complex. But surely we can detect now, more clearly than ever before, the harbingers of the dissolution of communism.

CHAPTER 2

EUROPE AND THE FUTURE
OF THE GRAND ALLIANCE

LAURENCE W. MARTIN

The Atlantic alliance is the proudest achievement of post-war Western diplomacy. Undoubtedly, the most salient feature of this achievement has been the progressive abandonment of American isolationism and the projection of the power of the United States into the European balance. Twice America has reluctantly become entangled in European conflict, and twice the same spirit of separatism that underlay that reluctance manifested itself in peace plans. These peace plans, even if no longer isolationist, contemplated sustained involvement in Europe's affairs only under a new system of international relations that transcended the traditional pattern. Only in 1947, in steps that were to lead us to NATO as we know it, did the United States undertake a role in a European system frankly acknowledged as a balance of power.

Initially, this projection took the form of a guarantee; the Russian atomic test in 1949 and the invasion of Korea in 1950 brought about NATO's emergence as an institution with standing bureaucracy and common structures. The United States' relations with Europe thus fell more or less in line with an apparent American predilection for trying to convert diplomatic problems into tasks of administration. Given American material predominance at that time, this was perhaps inevitable. The indifferent success of efforts to give concrete form to the military forces for which the many blueprints called, however, left some question as to whether the United States remained a guarantor of a client Europe or was progressively the leading participant in a joint effort to meet any military threat on its own terms within the European theater.

LAURENCE W. MARTIN is Woodrow Wilson Professor of International Politics at the University of Wales. He is co-author (with Arnold Wolfers) of *The Anglo-American Tradition in Foreign Affairs,* author of *Peace without Victory,* and editor of *Neutralism and Non-Alignment.*

This has not prevented the NATO structure from being generally credited with turning the tide of Soviet aggression that most observers assume—though without hope of proving—would otherwise have followed. This presumed achievement, and the importance of NATO as a symbol of unity used by every ally with demands to make on another, have made the institution seem sacrosanct in its own right. Yet in reality it was inevitable that the Western alliance, being largely, if not wholly, a product of the cold war, must change its shape as that sustaining tension relaxed, tightened, or shifted. Evolutionary crises have been a constant and natural feature of NATO. Like any traditional coalition of states, it has adjusted to alterations in the balance of advantages each member believes it derives from the association. Not unnaturally, therefore, a certain skepticism arises when each successive phase in the continual debate is ominously proclaimed a final crisis and fateful turning point. For all that, the juncture at which affairs have arrived in the mid-sixties does seem to mark what may well come to be regarded as the true end of the post-war era and the start of a new stage in relations within and beyond the West.

I

Several distinguishable ingredients contribute to what has been variously termed the end of bipolarity, the dawn of polycentrism, and the substitution of a balance of maneuver for a rigid confrontation of blocs. The novel development having most obvious direct relevance to organization within the West is the economic, political, and moral resurgence of Western Europe, defense of which was the immediate purpose of the original alliance. A second novelty is the recognition by both the Soviet Union and the United States, at least for the time being, of their vulnerability to nuclear attack, mutual if not equal, leading to a strategic deadlock and consequently to common declarations by the two nations that major war can no longer be an instrument of their active policy. Arising in part from this recognition has been a third and more superficial novelty of the world today: the emergence of a language of détente between Russia and America and the perception by many Europeans and Americans of an important change for the better in Russian behavior.

These developments combine to etch a distinctive pattern in affairs; each development also would have its own particular consequences, even in the absence of the others. The rise of Europe calls into question the balance of the alliance and would do so with or without recent changes in military technology. A nuclear stalemate, if such exists, would compel shifts in tactics however much underlying purposes remained unchanged and whether or not a sense of détente prevailed.

A quick appreciation of the changed posture of world affairs in the middle of the seventh decade can easily convey the impression of triumph and fulfillment for the architects of NATO. Russia appears contained; Western Europe is free, prosperous, self-confident, and more or less at peace with itself. Deeper reflection upon the hopes with which the alliance began, however, brings to light an underlying failure, for such preliminary successes were originally expected to produce a legitimate territorial settlement in Central Europe and liberation for Eastern Europe. A firm Western stand was to bring about the withdrawal of Soviet forces, whether from a slow change of heart or from necessity in the face of superior power exploited in ways that have never been very well defined. The United States would thus be freed from its European entanglement; either Russia would become amenable to a concert or a revivified Europe would become capable of containing Russia alone. Much current debate in the alliance really concerns the extent to which our partial successes justify our behaving as if these original hopes were fulfilled.

The stakes of such debate are high, for the East-West conflict is as yet frozen rather than resolved; the cold war is not so much liquidated as accepted with resignation as a tolerable way of life. This is perhaps natural in an era when large wars can be prepared but not fought. The process of dismantling a conflict under such circumstances is less akin to peacemaking than to negotiating an armistice with an adversary still powerful in the field. Such an undertaking is fraught with the dangers of disrupting alignment with one's allies and of unsteadying one's own resolve—thereby tempting the foe to new adventures.

Some have been quick to rate such dangers low and hasten to advocate rapid dismantling of the alliance in face of what they take to be radically changed circumstances.[1] Such a view presumes little risk of renewed Soviet pressure, and a high estimate of Europe's capacities. Those who are most bored with the burdens and clichés of the cold war, or who stand to gain most from relaxing the ties of alliance, naturally find their calculation arriving at these optimistic conclusions. From an American point of view, such calculation must comprehend not merely Europe's capacity to sustain a greater burden in implementing Western policy but the probability of its doing so in ways congenial to the United

---

[1] For a thoroughgoing statement of such a view see Ronald Steel, *The End of Alliance* (New York, 1964); cf. Coral Bell, *The Debatable Alliance* (London, 1964).

States. For of necessity the prospect of breaking step in the Western column and of revising relations with the East raises the possibility of separate deals and even of a distant reversal of alliances. In these circumstances, the very notion of "the West" may be called into question and revealed as a loose collective, embracing many interests that may no longer coincide. The more this is so and recognized as such, the more the United States, as leader and organizer of the alliance, will face choices between continuing to emphasize unity and making its own independent approaches to the East.

Such choices are naturally avoided as long as possible by the leader of a coalition in hopes that necessary accommodations with the adversary can be reconciled with the solidity of the alliance and the leader's own primacy in it. The United States, while certainly stressing the importance of reaching a tamer *modus vivendi* with Russia, has maintained that those who would dismantle the alliance are at best premature and underestimate the extent to which modifications of Soviet behavior arise from a Western position of strength to which American contributions are vital. Any stabilization and détente have not arisen from voluntary Soviet benevolence but have been built with laborious Western effort and that effort must be maintained. The nuclear balance is not a technological axiom but a skillful and continuous achievement; the fat and therefore peaceful Communist is not a present reality but a devoutly awaited prophecy. Soviet belts are not so loose they could not be retightened, nor are Russians presently too stout for all mischief. Multipolarity is thus the product of a continued underlying bipolarity. The newly found room for maneuvering enjoyed by medium powers is a function not only of their own regained substance but also, in large part, of the overriding Russian-American balance. It is therefore essential to ensure that efforts to adjust to changes on the diplomatic and strategic scene do not impair the conditions, and in particular the Western position of strength, from which these changes flow.

Thus has proceeded the American orthodoxy. It remains to be seen whether it serves the interests and satisfies the urges of American allies. But certainly there seems little reason to fear that a cautious response of this kind to relaxation of tension would in itself reduce Soviet interest in persisting with détente, provided of course that grossly provocative acts are avoided. For the most commonly identified sources of Soviet moderation—the economic and technological superiority of the West in depth, the growing demands of Soviet internal development, and the rise of recalcitrant China—are not trends readily reversible at Russian will. Thus while the nations of the West may well be advised to join in steps to stabilize and extend the effects of these incentives to Soviet moderation, it does not seem necessary to pay a price for the incentives themselves.

II

Unless the main course of American foreign policy since the war is to be sharply reversed toward isolationism or independent adventurism, the interest of the United States today would seem to call for preserving the coalition as a strong military equipoise to Russia in Europe and for continuing to seek a legitimate and stable settlement in Central Europe. It is also an American interest, however, that Western initiatives toward such a settlement are sober and that caution is observed throughout the alliance in the management of nuclear weapons. Outside Europe the United States needs all the help it can secure in discharging the worldwide responsibilities it has assumed for promoting economic development and maintaining a minimum of order.

There is in all these concerns an inextricable mixture of America's more direct, particular interests and those that pertain to its role as Grand Marshal of the alliance. In the past, the United States has frequently accepted injury to the former for the sake of the latter. But it becomes increasingly obvious that the burdens of global leadership can become unbearable even for a nation of America's strength. Unaccustomed infirmities in the trading position of the United States, however temporary, have provided an instance of strain and suggest that the day may soon pass when America could welcome sacrifices of its own welfare provided only that they strengthened or placated some other member of the alliance.

Patterns of relationship between America and its allies that might serve the common interest are infinite in detail but fairly limited in principle. First there is the familiar and established constellation of a dominant United States, disposing of most of the military power, and surrounded by a coalition of smaller, more or less compliant allies. Such a configuration could conceivably continue for a period, though some of the allies would be more powerful and probably more assertive than before. Second, the United States could become the relatively equal partner of a closely knit Europe behaving as a unit, a Europe almost certainly disposing of its own nuclear power. The connecting links between the two sides of the Atlantic could range from a sturdy, institutionalized union to loose, *ad hoc* cooperation. Similarly, the Europe in question might vary from the supranational or even federal entity, envisaged by enthusiasts for the European idea, to a looser coalition of fatherlands. Any of these Europes might embrace a greater or lesser number of nations, and those outside might maintain alliances or retire into a growing body of neutralists. There is, however, always the third possibility that quite novel patterns may emerge among the nations of the Atlantic and European area, with frameworks varying from function to function—now loose, now tight, now comprehensive, now limited to a core of states—and thereby leaving open the door for such presently undreamt of forms as may later manifest themselves for our emerging pluralist yet interdependent world.

The common element in all these patterns is the assumption that America needs Europe and Europe needs America. There is certainly no complete assurance that this assumption will continue to rule policy. It is alleged European desires for independence from American domination that suggest the possibility of a clean break with the trans-Atlantic solidarity of post-war years. There is even some speculation about a full or partial reversal of alliances and about French or German deals with Russia at American expense. Yet as soon as this notion is introduced, there is revealed the possibility that America might tire of its role as leader of the alliance and be tempted to withdraw or, more likely, to seek pre-emptive deals with Moscow—a possibility already suspected by Europeans in the context of arms control. Undoubtedly, if the United States' own relations with Western Europe do not provide reasonable assurance that Europeans cannot embroil America in conflict against its will, then the United States must be sorely tempted to seek such assurances in its own direct arrangements with Moscow.

It would indeed be unwise to take the Western Bloc for granted or to believe that the common interests of the whole must always override the conflicting purposes of the parts. The very notion of the West arises from the existence of common interests and only secondarily creates them. For the present, however, the task seems to be one of reshaping rather than abandoning the old habits of cooperation. The United States purports to have recognized the passing of its old unchallenged, if not unquestioned, hegemony and to be exploring ways of working out a more equal relation to Europe.

III

The symbolic and practical heart of the debate on how to amend these relationships has come to be the disposition of nuclear weapons. There are good grounds for supposing this is frequently neither the most relevant nor the most constructive context in which to proceed; but the

United States, having for so long put much of its discourse in nuclear terms, is scarcely in a position to protest. The key question is whether nuclear forces under American control, hitherto the mainstay of strategic theory within the alliance, can continue to be accepted by Europeans as a plausible deterrent and tolerable defense against direct aggression or indirect inroads upon European interests. In other words, how can the alliance meet the challenge posed by the Soviet nuclear power that has cast doubt on the American guarantee to Europe ever since 1949? This is not merely a question of whether an essentially American deterrent could be made technically efficient and politically reliable against Russia. It is also a question of what strategic relationships are compatible with the self-respect of nations now enjoying an increased sense of their own importance and with the degree of diplomatic liberty and influence they conceive to be their due.

The old question, latent since Russia first acquired a nuclear armory, as to whether nuclear weapons and alliances are fundamentally compatible, is thus posed with increased urgency. In outline, the strategical debate has been widely appreciated. American threats to retaliate with nuclear weapons upon Russia in the event of an otherwise irresistible attack on Western Europe decline in credibility as the United States itself becomes vulnerable. Many before General de Gaulle pointed out that suicidal threats are impressive, if ever, only when issued in the first person by entities with a strong sense of self identity. The response of American military leaders under Secretary of Defense Robert McNamara has been to prepare a flexible strategy with a scheme for counterforce bargaining by nuclear weapons short of massive retaliation, and with a build-up of conventional forces capable of meeting and defining the scope of sizable attacks without any nuclear measures at all. This strategic doctrine, however, already much modified since its first pronouncement, has raised almost as many doubts as it has allayed in European minds. Once flexibility is proposed it becomes exceedingly interesting to know who is going to be flexible about what. Europeans naturally fear flexibility may be secured at their expense. Their fears range from a general misgiving in some quarters that the very search for a flexible policy argues an infirmity of American purpose that might invite aggression, to the more refined anxiety that targets for counterforce action may be found in Western Europe, so that ultimately the tolerable use of nuclear weapons may come to be defined as employment against targets not within the boundaries of the two superpowers.

Similar misgivings surround the plan for an increased conventional force. Preparing a conventional defense means preparing to fight a destructive campaign on European soil. This is doubtless better than nuclear war, if either has to come, but it can never be as attractive an option for Europeans as for Americans. There are also fears that conventional preparations increase the risk of war by reducing credibility of the massive deterrent. Such fears of reducing the deterrent effect of the larger forces by achieving preparedness in the lesser, explain in part why some European nations have emphasized the early use of tactical nuclear weapons while maintaining a doctrine of ready escalation; the resolution of the paradox is, of course, that they rely heavily on nuclear weapons as a deterrent precisely because they believe their use as a defense would be intolerable.

The most direct solution for European uncertainty, the proliferation of an independent deterrent for each nation, is widely regarded in the United States as both undesirable and impracticable for reasons that have been freely advertised. Many of the allies are incapable of creating or sustaining such forces for technical reasons even if the will to do so existed. The capacity of even the larger allies to maintain nuclear forces large and secure enough to deter the enemy and independent enough to reassure the possessor is at best questionable. American pundits may have been too hasty in assuming that future technological developments will militate against the effectiveness of modest nuclear forces. Such an assumption is clearly congenial to Americans. But the prevailing opinion among many respected European as well as the majority of American students of the matter is that the nuclear programs at present projected in Europe are militarily ineffective and, worse than ineffective, dangerous as accident-prone interferences with the control of response that alone can preserve the credibility of deterrence.

The degree of danger in proliferating autonomous nuclear power in Europe has very possibly been exaggerated. No one can conclusively demonstrate a clear correlation between an increase in the number of nuclear centers and a greater likelihood of catastrophe. In any case the imminent danger of proliferation is less than the vigorous and continuing theoretical debate might lead one to believe. There are few signs that any new members of the coalition are contemplating such a departure. The most vexed question is the case of West Germany. The prospect of German access to strategic nuclear weapons, even in indirect forms, undoubtedly does arouse fears both in the West and, probably quite genuinely, in Eastern Europe and Russia. But the legal, technical, political, diplomatic, and geographical obstacles the Germans would have to overcome are formidable. Present German interest appears to be directed more to securing assurances as to the general nuclear strategy and diplomatic intentions of their allies, above all the United States, than to setting out on the hazardous road to nuclear sovereignty.

Nevertheless, the long term prospects must remain in doubt and, even if proliferation in Europe were not in itself destabilizing, it might ripple out as precedent for other areas. As to Germany in particular, it seems that the most powerful element invigorating German concern for a larger nuclear role may well be those outside well-wishers who so steadily reiterate the conviction that Germany cannot tolerate any inequality in these matters. There seems much force in the rejoinder that all nations suffer and enjoy the consequences of their own peculiar circumstances and that a certain special restraint in military matters should for some time be the result of Germany's geographical, political, and historical status.

On the other hand, the simplest solution from an American point of view, complete abandonment of Western nuclear efforts to the care of the United States, is almost certainly unattainable. In the first place, such is the imponderable nature of deterrent psychology that one can never completely demolish the belief that such independent nuclear forces as Europeans can achieve would serve their purpose as a guarantee against Russian attack or blackmail in the event of American betrayal. All the more is this the case when it comes to the indefinable influence that the distribution of nuclear power has on the course of routine or crisis diplomacy. Undoubtedly, the atmosphere of détente increases concern about the reliability of diplomatic support, for the détente paradoxically rests upon not raising certain delicate questions between East and West, as in Germany, while at the same time creating an atmosphere of movement within which some may hope these very questions might profitably be reopened, given a few adroit maneuvers or realignments.

A number of additional considerations serve to keep European interest in the control of nuclear weapons alive. So long as either exists, the French and British national programs feed on each other, for neither nation is eager to concede the role of sole European nuclear power to the other. Nor are European countries likely to give up completely the prestige that nuclear power is thought to convey to its owners, to surrender the access to negotiations on nuclear questions that it may confer, to forego the possible commercial advantages progress in nuclear technology may offer, or to lose the leverage on American policy that the capacity even to be no more than a nuisance in the nuclear sphere may provide. Above all, persistence in nuclear activity offers some assurance that the option of serious independent military effort may be more readily available to European nations should future technological or political changes yet unforeseen make the case against dependence on America more compelling than hitherto.

IV

Appreciating the force of some or all of these considerations, American administrations have busily explored hybrid alternatives to complete American monopoly within the alliance on nuclear matters. Crudely put, the task here from the American point of view is to give Europeans as much of the appearance of nuclear participation and as little of the substance of nuclear decision as will persuade them to comply with the essentials of American strategic doctrine. This carries with it the implication of considerable adherence to American diplomatic policy also.

No one can afford to be dogmatic as to what arrangements would satisfy such an essentially psychological purpose. So long as Europeans proceed rationally, however—and for each European nation the rationale will vary somewhat—they need assurance that nuclear weapons will be available for their defense when they themselves have decided the occasion has arisen, that the Soviet Union is impressed with the reliability of this assurance, and that, if the weapons ever have to be employed, they will be used in ways least harmful to European interests. This entails taking care of targets dangerous to Europe—Soviet medium and intermediate range missiles, for example—in a manner designed to minimize fallout and to avoid any unnecessary nuclear fire, from friend or foe, on Western Europe. Ideally, Europeans also need safeguards against American action in any part of the world, particularly nuclear action, that might expose them to attack when they do not themselves believe their vital interests are at stake.

Neither Americans nor Europeans are likely to achieve the full measure of their demands within a collective system. So long as they remain distinguishable political and moral entities it can never be wholly satisfactory to leave even a portion of vital decisions in other hands. Geography alone ensures that interests will diverge on innumerable practical points. Efforts to approximate a solution have ranged from sharing information on existing policy, to consulting on the design, deployment, and contingency planning of nuclear forces, and finally, to a part in deciding when to employ such weapons. Somewhere along this continuum the question arises as to whether it is necessary for others than the United States to own or have physical custody, shared or exclusive, of the actual weapons.

The ins and outs of schemes for collective nuclear activity are manifold and complex. Many forms of limited bilateral and multilateral sharing and coordination already exist. Perhaps not the least important of these, though rarely recognized, is the part European thought plays in molding the strategic assumptions of the United States and in defining the conception an American president has of his responsibilities as nuclear chief.

Most ambitious of the newer schemes for institutionalized sharing has been the vexed project for a multilateral, multimanned seaborne force of Polaris missiles. It seems fair to say that in its early forms this scheme remains within the traditional pattern of the alliance whereby the United States continues to be the dominant partner with substantial nuclear monopoly. Europeans secure a veto over use of the joint force but none of them secures any independent capacity or any control over the use made by the United States of its remaining and preponderant national forces. American hegemony would be complete if some of the architects of the multilateral force were vindicated in their scarcely veiled hope that its attractions may lead to existing European national forces withering on the vine.

Aware of the shortcomings, in many European eyes, of this military arrangement and of the political relationship it is thought to imply, other advocates of collective forces, devoted to the ideal of European unity, conceive of such ventures as the road to partnership rather than American hegemony. Hinting at control by majority vote, they present a multilateral force as the route to an independent deterrent under joint European control. This would indeed, they believe, have sufficient magnetism to kill off the national forces. In this perspective a multilateral force appears to envisage not the perpetuation of the old integrated alliance under American hegemony but the starting point of a truly dual alliance.

The single most effective public American encouragement for this notion was probably McGeorge Bundy's speech at Copenhagen in September, 1962, when he said, "We ourselves cannot usurp from the new Europe the responsibility for deciding in its own way the level of effort and of investment which it wishes to make in these great matters." [2] Some who endorse this attitude do so from the belief that a unified Europe not only can, but must, by nature, dispose of all the instruments of power. This notion has been voiced by Pierre Messmer and by such a non-Gaullist as Jean Monnet. One of the most detailed expositions came from Edward Heath when, in the full flood of negotiations for British entry into the European Economic Community, he declared,

[2] Speech before the Atlantic Treaty Association, Sept. 27, 1962.

We quite accept that the European political union, if it is to be effective, will have a common concern for defense problems and that a European point of view will emerge. . . . Of course, as the European Community develops, the balance within the Atlantic Alliance is going to change. In the course of time there will be two great groups in the West: North America and Europe. The growth of the European point of view in the defense field will not, we believe, be long in making itself felt.[3]

There is little doubt that Europe as a whole could support a considerable nuclear force. With American cooperation it could quite rapidly be realized. What makes the discussion academic is, of course, the fact that no Europe exists or is likely soon to exist, capable of creating, far less operating, a European deterrent. The existing "Six," and still more the Six with Britain and her followers added, are unlikely to have more than a rudimentary political organization in the near future, and the whole problem of the alliance is the incompatibility of loose political structures and nuclear policy. It is certainly conceivable that a nuclear force could be the center around which community might be built. But it seems unlikely. Past experience suggests nuclear matters are often more divisive than solidifying and, as the experience of the alliance as a whole has shown, federal structures demand explicitness in areas sometimes best spared too minute a scrutiny.

V

What calls for more detailed examination is the vision of a future political structure for the Western Bloc that underlies the advocacy of a Europe, united, including Britain, and acting as a diplomatic, economic, and military unit at the highest level. Many have been attracted by the idea of America acquiring a single European partner, thereby basing the alliance on what have been called the "two pillars." Such a dualism, indeed, usually seems to be what is meant by the slogan of "partnership," and many of the advocates of Atlantic community complete with institutions believe it can come about only by the approximation of Europe and America as equals.

This prospect suits those in America whose view of Europe, consciously or not, is a projection of American experience so that their solutions for problems of cooperation in the free world partake of the nature of state-building with an ultimately federal mold for the whole

---

[3] Speech to the Council of Western European Union, April 10, 1962.

Atlantic area. Others believe that only equals can wholeheartedly cooperate, and that a united Europe offers the sole prospect of an equal associate for America. The solution to the problem of American predominance must be the end of predominance, though perhaps not all advocates of the two pillars phrase it this way themselves. Creation of Greater Europe also has the definitiveness and tidiness that appeals to many Americans in their approach to political questions, for there is a strain in American foreign policy that thinks of diplomacy in terms of establishing organizations and running operations rather than manipulating autonomous entities. In this sense, pushing Britain into the European Economic Community would have removed the complication of dealing with an important unit that did not fit the preconceived scheme. Nor can it be forgotten that for some the vision of a united Europe revives the prospects of an ultimate disengagement from trans-Atlantic problems that originally underlay NATO and the Marshall Plan.

The merits of the two pillars design for the Western Bloc depend in large part on the nature of the pillars and the arch uniting them. Events have made it clear that, for the time being, the design fails—as in the strategic field—because there is little prospect of the European pillar being quickly erected. The problems the Six face with their existing degree of cooperation make the idea of Europe capable of acting with cohesion comparable to the United States seem even more remote than when the ideologues of Atlantic communiy first seized on it. Real though the achievements of the unification movement are, the dominant realization of the last two or three years has been that of the continued robustness of national consciousness. Nor have the various states of Europe yet demonstrated that they identify their interests and preferences any more regularly with each other than with those of outsiders, including the United States.

This leaves open, however, the question of whether the United States should continue to put pressure on Europe to unite with a view to producing a political partner in the future. Events have made it difficult not to notice that Greater Europe might prove a recalcitrant partner. Concern about one aspect of this is expressed in the frequent exhortations that Europe be "outward looking," a rather loose phrase signifying that she should be a liberal trader and a reasonable negotiating partner willing to shoulder burdens of the alliance and to tailor her policies to the broader concept of a free world. A cynic might more briefly define outward looking as ready to fall in with the Grand Designs of Washington.

It is now obvious such complaisance is not to be taken for granted. Most now agree that, whatever his idiosyncrasies, General de Gaulle's self-assertiveness represents a pervasive though by no means inevitably dominant streak in European opinion. To his way of thinking "interdependence" is an abhorrent idea, especially if it is a euphemism for American leadership. Even a cautious Canadian observer, trying to promote cooperation, comments, "It is strange how few Americans have recognized the deep-seated anti-American aspects of the European movement, the urge to be independent of American aid and American policy. . . ." [4] One source of this blindness seems to have been the impression that the E.E.C. was chiefly concerned with the promotion of free trade as a good in itself. Even in theory, however, it more closely concerned economic growth, political integration, and self respect, while in practice it involved as mixed and frequently devious a set of motives and participants as any public enterprise usually does. The question therefore becomes whether a European political community can be created that is capable of equal partnership yet compatible with that degree of coordination regarded as essential by the United States. This being far from certain, it is not impossible that a loosely knit Europe might be more serviceable than a coherent but recalcitrant unity.

One theory behind partnership is that only equals can cooperate freely. But it can be argued with equal force that there are real differences of interest between Europe and the United States—some economic, some arising from the tasks of community building, some from competition for primacy in dealing with the single adversary, yet others from inevitable divergencies of strategic view that geography imposes—and that these would be compounded by synthesis of Europe into a single center of responsibility disposing of the resources to attempt an independent course. The argument that only equals can cooperate can thus be countered with the thesis that divergent interests become irresistible when the parties concerned have pretensions to self-sufficiency. All this leaves unexplored misgivings expressed about the effects of uniting Western Europe on the chance of moving closer to Eastern Europe, and in particular of rendering relations between the two Germanies more intimate.

As such possibilities emerge, Washington displays increasing concern for the strength of the link between the two halves of the partnership envisaged. The machinery for this link is rarely detailed but the substance of the relationship seems to be that views acceptable to America as to how to conduct world affairs should prevail in the Western camp. Since it is hard to conceive of ways in which even good behavior in the

---

[4] John Holmes, "Implications of the European Economic Community," *Atlantic Community Quarterly,* March, 1963, p. 31.

present could guarantee conduct in the future, it is easy to see why many Europeans suspect that the institutional arrangements proposed are intended to enshrine American predominance.

Doubts about the amenability of Europe are now fairly widely entertained in America. Much less often is it acknowledged that America may also be unready for the partnership. The existence of a great American center of power and decision is not of course in doubt. But it is equally clear that the United States has no real intention of trammeling its formal independence or reducing itself to merely an Atlantic partner. That is to say that, while the United States would like a firm arch between the two pillars to constrain Europe from using its newly united power in ways inimical to American interests, it is unwilling to restrict its own freedom reciprocally. Traffic on the arch would be one-way. All the more remote then are elaborate schemes for true Atlantic federalism on other than the most rarefied, symbolic level.

A question arises therefore as to whether it is even wise to encourage the development of such symbolism as the proponents of Atlantic community have done. America is an Atlantic power only in an inclusive and certainly not an exclusive sense. The United States has a global role peculiar to itself, in which it has no presently conceivable equal partner, and in which for the moment its only true opposite number is the Soviet Union. Regardless of all the nuclear possibilities discussed previously, the United States remains the Grand Deterrer. Whatever progress the Europeans may make in the next few years, the possibility of American nuclear action, however watered by doubt, will pose by far the most weighty uncertainties faced by Soviet strategists in Europe. All European plans, including those of General de Gaulle, accept this as part of the world within which they intend to pursue their own policies. Thus one can probably take seriously—all the more for its tart phrasing—the General's remark in a press conference on July 30, 1963, that "en cas de guerre générale la France, avec les moyens qu'elle a, serait aux côtes des États-Unis, et je crois réciproquement." In addition, America's power is engaged in many areas of the world where few Europeans are still concerned. The United States cannot submit its actions in these areas to European consent without encouraging a lowest common denominator of resistance to Communist initiative that would gradually permeate all diplomacy as well as the directly military confrontation.

As the great deterrer, as a Pacific power, indeed as the only truly world power now existing in the democratic camp, the United States cannot accept Europe as an equal partner so long as it remains essentially local. Indeed, does encouraging the coagulation of Europe render an unqualified service to the American goal of a pluralistic order for the entire non-Communist world? Is it wise to encourage the remaining European nations that profess a concern for global affairs to submerge their identity in a more parochial community; to insist, for instance, on extinguishing a distinct British voice in the alliance? Might it not be more valuable to preserve an associate, however junior, with a world-wide presence to share in the public accounting for such operations as military aid to India and to act as an informed critic on matters so removed from the concerns of Brussels?

It is difficult not to conclude that dominant American leadership is henceforth inevitably open to question and that solutions centered around the Atlantic alone, especially on federalist models, are both remote and of doubtful merit. Consideration of economic policies or of the details of diplomatic tactics in the cold war lead to much the same conclusions as are drawn from the military realm. For the reasons sketched here, and for many others, the United States cannot resolve the tensions occasioned by its primacy in the alliance by conjuring up Europe in an effort to shed its predominance. On the contrary, America must remain the prime and most widely extended member of the Western grouping for the foreseeable future, and this will be symbolized by its retention of overwhelming nuclear force.

On the other hand, the Europeans are not about to agree that, just because America has primacy, that primacy is as great as it once was and can be expressed in a continuation of the relationship begun in the immediate post-war era and embodied in a lightly retouched NATO. For its part, it would be foolish for the United States to deny itself the fruits of a valuable relationship merely because it can no longer be maintained in traditional forms.

The United States must therefore resign itself to an untidier coalition than is perhaps congenial to the American political genius. In a sense the design for Atlantic community fails, not because it is ahead of its time, but because it reflects too much the shape of the past. It seeks to perpetuate the pattern of the last two wars in which America has come to help the Western extremities of Europe in an essentially European conflict. Even in the last war this perspective called forth charges of neglect for other theaters. If Europe is still undoubtedly the most important player, stake, and area in the game, it certainly is not the whole picture. Already the various neutrals, the Commonwealth, the incongruous appearance of Japan in O.E.C.D., all serve as reminders of the loose ends a solely Atlantic formula entails.

VI

Perhaps we must fall back on the third alternative mentioned at the outset, abandon the discourse of pillars and communities, with their connotation of well-defined structure, and work toward *ad hoc* functional systems—some military, some economic, some tight, some loose—not as a mere second best but as a flexible framework that would do most to meet the demands of the present without prejudicing the possibilities of the future interdependent world. Such a framework might avoid the demands for logical precision which constitutional schemes make but which are not necessarily well suited to the uncertainties and probabilities of modern strategic systems or the ramifications of international economic relations.

As a limited expedient for solution of Germany's peculiar problem and as a vehicle for expanded cooperation and consultation, a multilateral force, for example, may well prove to have a place in such a framework. But there is no need to regard it as a blueprint for the future of the West. It is not yet obvious that the groupings available for particular military purposes are those best suited to the long-term political future. Yet unless this is freely recognized, hastily erected structures may become obstacles to other ventures. Even as a strictly military matter, elaborate schemes need not entail rejection of more limited forms of cooperation. The best hope may therefore be for something in the nature of a multilateral force to accommodate Germany and others, with the British and French forces surviving, formally independent, but in practice increasingly integrated as a specialized contribution to common power. In the same spirit, improvements in the consultative arrangements for broader matters and for the formulation of strategic doctrine could be built by those who chose to do so. Perhaps quite as important as formal machinery is the cultivation of free interallied debate, private as well as official, on strategic matters to develop the common set of assumptions without which efforts to convince allies that American leadership comprehends and serves their interests can hardly attain an enduring success.

A loose constellation of this kind would call for more, rather than less, quality in American leadership. Leadership must mean resignation to interminable frustration and the final abandonment of the belief that somewhere there exists a way to transcend the perpetual wrestle with problems never susceptible to complete solution. The right to cut the knots of allied indecision in the last resort can be gracefully retained, if at all, only by virtue of inexhaustible patience with associates, deference for their views, and tenderness for their interests.

Analogies with the deference of the superior to the inferior in the Commonwealth that resulted in the free entry of the Dominions to two world wars are tempting but perhaps farfetched. One feature of British experience is relevant however. The now much derided "special relationship" was no complete illusion, as any familiarity with the intimacy and mutual confidence of British and American officials, compared to their continental opposites, will confirm. In essence, by cooperation, the British purchased a close hearing whenever they felt obliged to dig in their heels on a truly vital interest. The skill the British showed in cultivating this relationship is often acknowledged. Curiously, Americans have been slow to recognize it as a considerable achievement on their part too.

By its nature, a special relationship cannot be extended to others without dilution. But the adjective and the noun are not completely inseparable. If "specialness" is not very extendable, the substance of the relation may be more elastic. It should not be impossible to develop among the leading allies something of the same sense of being less than foreign to each other, the confidence that their major interests are consistently and sympathetically taken into account, not from time to time, but as a natural part of the daily workings of American government. Some, it is true, would reject such intimacy, but it is not easy to believe we have yet exhausted the possibilities of this direction. Should the United States succeed in establishing such patterns it might find itself, as Sir Winston Churchill once envisaged Britain, at the intersection of a set of varied circles describing the wide orbit of its interests.

CHAPTER 3

COLONIAL LEGACIES TO THE POSTCOLONIAL STATES

ROBERT C. GOOD

Nothing quite like this postcolonial era of independence-for-everyone has happened before. As the Western colonial system was unprecedented in scope, unprecedented too has been the impact of its collapse. Almost fifty new states have joined international society since 1945, creating a "new" United Nations and new dynamics in international politics. But we do not understand this new era at all unless we also understand its links to the declining colonial order.

The most significant legacy of the old to the new era—the one on which all else is founded—is, quite simply, this: the postcolonial states owe their existence to colonialism.

In certain respects, colonialism produced the postcolonial era (and its own demise) quite unwittingly. A paraphrase of Karl Marx's famous thesis is to the point: "But not only has the [colonial power] forged the weapons that bring death itself; it has also called into existence the men who are to wield those weapons. . . . What [colonialism] therefore produces, above all, are its own grave diggers. Its fall and the victory of [anti-colonial nationalism] are equally inevitable."

This is a remarkably vivid description of the process by which the colonial order has given way to the postcolonial era; what Marx would have called "contradictions" in the former have brought the latter into being. The Western metropoles (Britain, France, and the Netherlands, in particular) summoned the ablest of their colonial wards—Nehru to Cambridge, Bourguiba to the Sorbonne, Ayub Khan to Sandhurst—and

---

Robert C. Good is U.S. Ambassador to Zambia. He was previously director of the Office of Research and Analysis for Africa, Department of State. He is co-editor (with Harry R. Davis) of *Reinhold Niebuhr on Politics* and a contributor to *Neutralism and Nonalignment: The New States in World Affairs.*

schooled them in the doctrines of political liberalism. The result? "When Indians attack our rule," observed Clement Attlee, the Labor Prime Minister who presided over the liquidation of Britain's Asian empire, "they base their attack not on Indian principles but on the basis of standards derived from Britain." In the same vein, Bertrand de Jouvenel has remarked that "the main rebels against French rule in the French overseas territories are also the personalities least foreign to France; they can be recognized as conscious replicas of Lafayette, Mirabeau, or Robespierre. They are playing a role against France which is taken from a French script."

The historical process is complex. Again in dialectical terms, we not only have a thesis—colonialism—and an antithesis—anti-colonialism—but, in a sense, a synthesis—postcolonialism. Postcolonialism is a prototypical "synthesis," for the postcolonial era marks at the same time the death of Western colonialism and the universalization of the Western state and the Western state system—if not as accomplished facts then as generally accepted goals and norms. At least in part through its colonial establishment, the West has succeeded in reproducing itself everywhere.

This, incidentally, is a phenomenon that Marx's collaborator, Friedrich Engels, would have found baffling, at least with respect to some parts of tropical Africa. "Peoples which have never had a history of their own," he once wrote, "which from the moment they reached the first, crudest stages of civilization already came under foreign domination or which were only forced into the first stages of civilization through a foreign yoke, have no vitality; they will never be able to attain any sort of independence."

Clearly, Engels was wrong. What he did not foresee was the ability of peoples "which have never had a history of their own" to create or appropriate a "national" history convenient to their needs. Nor did he understand that a colonial power, by the imposition of alien forms, by a combination of force and tutelage, and by making itself the object of an animus that brings otherwise disparate subject peoples into a kind of unity, might produce a state where none had existed before.

This is what the colonial order did. The new states themselves are its legacy to the postcolonial era. Not just the principles of political liberalism—the notions of self-determination, nationalism, and equality of rights—but the very form and structure of the modern state are the bequests of the Western colonial powers to their colonial wards. "What powerful reality those lines drawn on a map possess," the eminent French scholar Robert Montagne once wrote, "lines which neither nature nor the inhabitants, left to themselves, could have brought into being. The West is there, in these invisible frames which it has drawn on its own maps. . . ." It is there too in the institutions and the ideas with which it has filled these frames.

The modern state has several attributes. These relate to the precision of its boundaries, the completeness of its jurisdiction within those boundaries, the cohesiveness of its population, and the capacity of its government not simply to maintain order but, acting through institutions designed to represent the will of the people, to formulate and execute policy vitally affecting the welfare of the national community. When we speak of the "Western" or modern state, we mean, thus, the territorial state, the integral (or national) state, the democratic state, the welfare state. However imperfectly this complex model of the modern state may be realized in the West, these are its hallmarks; they are accepted without question by the leaders of most of the new countries; they are guideposts by which the postcolonial state must measure its approach to modernity.

The colonial era not only willed these notions of the modern state to its legatees; it also made certain advances in satisfying the prerequisites of modernity. It is difficult to generalize, for performance varied widely from one colonial administration to another, and within any given colonial administration over time. But everywhere colonial authority did prescribe boundaries and did make some contribution to the cohesiveness of the subject society: positively through the integration of administrative services, the creation of an internal exchange economy, the introduction of a common language; and negatively by imposing internal peace and offering sufficient resistance to reform movements to oblige them to become increasingly effective and, in the end, both national and political in character. Toward the close of the colonial era, though in sharply different degrees in different colonies, the metropole frequently arranged apprenticeships in public service and, usually under considerable duress, provided gradually expanding opportunities for the initiation and development of the institutions of self-government.

Viewed however in its entirety, the colonial order was *not* aimed at achieving cohesive, self-sufficient and self-governing political communities. On the contrary, the political order imposed by colonial rule was often a product more of accident or expedience than the application of policy or plan. The impact of the colonial era has been deeply ambiguous. However unwittingly, the colonial powers called the new states into existence. But they were often unwilling, and indeed in large measure unable, to bequeath the capacities of statecraft or the qualities of the modern nation.

I. The Territorial State

The role of accident and expedience is nowhere more apparent than in the territorial demarcation of the colonies, which today determines the boundaries of the postcolonial states. The new states must organize themselves within the mold of the old empires, and often the very shape of the mold adds to the complexity of the task.

Administrative units under colonialism frequently bore little relation to the distribution of ethnic or linguistic groupings, or even to the logic of geography. It is true of course that there is no such thing as a "logical" boundary for demarcating a modern state in a fissiparous, traditional society. But colonial boundaries were even more capricious than most. They were determined by competition with other metropolitan powers, by the resistance offered by local populations, or by the skill with which a colonial adventurer made treaties with local rulers.

Whatever the combination of factors that brought them into existence, however, these geographical inventions of the West were imposed, in Margery Perham's image, "like a great steel grid over the amorphous cellular tissue" of isolated and often hostile communities which were then "held within its interstices in peace." Montagne is right when he tells us that these "invisible frames" drawn by the West on its maps, frames that both encompass extraordinarily divergent groups and divide homogeneous ones, represent a "powerful reality." They will be changed only slowly. But this does not mean that they are not often resented. There are many postcolonial states unwilling to accept the legitimacy of boundaries inherited from a colonial dispensation; there are many still in search of their proper frontiers.

II. The National State

Government under colonial rule was far more administrative than political. In no important sense was the colonial viceroy accountable to the local population or to local institutions. Rather he was answerable to a foreign parliament and to a foreign public. The success of his governance depended not so much on the development of indigenous political institutions or the cultivation of a political will among the colonials, but upon the apathy of traditional society, upon the skill with which he manipulated and balanced off local rulers, and upon the constant presence and the occasional use of military force. By these devices he held in check the centrifugal forces of the society placed under his control. In short, the first task of colonial administration was to maintain order, not to create a "nation."

When the tight mold of colonial rule is removed, long suppressed divisions and tensions once again emerge to threaten the fledgling state with chaos. To return to the precolonial feudal or tribal polity is unthinkable because the mystique of the modern state has now possessed the indigenous leadership, and because only centralized political authority can provide the services and the panoply of prestige and power that the politically articulate, and even the inarticulate, increasingly demand. "We cannot go back to the tenth century," Egypt's Nasser has written. "We cannot wear its clothes, which appear strange and exotic to our eyes, and we cannot become lost in its thoughts, which now appear to us as layers of darkness without any ray of light."

What does all this signify? It means that the postcolonial era is thickly settled with partially formed political communities each engaged in a desperate struggle to become a nation, a community coterminous with the boundaries of the state and commanding the loyalty of a sizable majority of its inhabitants. In case after case the familiar sequence of political development has been foreshortened—in a sense even reversed. First comes nationalism, an emotional-intellectual ferment among a small elite. Then comes independence, precipitately and for many new states without a national struggle of any significance. Only last comes what should have been concurrent with the first two stages, the long and difficult task of building something like a national society to go with the newly won juridic status of nationhood. The problem is capsuled in a line taken from the introduction of Congolese Prime Minister Cyrille Adoula to a mass meeting in Stanleyville: "Adoula is a great nationalist and he will explain nationalism to you."

The point concerning the achievement of independence without a struggle is worth pondering. One would suppose that the toughness and resiliency of the postcolonial state would relate importantly to the manner in which it has gained its independence. Did it mobilize and fight for liberation? Or was independence wafted effortlessly on the winds of change? It is probably too early to assess the evidence. But significantly the importance of the *idea* of national struggle is widely accepted. It is symbolized in Guinea, where independence was achieved by a peaceful referendum arranged by the metropole, but where today the mythology of the nation's struggle against the colonial oppressor is on the lips of every leader and is memorialized in a national monument bearing the inscription: "The Republic of Guinea to all the martyrs of colonialism." This suggests that many postcolonial states, having won independence too easily, will find it necessary following independence to perpetuate the struggle or to recreate it in some sublimated form.

The course of nation-building is not easy. Even a successful independence movement creates its own trauma, for success cancels the most important cohesive force the aspiring nation has known. A former Prime Minister of Ceylon, Sir John Kotelawala, once observed that Ceylon was a nation when its people were colonial subjects, but that national unity in independent Ceylon was in grave danger.

The sense of "we-ness" in the new state is frail. Objects of primary loyalty remain parochial, determined by family or tribe or language or religion, not by this new fiction, "the state." The effective jurisdiction of the state is badly frayed; sometimes it is nonexistent, as when dissident groups break the state's monopoly of the means of coercion and maintain an order hostile to central authority. The problem is complicated by the habit, inculcated during the colonial era though arising from traditional resentments long predating the advent of colonialism, of inveighing against established authority: he who is the master is the enemy. The habit is hard to break. Government, even after independence, remains the "they" standing against the "we." The postcolonial state has not been fulfilled, Charles Burton Marshall has observed, until men have learned to choose the right pronouns.

The establishment of effective polity is also inhibited by a shortage of trained native personnel, and by political pressures to "nativize" the civil service at a time when new government programs (expansion of services, economic development, literacy drives, and so forth) make a greater demand upon the available resources than ever before. The situation is further aggravated when antagonisms develop between the civil service, tutored by and thus identified with the colonial regime, and the politicians, whose notions of legitimacy derive from the struggle against that regime.

The effort to create an integral state—to bring into being a truly national community, to consolidate power, and to make the jurisdiction of the state complete within its prescribed boundaries—is not limited to the new nations. In some degree it is the continuing problem of every state. In Latin America, where the colonial era ended over a century ago, the problem is still acute. The struggle to build viable states is not unique to the postcolonial era; but with the dismantling of imperial modes of order, that struggle has today been universalized.

III. THE DEMOCRATIC STATE

It is hardly surprising that representative institutions, designed according to the specifications of Western democracy, undergo the severest strain in the new state. Democracy is based upon restraints on the exercise of power. The problem in most new states, however, is not to restrain but to accumulate power sufficient to make the writ of the government effective throughout the land.

Democracy presupposes countervailing power, the capacity to bring the government to account in its management of the public's business. But in many new states the social and economic resources are too thin to construct more than one pinnacle of power—that of the party and the government it controls. Only loyalty to the ruling party can give access to influence and wealth; comparable rewards are quite unattainable outside of it. In Senegal, a major oil company selected twenty-seven of its brightest employees for executive training. Twenty-four months later all but two had voluntarily left to take positions in the government.

Democracy demands a sense of the commonweal so compelling that the ruling elite and those who compete for leadership see themselves and each other as trustees of an interest larger than that of class or section. Yet, as we have seen, the "opposition" in the postcolonial state frequently does not participate in this "commonweal," for it tends to express not national, but tribal or sectional loyalties and interests. The line between "opposition" and "sedition" becomes difficult to draw.

The legitimacy of "opposition" is often not recognized at all. "The foes of the National Union," editorialized the party organ of Morocco's National Union of Popular Forces (U.N.F.P.), "are the enemies of the people. They make up the Fifth Column of the country. We must denounce the Fifth Columnists and wage an open battle against them." This extreme view, which equates loyalty to the party with loyalty to the state, has links with the colonial era in which effective opposition to viceregal authority *was* seditious. It has equally distinct links with the transitional era: the struggle for independence brooked no deviants. The movement gathered to itself *all* patriots and insisted (reasonably enough given the stakes and the nature of the struggle) that those not for independence were against it. With victory, the mantle of legitimacy is worn by those who consider themselves the true leaders of the struggle; they alone have inherited the right and the duty to rule; only they can consolidate the national revolution while defending its gains against the forces of reaction. To part company with the revolutionary leadership is *ipso facto* to place oneself in the camp of the counterrevolution.

Finally, there inheres in democracy the idea of responsible, as opposed to arbitrary or capricious, politics—politics, that is, under constraint. The political incumbent is constrained by the knowledge that his constituents will hold him accountable for his actions and will turn him out unless he can evoke their continuing support. The politician out of office is constrained by the awareness that his hue and cry, his protestations, must be measured against acts and decisions for which he will be held accountable should he gain office

No one has analyzed these requirements of democratic politics as they bear on the new states more aptly than Charles Burton Marshall. Evocation and action must be united if politics is to be responsible. Yet, Marshall reminds us, colonial administration compelled a disjunction between them. Those who wielded power, who decided and acted, were not required to justify their actions in public forums or to evoke public support. And the revolutionary leaders, those who engaged the public, who mobilized public sentiment by their protests, were removed from the responsibilities of action and decision within the framework of government. In most instances the politics of protest is the only role available to the aspiring colonial politician. It is a role as conducive to "irresponsibility" as is that of the colonial administrator, a point not frequently enough observed. Over one hundred years ago Lord Durham wrote:

> The colonial demagogue bids high for popularity without the fear of future exposure. Hopelessly excluded from power, he exercises the wildest opinions, and appeals to the most mischievous passions of the people, without any apprehension of having his sincerity or prudence hereafter tested . . . and thus the prominent places in the ranks of the opposition are occupied for the most part by men of strong passions, and merely declamatory powers, who think but little of reforming the abuses which serve them as topics for exciting discontent.

With independence, the difference between arousing a populace and running a government often seems to remain unclear. Declamation continues to be a substitute for action. The policy process is confused with the coinage of slogans. Moreover those in power tend progressively to isolate themselves from the arena of political competition. Competitors are placed under severe restraints or eliminated entirely. Government continues, as in colonial times, to be largely a matter of "administration." Only the leaders have changed.

The gap between the notion of an integrated state and the realities of the postcolonial situation is, if anything, exceeded by the gap in most of the new states between the theory and the practice of democracy. Yet so compelling is the image of the democratic state that almost every leader is by his own assessment a democrat—whether a "guided democrat," a "basic democrat," or in the case of the Communist, a "people's democrat."

IV. The Welfare State

The modern state is defined, finally, in its welfare aspect, in its capacity for progress measured in specific and quantifiable terms: growth of national income, increments in per capita income, numbers of classrooms, literacy rates, import and export levels, expansion of power production, increases in acreage under cultivation. The state's involvement in the welfare of the national community is, however, broader than the notion of progress. It encompasses also the idea of equity, and this necessarily means a frontal attack on the traditional structure of society. These two concepts, technological progress and social equity, add up to the process we have come to identify as modernization.

Here again is a legacy of the West to the new era. It has been imported through the colonial system as well as through those countless other contacts that have brought traditional societies everywhere into communication with the modern world. The legacies of progress and equity, like those of the territorial, national, and democratic state, represent aspiration rather than capacity. The gap between the two, and the problems created thereby for the new country, are enormous.

Of course the West bequeathed to the postcolonial state something more substantial than just the concept of progress and the demand for improved welfare. During the terminal phase of the colonial order, a form of "welfare colonialism" appeared. The flow of capital and talent from the metropole to the colony in some cases reached such proportions that observers have called it "inverse colonialism"; the colony was exploiting the mother country. A Liberian ambassador to the United States once complained that his nation lagged behind Ghana in the race to modernize because, having been independent from the outset, Liberia did not enjoy Ghana's considerable colonial inheritance.

But the economic and social legacies of colonial rule (and indeed of the West's impact on the social fabric and the economic institutions of all underdeveloped countries) have been uneven and in some cases detrimental. The colonial economy cultivated primary products designed for export rather than a balanced economy designed for domestic growth and stability. It depended upon cheap mass labor (imported when necessary, and thereby creating in some areas severe minority problems) rather than labor-saving capital equipment. It recruited from the mother country most of its technical, managerial, and entrepreneurial personnel, instead of promoting these specialized capabilities within the indigenous population.

As a result, the post colonial economy suffers from the economic instability brought about by fluctuations in world prices for its relatively few primary products. It remains dependent upon the economy of the former metropole, which renders difficult economic diversification at home and the development of economic complementarity with its neighbors. Finally, the postcolonial economy finds expansion seriously impeded by a shortage of trained personnel and by a subsistence economy that, short of totalitarian methods, cannot yield the necessary investment capital.

These difficulties are compounded by the flight of foreign capital that frequently follows independence, and by acute balance of payments difficulties as imports rapidly rise to meet demands for increased consumption and larger welfare programs. It is curious, incidentally, how the pursuit of the "social revolution" frequently slows down the completion of the "national revolution." Seeking to free itself from dependence upon protected markets in the former metropole, the new states must lower production costs to compete in the world market. But welfare programs must be financed—through taxes or inflation. In either case, production costs increase and further frustrate the attempt to escape the metropolitan market.

The impact of colonial rule was uneven in other respects too. Education was often encouraged, but it was education designed to facilitate colonial administration, not to replace it. A high priority was given to clerical and other skills appropriate to the lower and middle rungs of governmental and commercial ladders. But the range of specialists needed in an independent and rapidly developing society was not generally among the legacies left by retreating colonial administrations.

The introduction of the cash nexus and the law of contract, the opening of avenues of commerce and the provision of infrastructure necessary for the exploitation of natural resources, created a base for economic development in many colonies. But these contributions also tightened the financial and commercial bonds between the colony and the metropole and created within the colony islands of economic modernity that could be maintained only by foreign skills.

Rapid progress might be obtained most efficiently by permitting, and even encouraging, the continued "exploitation" of resources, markets, and services by foreign capital and skills without worrying too much about "uneven" development. But the new state, sensitive to the demands of sovereignty and inordinately suspicious of foreign interests, often weighs these matters more with its political heart than its economic head. It must progress; it must also complete its national revolution. And the two requirements are not always easily reconciled. The temptation is great, therefore, to close the foreign schools before new national schools are ready to open, to cut back the numbers of expatriate civil servants before their replacements are adequately trained, to curtail the role of foreign enterprise before domestic managers, entrepreneurs, and investors are available—in short, to reject as quickly as possible every hint of foreign tutelage. The consequences for progress can be devastating.

We remarked earlier that the legacy of the welfare state encompassed more than progress, that it involved also the idea of equity. "There is no point in the Moroccanization of exploitation," that country's most prominent labor leader once said in an interview. "We must seek a society free from exploitation whether French or Moroccan."

To a colonial revolution is thus added incipient civil war—a struggle against the domestic institutions of feudalism and traditionalism. Motivations vary. Justice is involved. But a modernizing elite bent upon consolidating its power must also break the authority of traditional leaders; and if rapid progress is desired, men must be emancipated from the strait jacket of immemorial custom. For all these reasons the established order comes under attack—the land owner, the tribal chief, the feudal lord. Every aspect of life is affected. Change beckons; it also threatens. Tension rises between rural areas and urban centers. Men are torn between old habits and new methods, between ancient loyalties and strange new allegiances. There is the story of Addi wa Bihi, governor of a province in Morocco, who was sentenced to death in 1959 for leading an armed revolt against Rabat. "I took up arms against the State," he explained in his trial, "because I was told the King was in danger."

The new state is cut adrift not only from its imperial moorings but from its traditional ones too. In his *The Philosophy of the Revolution* Gamal Abdul Nasser expands on his notion of the two revolutions, national and social: "Peoples preceding us on the path of progress. . . . have not had to face both simultaneously. . . . The terrible experience through which our people are going is that we are having both revolutions at the same time." Nasser goes on to point out that the one revolution gets in the way of the other. The national revolution, he says, ". . . must unite all elements of the nation, build them solidly together and instill in them the spirit of self-sacrifice for the sake of the whole country. But one of the primary features of social revolution is that it shakes values and loosens principles, and sets the citizenry, as individuals and classes, to fighting each other."

Frequently the contradictions run deeper than this, deeper even than the incompatibility referred to earlier between the requirements of economic progress and the need to complete the national revolution. The fight against colonial rule calls forth the necessity to "re-discover" and to assert the uniqueness of the nation. The past is venerated. Ancient customs are recalled. Movements arise to further the use of indigenous languages. There is a quickened interest in religious tradition. The "national personality" is celebrated; non-national values are condemned. This infatuation with the national tradition threatens to contravene the social revolution, which demands the rupture of tradition, and to blunt the modernizing process, which depends upon the development of non-indigenous institutions. The problem is compounded because these non-indigenous institutions—like the ideologies of progress and equity which undergird them—are derived from the "imperial" West.

Thus there arises for many new states an ideological crisis. The uniqueness of the nation is both asserted and denied. The West is condemned even while Westernization is desired. Impaled upon this contradiction, some new states seem unable to get on with the task of effective state-building. The West is ridiculed; colonialism is vilified; foreigners are sent home; world conferences are convened and slogans coined. But the business of becoming a state remains at dead center.

"The West has set the pattern of our hopes," Ghana's Kwame Nkrumah once observed, "and by entering in strength it has forced the pattern upon us." Nkrumah's "pattern of hopes," arising from the impact of the imperial West, is an apt phrase. For though the Western-derived, postcolonial state is a recognized legal entity, often it is still, politically speaking, more a hope than an actuality. The legacy of the colonial order to the postcolonial era has been the form of the state, and not necessarily its prerequisites; it is a legacy of expectation, not realization; of aspiration, not capacity. The gap between the "pattern of hopes" and their fulfillment, between the requirements of sovereign statehood and present political, economic, social, and psychic realities in the new states, between the drive for "modernization" and the tools available to do the job, constitutes one of the gravest sources of tension in our times.

CHAPTER 4

NONALIGNMENT REASSESSED: THE EXPERIENCE OF INDIA

CHARLES H. HEIMSATH

The argument to be presented in this essay is that from the end of World War II to the present India's power—its ability to influence the policies of other states—has rested chiefly on certain intangible bases which are no longer adequate to support all of its national interests. I propose to examine the record of India's impact on world affairs since 1945 in order to discover the source of India's power in the decade of the 1950's. I also wish to examine the reasons why India's international prestige, which was partly dependent on that power, has declined during the past several years, rapidly after the Chinese military advances of the autumn of 1962. Finally, I plan to explore the possibility that India might reconstitute the base of its power to meet the new and different challenges to Indian national interests and to democracy in Asia in the decade of the 1960's.

I

One of the great international issues which remained unsolved at the end of World War II was the independence of India. Its postponement until the end of hostilities had been a source of wartime friction between the United States and Britain. Some American leaders had insisted that the prosecution of the war, especially against Japan, was hindered by Britain's failure to associate Indian nationalist leaders with the war effort. They also believed that the political objectives of the United Nations could not stand scrutiny in the light of the continuing reluctance

CHARLES H. HEIMSATH is associate professor of South Asian studies at the School of International Service of the American University in Washington. He is the author of *Indian Nationalism and Hindu Social Reform*.

of the Churchill government to dismantle the empire in India. Not only in the United States but throughout the world, India's case had wide public support, largely because of the publicity that Mohandas K. Ghandi had given to an India subjugated and striving for its political and spiritual freedom. In 1945 the Labor government came into office in Britain, not only committed to a policy of reform of Imperial affairs but also sensitive to the support that India's freedom movement had aroused abroad.

Thus, India's independence in 1947 was in some measure the outcome of the international support that its nationalist movement had elicited. India's ability to influence political decisions elsewhere and to create support for its interests in other parts of the world, by psychological or moral suasion, was thereby demonstrated at the time of independence. This ability became the foundation of India's power in the post-independence period.

After almost three decades during which powers were gradually being transferred from Britain to India, the Indian Interim Government in 1946 assumed control over its own external affairs, and the following year India moved calmly into the international arena as a sovereign state. Its continued attachment to the Commonwealth, even after the proclamation of the Republic in 1950, had the advantage of reinforcing its influence among certain states, but it also led many governments to discount the independent importance that Prime Minister Nehru sought for his country in world affairs. In any case, while critical international developments from 1947 to 1950 in Europe and China were occupying the attention of statesmen and military leaders of the major powers, India's foreign policies were not of great importance in world politics. In addition, India's domestic problems and its conflict with Pakistan over Kashmir helped to postpone its assuming an influential position in the international scene. Indeed, India's influence in those years was scarcely effective enough to defend satisfactorily one basic national interest—its legal rights in Kashmir. As a result of inadequate diplomacy in the United Nations and a failure to expound convincingly its Kashmir policy to interested states—the Nehru government itself did not fully comprehend its position in Kashmir—India suffered its first major defeat in international politics, when the Security Council adopted a pro-Pakistan approach in debates on the disputed ex-princely state.

During these early years of independence India had few opportunities to establish and exert power internationally. Its position in world politics, as an independent, nonaligned state, had not yet created a forceful enough impression on the major foreign offices to cause them to adopt special policies toward New Delhi. The rapidly emerging alignment of states into a bipolar system preoccupied the attention of the major governments; and nonalignment seemed to have no place in the evolving scheme. Both the Soviet and the Western coalitions tended to view nonalignment as merely a verbal exercise, not a policy that by itself could alter India's basic commitment to the West—a commitment rooted in economic necessity and the need for political support from those countries whose constitutional systems India was endeavoring to emulate.

The United States, failing to recognize that a government's commitment to democracy does not always result in a pro-American foreign policy, initially looked upon India as a candidate for the Western alliance. After the defeat of the Chinese Nationalists, India appeared to some American officials as the strongest potentially anti-Communist force in Asia. American efforts to associate India with a series of anti-Communist measures, including resolutions in the United Nations, led to harsh rebuffs from Nehru's government. The more pressure applied from the West and the greater the Western expectations for involving India in an anti-Communist bloc, the more vigorous became Nehru's insistence on nonalignment. (The psychological need of Western-trained Indian leaders to free themselves of their cultural reliance on the West and to be acknowledged as independently Indian reinforced their repudiation of a pro-Western alignment in foreign policy.) Simultaneously, Soviet leaders rivaled their Western counterparts in disbelieving Indian nonalignment and also acted on the assumption that Nehru's government, all verbal protestations not withstanding, was linked to Western interests. Therefore they failed to foster the close ties with New Delhi that Nehru might have expected, gave support to the revolutionary Communist party of India, and apparently awaited the "inevitable" transfer of power into truly "popular" Indian hands.

Under these conditions, wherein neither of the great coalitions was prepared to recognize nonalignment as a significant factor in world politics, India's power remained weak, in global terms.[1] In relation to nearby states in Asia, India at that time, because of its geographic size and position, its huge population, its tangible economic and military strength, and the inspiration that its nationalist movement had extended

[1] We use the term power when referring to international politics, to mean influence on the policies of other states. See Harold D. Lasswell and Abraham Kaplan, *Power and Society* (New Haven, Conn., 1950), pp. 74f. R. H. Tawney's use of the term, as quoted therein, is: "Power may be defined as the capacity of an individual, or group of individuals, to modify the conduct of other individuals or groups in the manner which he desires. . . ." From his *Equality* (New York, 1931), p. 230.

to all dependent peoples, exerted influence and was assumed to be potentially (or feared to be already) the dominant state in the Indian Ocean area.

The Korean War transformed Indian nonalignment from a verbal assertion into a global posture which served as an effective instrument of power. The necessity for the United States to obtain United Nations sanction for its Far Eastern containment policy gave India, as leader of the so-called Arab-Asian grouping of states, a new importance to the West. As Indian delegates in the United Nations increased their country's involvement in the diplomacy of a global crisis and Nehru maneuvered his government into positions of mediation between the Soviet and Western coalition, India's nonalignment evolved into a sophisticated means of influencing the decisions of other governments. Its policy in the Korean crisis was rooted in a careful assessment of its national interest: to remain uninvolved, which seemed especially compelling after the Chinese intervention, and to assist in bringing about a settlement. But that policy produced the added, and longer-term, benefit of forcing the great powers to recognize the significance of nonalignment. That posture received its pragmatic test when Indian troops presided over the operation climaxing the Korean armistice negotiations, the exchange of prisoners of war, which won reluctant praise from all sides for the Indians' disciplined and courageous impartiality. As a result of Korean War diplomacy, the essentially negative and passive character of nonalignment was altered. India proved its ability to assume the role of mediator and impartial arbitrator, and no further demonstrations of its unique posture were needed to establish in fact what Nehru had been proclaiming in theory. The Soviet Union, somewhat more tardily than Western states, began to revise its assessment of India's foreign policy and even before the death of Stalin in 1953 recognized nonalignment as a fact of international politics.

At the Geneva Conference in 1954 Indian influence was a recognized, though unofficial, factor in the Indo-Chinese settlement, and Indian representatives were accorded the pivotal positions in the International Control Commission teams for Vietnam, Cambodia, and Laos. (The precedent of the Neutral Nations Repatriation Commission for Korea was obviously being followed in the arrangements for the Indo-Chinese Commission; in both cases Indians acted as chairmen of groups made up of equal numbers of Communist and non-Communist representatives.) In 1953 an Indian was named head of an international commission to supervise elections in the Sudan, thereby satisfying the demands for impartiality made by Britain and Egypt. Indian diplomacy was welcomed at the time of the London Conference dealing with Egypt's nationalization of the Suez Canal Company and might have helped in bringing the parties to a settlement had not Egypt been attacked. More recently, when disorders in the Congo threatened to destroy the new state and to attract direct intervention by major states, India dispatched troops again for overseas duty in a region of crisis, this time as part of an international force. Eventually Indian soldiers made up one-third of the United Nations Congo force. Less publicized Indian efforts to reduce international tensions were New Delhi's negotiations in behalf of the release of United States airmen held in Communist China; Nehru's appeal—the first of its kind from any foreign office—to the United States and the Soviet Union to cease testing nuclear weapons; and India's participation in the Geneva disarmament conferences. Except for the problems of Germany and Berlin, there was no international issue or crisis of major importance after the Korean War in which India's influence was not felt. In the United Nations General Assembly, the specialized agencies, and the Secretariat, Indian representatives and international civil servants added much to their country's stature and occasionally markedly influenced decisions on crucial issues, as for example the defeat of the Soviet Union's "troika" proposal for the Secretary Generalship.

The power which India derived from establishing itself firmly as a nonaligned state was exerted most effectively on the major contenders in the bipolar struggle, the United States and the Soviet Union. These also happened to be states whose territorial, economic, or military interests in no way conflicted with those of India. In relations with neighboring states, notably Pakistan and China, India's power had to be calculated in tangible terms. During the 1950's that power, measured by India's ability to influence in its favor the foreign policies of nearby governments, declined. In 1954 Pakistan and China pressed forward policies which were aimed primarily at weakening India, and New Delhi in turn was unable to advance successful countermeasures. Pakistan concluded a military aid agreement with the United States that assured it a more rapid rate of military modernization than India could maintain without sacrificing either its nonalignment or its economic development programs or both. China succeeded in restricting Indian contacts with Tibet and gained India's formal acknowledgment of Chinese sovereignty over Tibet by means of an agreement which also included the controversial Panch Shila (peaceful coexistence) clauses. New Delhi recognized the hostility underlying the Pakistani and Chinese moves but lacked the will and the kind of power needed to check them. The Asian-African Conference at Bandung in 1955 demonstrated the fact that India would have to share any ambitions for leadership in that area of the world with

China, and further that the non-Western countries were a seriously divided group—Communist, anti-Communist, and nonaligned—unlikely to lend support to India's national interests.

Even a glance at the record of India's declining influence in the southern Asian region was cause for distress in many Indian circles. Pakistan's military build-up created risks to Indian security which New Delhi interpreted as necessitating the continued deployment of the bulk of India's army on the West Pakistan and "Azad" Kashmir border. Simultaneously the need was apparent for increased defenses on the Himalayan frontier, but the Pakistan threat was regarded as more pressing. India could do nothing to inhibit Pakistan's joining SEATO in 1954 and the Baghdad Pact in 1955.

After its independence in 1948, Burma, unlike Pakistan, established and maintained a posture of nonalignment similar to India's. But by the mid-1950's the Rangoon government began to formulate a foreign policy in accordance with its own peculiar needs, most crucial of which was an understanding with China. Despite basic agreement between the Indian and Burmese governments on many global political issues, Burmese policy toward China did not take Indian interests fully into account. Undoubtedly recognizing the evidences of Chinese expansionist aims in the direction of India and countries of southeast Asia and seized with its own border difficulties with China, the Rangoon government in 1960 signed a boundary treaty with Peking. At once the Chinese made use of the treaty to embarrass India, which refused to come to a similar agreement with China. The Burmese government was cautious in not lending support to India's Himalayan boundary claims and committed itself by a 1960 nonaggression treaty not to take part in any alliance against China. The Chinese became Burma's leading customer for rice exports, economic relations between the two countries increased, and by the early 1960's Burma provided for Chinese diplomacy a significant access route into the political life of mainland southeast Asia. The Nehru government acquiesced in the increasing Burmese rapprochement with China, despite its need for external support for its China policy from all of its neighbors. New Delhi was unable, or unwilling, to counteract the growing isolation of India from other southern Asian countries that Chinese political and military measures were bringing about.

Ceylon in the 1950's, although not faced by a Chinese presence on its border, sought closer relations with Peking, possibly in part to counteract the great influence of its neighbor to the north. Between India and Ceylon the issue of Indian immigrants in the latter country continued to cause misunderstanding and even bitterness. Several agreements were reached on the status of the immigrants, on procedures to deal with illegal entry into Ceylon, and on remittances to India. But each government continued to distrust the other, and no reconciliation could be reached. Even before the leftist Bandaranaike government came to power, Ceylon entered a five-year barter agreement with China to exchange rubber for much-needed rice. In 1957 the agreement was extended to provide for Ceylonese imports of Chinese textiles, and China soon became a strong competitor of India and Japan in Ceylon's textile market. Peking began to assist Ceylon's economic development schemes, and closer political and cultural relations between the two countries ensued. Because of its new ties with China, the Colombo government adopted a policy of virtual nonalignment on the Sino-Indian boundary conflict in 1962.

The Nepal government in the mid-1950's began to recognize the possibilities of reducing Indian influence on its internal and external policies by accepting overtures from China. In 1955 Nepal and China established diplomatic relations and the next year signed a treaty on Tibet which permitted Chinese trade missions to be permanently stationed in Nepal in return for the Nepali missions already in Tibet. Chinese economic aid and accompanying technicians began to move into Nepal; Chou En-lai visited Kathmandu in 1957; and further agreements were signed on boundary demarcation and diplomatic representation. The building of an all-weather road from Kathmandu to Lhasa was begun by both countries. Toward Sikkim and Bhutan Chinese moves were less immediately successful, but the pull toward Tibet and China on the Himalayan border peoples was undermining India's long-standing dominance in those regions.

Power in international politics is a relative concept, and the decline in India's power in southern Asia was the result chiefly of the military and economic advances being made by China. (Because of the fundamental inferiority of Pakistan in relation to India, the United States military aid program to Pakistan did not crucially affect India's influence in the region.) Chinese military movements on the Himalayan frontier continued from 1954 (the year of the Panch Shila accord) and increased sharply in 1958 and 1959, when internal disorders in Tibet led to extreme measures against the Tibetan people. After the flight to India of the Dalai Lama, Chinese troops attempted to close the Tibet-India border to prevent mass escapes, and the Chinese administration in Tibet took steps to eliminate all Indian contacts with that country. Chinese road-building activities in Indian-claimed Kashmir and border clashes in the late summer and autumn of 1959 finally alerted the Nehru government to the immediate and long range dangers from China. But no effective military steps were taken by India to secure its control over the North East

Frontier Agency or to reassert authority over the traditionally non-administered Aksai Chin region of Ladkh in Kashmir. If India could be said to have had a farsighted plan for checking China in the Himalayas and Chinese influence in southern Asia, that plan must have been to develop the industrial resources of the country in order to support a military establishment powerful enough to hold the border areas and an economic policy which would attract the underdeveloped countries in Asia. But immediate measures could accomplish little to offset Chinese moves; the strengthening of the border posts and the diplomatic talks with Peking, which began in 1960, provided no real basis for Indian confidence. Meanwhile China increased its efforts to isolate India politically from other Asian states by negotiating border settlements with Nepal and Burma and a nationality agreement with Indonesia; Pakistan was to come later.

The decline of India's power in southern Asia was in part also the result of India's "diplomatic style," which offended many southern Asians who were sensitive to notions of Indian cultural superiority and political leadership. Whether or not it was aware of that sensitivity, the Indian government gave little evidence that it was interested in improving its diplomatic means of influencing southern Asian governments.

While the gains made in Chinese power at the expense of India's power in the decade of the 1950's were relatively impressive, one must understand that the main thrust of Indian diplomacy during that period was aimed not at the countries of Asia, but toward the great powers. The game of regional politics, in what Michael Brecher has called the "subordinate state system of southern Asia," [2] has always been a concern of New Delhi secondary to the acquisition of prestige and support from the great powers and the Commonwealth. There are several facts which explain this. One is the tradition of close ties with the West, which under British rule produced security for the Indian subcontinent and precluded the development of ties with Asian states. Another is the fact that Indian officials with foreign policy responsibilities, unlike those of some other Asian states, are men and women whose understanding of the West is far greater than their understanding of (or even sympathy with) Asia and Africa. But of much greater importance than either of these in determining the priorities of Indian foreign policy objectives was the need for large-scale and continuing economic aid from the industrialized countries. In 1955 Russia joined the countries which were extending massive capital goods assistance to India, thereby demonstrating that India's unique influence operated on both sides of the bipolar struggle. It

[2] Michael Brecher, "International Relations and Asian Studies: The Subordinate State System of Southern Asia," *World Politics*, XV, No. 2 (Jan., 1963).

could be argued at the end of the 1950's, that despite its weakness in Asia, India's nonalignment was still an adequate instrument for the pursuit of its most vital national interest. But the decade of the 1960's revealed altered political patterns in world affairs and presented problems for India with which nonalignment alone could not cope.

II

India's posture of nonalignment, which achieved its greatest effectiveness in the 1950's, was not designed with the physical security of the country chiefly in mind. In fact, when Nehru first enunciated India's desire to remain aloof from major power groupings in world politics, in the mid-1940's, Britain still ruled the country and provided for its defense. In later years the most that could be said for nonalignment as a defense policy was that an India which refused to take sides might hope to escape involvement in a major war—a very doubtful proposition and never very strongly put forth by the Indian government. Nonalignment was aimed at achieving two cardinal national objectives: full national independence, which meant recognition by all states of India's freedom to define its own interests and policies; and a stature of great significance in world affairs whose acknowledgment by established states would assist in the downfall of colonialism and racialism, strengthen the "resurgence of Asia" (in Nehru's words), and lend support for India's modernization. A third objective, whose relationship to national interest in the minds of Indian policy makers was debatable, was the maintenance and extension of a "third area" (Nehru's phrase) which could act in behalf of world peace by offering mediation and providing a kind of buffer between the conflicting power groups. All those objectives were substantially realized in the brief span of a single decade and might not have been, to such a degree, had India committed itself to one or the other coalitions.

Nonalignment was a declaration of independence in world politics, a logical culmination of the Indian nationalist movement's struggle for internal self-government. Beyond that, nonalignment brought recognition to the largest of the newly independent states and a realization, unprecedented in modern times, of the needs of the pre-modern countries and of the responsibilities towards them on the part of economically advanced countries. Furthermore, there can be little doubt that the efforts of India and other nonaligned states to produce peaceful settlements of international disputes and to reduce the level of international tensions made real contributions toward world peace.

Although nonalignment was not a posture requiring vigorous assertion of national capabilities, as a predominantly military posture would have been, it was not at all a passive, inactive retreat from political involvement (hence, the misunderstandings engendered by the word, neutral, applied to India). Nonalignment, as India pursued it, was incessantly active in the political sense of constant and rapid maneuvering. The fox-like alertness, the diplomatic aggressiveness, and the temerity to engage in novel political procedures which characterized V. K. Krishna Menon at his best set the standard, which few other nonaligned states could match. In contrast, the international political behavior of those small states that had associated themselves with a great power, often for well-considered reasons of enlightened self-interest, could be described as passive, or at least highly predictable.

India's nonalignment, as we have seen, has been the main source of its power in international political relations. Credibility is an indispensable attribute of effective power. Military capability, for example, must be believed to exist by the state against which it is to be directed as a threat; otherwise obviously it cannot influence policy. Unlike military capability, which may be directed against any state provided it is within physical striking range (all governments understand the threat or use of force), the power derived from nonalignment exists only in relation to those states whose peculiar interests are held to be affected when that posture is assumed by another state. This came to be the case with the United States and the Soviet Union. Other states, such as Pakistan and China, were left unmoved by India's nonalignment because the interests of these states were not substantially affected by India's assumption of that posture.

The governments of the United States and the Soviet Union, as the leaders of powerful coalitions seeking adherents to their respective causes, recognized by the early 1950's India's important position. (That position was admirably illustrated by events of the winter of 1950–51, when India, while never retracting its support for the United Nations resolutions condemning North Korean aggression or withdrawing its ambulance corps serving with United Nations forces, provided defensible arguments for the Chinese intervention, actively tried to mediate between the two sides, and urged Peking's admission to the United Nations.) Both sides in the bipolar struggle for global dominance recognized their need for India's support (or at the very least the importance of preventing India from giving its support to the opposing side). Neither side, however, was able to obtain any sort of commitment from New Delhi to provide that support, and therein lay India's power. Because India's policy on many issues could not be predicted and in a larger sense because India's long term or ultimate attachment to one or the other of the competing structures of society and government was uncertain, both the United States and the Soviet Union were induced to modify their policies in certain instances so as to better attract Indian support. In regard to issues such as colonialism and racialism in international affairs, on which India's policies were generally consistent, the policies of the great powers were also affected by India's stands, because to offend Indian interests in one situation might lessen the chances of gaining Indian support in the next.

This is not to suggest that India was ever capable of altering policies of the major states in violation of the latters' important interests; in fact on numerous occasions India's interests (as in disarmament negotiations) were blatantly ignored or repudiated by those states. What seems clear is that the United States and the Soviet Union recognized the importance of Indian support for, or opposition to, many of their respective interests and policies. When those states understood that the chances of such support or opposition grew or diminished partly in response to their efforts to satisfy Indian interests, and when they acted in order to produce a favorable Indian response, the power of India was an established fact.

In short, India's power rested on the acknowledgment by other states that India had something to offer and could be induced to supply it. The achievement of that acknowledgment, which occurred in the early 1950's, was the outstanding success of the Nehru government in foreign relations. By the mid-1950's India's nonalignment had passed through the period of rebellious, sometimes irresponsible, youth into the confidence of middle age, and its posture was regarded as a stable and relatively permanent feature of international politics. Both power coalitions came to regard that posture as a beneficial state of affairs, and henceforth their respective policies toward India were directed toward the preservation of its special relationship to both sides.

A comparison of India's nonalignment with the classical posture of a buffer state might clarify further the reasons why the great powers first tolerated, then respected, and finally supported India's international stance. As a buffer state traditionally acts to maintain between opposing states, and by their mutual consent, a zone where contending interests are kept from open conflict, so India's nonalignment (and that of other smaller states) maintained an area free from direct great power conflicts. This was Nehru's "no-war zone," which he hoped to extend to all of south Asia (and if possible beyond) until Pakistan's military agreement with the United States made that ambition impossible. At first this zone existed, to be sure, at the sufferance of the great powers as a possibly temporary feature of world politics. But as India proved itself agile and occasionally fearless in respect to great power controversies, such as in Korea and Indochina, tolerance merged into respect for India's ability to sustain its posture in the face of definite risks. (India's fearlessness may have been largely verbal and was certainly enunciated with the confidence that the powerful states had no intention at that time of coercing India into positions of alignment. But economic assistance from the United States—for example, the $190,000,000 grain loan negotiated in early 1951—and later from the Soviet Union might have been withdrawn in retaliation against certain Indian policies; the Indian government recognized those risks and pressed its own independent policies despite them.) Governments of smaller states gained the courage to remain or become nonaligned on the Indian model, which appeared eminently workable and profitable. After 1958 the emerging African states, one after the other, made debuts in world politics with Indian-sounding pronouncements about nonalignment, and the global buffer zone was extended, though not under India's leadership.

In a manner analogous to a buffer against military and political conflict between more powerful states, India acted as an ideological buffer by refusing to commit its 400 million people to either of the two great global causes. This meant that the lines of ultimate confrontation between Western and Soviet values could not be drawn: India had not yet made its choice; and thus the test of the strengths or persuasive powers of the two systems in an important theater of world politics could not take place. The possibility of serving as an ideological buffer arose from the bipolar competition between the value systems—as distinguished from the tangible powers of the Western alliance and the Soviet Bloc. Both sides sought to add the support of numbers of adherents to their respective ideological positions. This so-called "competitive coexistence" became especially beneficial to India when the Soviet Union joined the United States in offering massive economic support for its industrialization program. Both sides were engaged in exporting economic assistance for basically the same reason, to try to influence the course of India's future development in the direction of a certain structure of values.

To the extent that the long range goals of the United States and the Soviet Union were understood by both sides to be *primarily* ideological—a doubtful premise, but one which probably underlay many foreign policy decisions of the great powers, especially toward nonaligned countries—India, in a buffer status, assumed in addition certain of the characteristics of holder of the balance of power. A buffer state is obliged to balance the influence that one state seeks to exert upon it against the influence sought by another state, in order to maintain its relative free-dom from direct interference by stronger outside forces. Such a balanc-ing can often be accomplished without the exertion of positive power against other states, and India often found itself in just such a position with regard to the economic, military, and certain political objectives of the great powers. When, however, India became the object of great-power competition for ideological or moral support, a more positive balancing posture could be adopted. In these terms India was not merely a passive spectator in a great-power struggle endeavoring to stay clear of the conflict and occasionally dampen it, but had the capacity to influ-ence the outcome of that struggle by throwing its ideological weight to one side or the other. While India's economic and military support could not have been crucial to either side—its capabilities in these areas were pitifully limited—the support that it could provide by assuring that its future development would be in the direction of adherence to one or the other of the major value systems was potentially immense. Within the frame of reference suggested by the ideological competition between the Western and the Soviet systems, therefore, India's position was analo-gous to that of a classic holder of the balance of power. The possibility of committing its people to one system or the other gained for India the capability of influencing the policies of other states.

To contrast India's posture vis-à-vis the great powers with its rela-tions with the important states in Asia is to juxtapose ideological interests against the realities of tangible power. Neither Pakistan nor China—nor, for that matter, the other Asian or Middle Eastern states—interpreted the long term struggle between the Communist and democratic systems in a manner that made India's nonalignment crucial to their respective national interests. Because of its military, economic, and geographic inferiority in regard to India, Pakistan formulated its Indian policies on the narrow, but logical assumption of permanent geopolitical insecurity. China, on the other hand, sought dominance in Asia and regarded India as a rival which had to be subdued. India's capabilities to influence these states, i.e., its power, lay in *their* recognition of the ways in which India could affect their respective interests. Almost all of these ways could be equated with India's economic and military capabilities, although Indian political decisions at certain times (as in negotiations with Pakistan on Kashmir) carried some weight. Much the same analysis could be ap-plied to India's relations with other states in southern Asia.

With regard to newly independent states in general, including those in sub-Saharan Africa, India's influence waned as each of them sought to establish its reputation in world political affairs and no longer viewed India as a major champion of anti-colonialism and nonalignment. At the

Belgrade Conference of Nonaligned Countries in 1961 Nehru declared, in effect, that India was no longer primarily concerned about colonialism and urged the governments represented to turn their attention to the problem of escaping global war. His remarks could be interpreted as an admission that India was no longer making an effort to lead the nonaligned countries, whose common political interest was anti-colonialism. (In its relations with sub-Saharan African countries in particular, Indian diplomacy was never very successful, for many reasons, one of which was the obvious sense of cultural and intellectual superiority which many Indians displayed when dealing with Africans.)

In summary, the general perspective suggested here supports Michael Brecher's contention that India operates in at least two "state systems," the "dominant state system" and the "subordinate state system." The nature of India's effective power differed (and still does) according to the "system" of states in which India operated. Its power in the "dominant system," that is, the one controlled by the United States and the Soviet Union, was greater than in the "subordinate system," because India chose not to stress military and economic capabilities, but rather to rely on the diplomacy of nonalignment to support its international objectives—except at various times in relation to Pakistan when direct military and economic policies were adopted. Such reliance resulted from a conscious decision to allocate all available resources, internal and external, to economic development and to avoid as far as practicable displays of tangible coercive power, which many Indians regarded as unworthy of their nation's image as a peacemaker. Also the Indian government was directed by men who had participated in the demise of British rule in India, which was brought about primarily through the psychological power of the nationalist movement. The National Congress had discovered moral suasion to be a perfectly adequate substitute for physical might, and perhaps superior to it. The Congress leadership in independent India, perhaps unconsciously, placed great reliance on a similar kind of power in international politics.

III

The decline in India's power, signs of which were noticeable in the mid-1950's in southern Asia and the Himalayan region, reached alarming proportions by the 1960's. That decline was most clearly defined by the intensification of India's confrontation with its most powerful neighbor, China, a state whose politics could be influenced only by India's assertion of tangible national power. In a move partly aimed at reestablishing some of its lost prestige, at home and abroad, the Indian government sent its troops into Goa in December, 1961, and terminated the four-centuries-old Portuguese sovereignty over that territory. Indian motives for seizing Goa, after Nehru had frequently promised not to use force to settle that issue, surely included India's desire to reinforce its anti-colonialist *bona fides* among African governments. Those governments saw no sense in a foreign policy based on nonviolence and were beginning to view India as a supporter of great power interests in Africa, partly because of its role in the Congo and partly because of a seldom concealed disdain which many Indians displayed toward African culture. Another likely reason for the Indian action was the need to demonstrate the Indian army's capacity to carry out a successful operation, after numerous setbacks in the Himalayas. Neither of these objectives —or any other foreign policy objective beyond that of gaining control over a bit of alien-held territory with a good harbor—was unconditionally realized, but an estimate of the gains minus the losses to India's prestige resulting from the action yields a net advantage to Indian national interest. (The impact on the prestige of the United Nations of still another flouting of the Charter—this time by one of its important defenders—would, of course, also have to be weighed in the balance.) India got support and praise for its action from the newly independent states and from Communist governments, while the only vociferous criticisms were issued from the press and governments of Western and Western-allied countries. The policies of the West toward India, however, changed not at all, and the issue was regarded as unimportant after a few months.

One significance of the Goa action in the broader perspective of Indian foreign policy should be mentioned. The Indian government demonstrated at Goa that it was becoming more concerned with its prestige, i.e., its predictable power, among Asian and African states than with its standing in the eyes of the non-Communist West. Reportedly rejecting a United States mediation effort just before the invasion of Goa, Nehru was prepared to exchange the image of an India upholding the principle of peaceful settlement, built up by diplomatic efforts for a decade, for an initial installment (apart from Kashmir defense) on a reputation of using force successfully to advance its legitimate external interests. The latter reputation badly needed fostering, especially since the Chinese occupation of Aksai Chin, if India were to realize its potential of power in southern Asia.

The dramatic declaration, in the form of the Goa action, that India no longer wished to be regarded as relying on intangible power to achieve its major objectives was followed by a stunning setback less than a year later when the Chinese moved into the North East Frontier Agency. Disregarding the known weaknesses of the Indian army's position in N.E.F.A., the Indian government ordered its forces to eject Chinese troops from an area two miles south of the McMahon Line, in September, 1962. The Chinese, poised to take advantage of any such Indian "provocation," advanced rapidly into N.E.F.A., capturing 4,000 Indians and killing over 2,000 and leaving the plains of Assam almost totally defenseless. As if the military defeat were not enough of a humiliation for India, the Chinese compounded it by inflicting an almost equally decisive diplomatic victory. They unilaterally halted their advance, withdrew their forces to previously held positions, and assumed the posture of an aggrieved state willing to negotiate but overwhelmingly powerful in defense of its interests. India found itself outclassed militarily and without strong backing from the nonaligned states of southern Asia; the latter clearly did not regard common interest in nonalignment as sufficient reason to support India when such support meant antagonizing China. Offers of military assistance came from the Western alliance countries at once and later from the Soviet Union, states whose friendship India had long cultivated at the cost of neglecting efforts and skills that would have produced allies or supporters elsewhere. Great-power assistance was welcome, but it could not overshadow the striking image of defeat and weakness that India presented especially to smaller states which had once held high estimates of India's capabilities. Indians themselves suffered demoralization while trying to explain to others and to themselves what had happened.

India's reliance on outside military aid *in extremis* to defend its own territory emphasized its weakness and cast the deepest kinds of doubts on the validity of the nonalignment posture as an instrument capable of protecting the basic national interest of self-preservation. In terms of building military strength in advance of an attack, India's foreign policy over the previous decade was proved to be an almost total failure only partially offset by the promises of future military aid from both the United States and the Soviet Union. Its natural ally for defense of the subcontinent, Pakistan, promptly took advantage of India's difficulties by pressing for a favorable Kashmir settlement. While failing in this, Pakistan at the same time saw the possibilities of exerting further pressure on India by negotiating a border agreement and an airlines accord with China and by seeking to hinder large-scale military aid from the United States to India. (These were rational moves by Pakistan to increase its power vis-à-vis India, once Pakistan had adopted the possibly mistaken premise that India, not China, was its long term opponent.)

Even without the dramatic illustration of India's weakness provided by the Chinese advance in October, 1962, a good case could be made that during the 1950's Indian leaders had become complacent about their country's power position. No vigorous new policies were being formulated to meet the rapid movement of China into a position of dominance in southern Asia; India appeared to be counting on the United States and the Soviet Union to provide the force necessary to contain Chinese ambitions. Although the Goa take-over signified a desire by India to enhance its power position, the action was crudely handled and was an illustration of the waning imagination and vitality of the Nehru government in foreign relations. A decade earlier Nehru spoke of the "inevitability" of India's leadership in Asia and perhaps in the world, because of its size and rich heritage. By the early 1960's the Indian government was no longer persisting in any endeavors to demonstrate its capacity to lead. It no longer assumed the leading role in meetings of the nonaligned countries; its position vis-à-vis the great powers was so stable and predictable that nonalignment no longer provoked an anxious wooing from both sides. It seemed resigned to a permanently hostile Pakistan, and, above all, it was unable to check the drift of Himalayan and southern Asian states into closer relations with China. Satisfied with its truly remarkable rise to importance at an earlier period and the concomitant benefits received from the United States and the Soviet Union, India seemed prepared to accept a permanent status of third rate power, even in its own sphere of geographic influence—a status granted it, so to speak, *in absentia* from the struggle for tangible strength.

India's striking inability to meet the threat of China alone and overcome the frustrations to its diplomacy and to its military strategy presented by Pakistan should not, however, be judged without regard to certain advantages that the nonalignment posture had produced. Nonalignment was never intended to compensate for a military policy, and it should not be evaluated in that perspective. But even in military terms it brought the distinct advantage of leaving open the possibility of assistance from both great powers against China—provided both sides sought simultaneously to hamper Chinese aims. Of greater importance, nonalignment provided and does still provide the reinforcement by the great powers of Indian economic and political objectives. India's military setbacks do not impress the American and Soviet governments, in whose eyes India is a third rate military power at best. Neither the United States nor the Soviet Union expects India to provide the military balance in Asia against China, at least for some time to come; that is a task that both sides have themselves apparently undertaken. India still obtains favored treatment and recognition of its importance by both great powers, and despite a tapering off of the bipolar struggle that situation is likely to continue. Finally, India's preoccupation with economic development during the fifties, in many ways made possible by its abjuration of the military build-up that alignment would have required, may well have placed that country in a better position in the long run to undertake its own defense than it would have acquired by injections of military aid from outside unsupported by broad-based domestic economic development.

In short, we cannot assert with certainty that on balance Indian foreign policy in the 1950's was proved unwise by the Chinese military and political successes in the autumn of 1962. The 1950's brought some striking successes and a number of profound setbacks, and India will for many years be experiencing the results of both. What should be clear, however, is that India's posture of the 1950's will require radical amendment to meet the conditions of the 1960's. Specifically, India will require the tangible varieties of power that countries other than those participating in the global ideological struggle will understand. Furthermore, it may conceivably be able to do this without sacrificing its favorable relations with both sides in the bipolar ideological struggle.

India is being challenged in the 1960's to contain the military power of China in at least one region and thus achieve a status of a major state within the "subordinate state system" of southern Asia. To accept this challenge would appear to mean that New Delhi reject openly and entirely the myth that nonalignment and the attendant veneration of peaceful coexistence is a posture which must determine its relations with *all* states. (Refusal to discuss the proposal of Ayub Khan of Pakistan, made in April, 1959, for a joint defense of the subcontinent was partly based on the conviction that any agreement would necessarily involve India in Pakistan's military alliances.) Already India has been forced into recognizing its predominantly military posture vis-à-vis China and is receiving outside military assistance. This new recognition could be expanded into a general policy of tangible power build-up aimed at the ultimate achievement of a military capability sufficient for defense of Indian interests in the Himalayas. If India does not achieve that position it may lose the independence that was the genesis of nonalignment and remain reliant on other states to defend its security interests. (The unique situation in which both the United States and the Soviet Union follow policies aimed at containing China may not persist, and in any case it is a risky premise on which to base Indian defense.)

In order to create the military and economic power requisite for its present obligations to check Chinese expansion, India not only needs aid from the industrial states but, equally, she needs trustworthy allies in

Asia and throughout the underdeveloped world. The Indian government may come to realize that the formation of alliances is not the prerogative of the great powers, and that participation in an anti-Chinese coalition in Asia might not compromise its nonalignment vis-à-vis the great powers. It may not be impossible (especially given the present hostility between the Soviet Union and China) for India to construct an alliance system of its own against China and still remain outside of the Western military arrangements in Asia. India's scorn for military blocs could be clearly understood to apply only to coalitions dominated by the United States or the Soviet Union.

Nonetheless, such a policy would require a radical shift in the thinking of the External Affairs Ministry. That policy would concentrate on winning support for India among those Asian states which already have adopted anti-Chinese positions, on reaching a military agreement with Pakistan for joint defense, and ultimately on assuring the neutrality, at the very least, of those states which refuse to align their policies with an anti-Chinese coalition. A plausible first step that pursuit of such a policy would require would be an attempt to reach certain understandings of a military and political nature with Japan, Formosa, the Philippines, Malaysia, Thailand, and South Vietnam—understandings which would not commit India to Western strategies but would define common interests of Asian states alone.

If India's own military power is more fully mobilized, and a policy of military and political alignment with states in Asia that also oppose Chinese encroachments on their independence is pursued, India could regain much lost prestige. Tangible power would replace the unconvincing posture of nonalignment as the basis for India's relations with Asian states, and it might be hoped that recognition of India's new position would influence the governments of Nepal, Burma, Cambodia, Indonesia, and Ceylon to adopt pro-Indian positions, or at least hinder any tendency on their parts to move into closer relations with China. There would be risks also in the adoption of such a policy. The most serious risk is the possibility of increased hostility from China and even a preemptive attack in the face of India's clear intentions to improve its military position. It could be argued, however, that this risk should be taken; otherwise Chinese ambitions in the Himalayas and in southern Asia may not be properly checked and India may ultimately be threatened with a hostile envelopment which would curtail or even terminate its independence. A second risk is that the involvement in an anti-Chinese coalition in Asia might compromise India's nonalignment posture vis-à-vis the great powers; such would certainly be the case if the Soviet Union and China resumed cordial relations. Every effort could be taken by India to maintain its nonalignment in the "dominant state system," so long as that posture provides it with power and benefits. But if the creation of new instruments of power to protect Indian interests in Asia should lead inevitably to a reduction in the power and attendant benefits derived from nonalignment, it can be argued that such a policy might nevertheless be followed, again on the grounds that security interests must dominate in any evaluation of national objectives.

Apart from these and other risks that a policy of military build-up and alliance would entail, domestic economic and political consequences would have to be faced. The effects of rapid increases in defense forces, with or without external assistance, on India's economic development would be great. Although it is true that economic progress would be hindered by popular uncertainties about the security of the nation, it is equally the case that a military build-up (which even now is causing cutbacks in development plans) cannot be carried forth on a weak industrial base. Politically, the encouragement of militancy in foreign policy would be likely to increase the influence of the Right wing parties in the country, which constitute threats to communal harmony and even to constitutional procedures. A further problem would arise from the nature of the responses that India might receive from Asian governments which it approached for discussions on security issues. Many of those governments are already aligned with the West and are possibly anxious not to acquire new obligations that could undermine their relations with the United States. The issue here would probably hinge on the reaction of the United States government to a realignment of Indian policy.

The scope of this essay does not permit a satisfactory analysis of any of these problems. The purpose here is merely to acknowledge their existence and to suggest nevertheless that fresh consideration may be given to India's foreign policies in the light of its present and future defense problems. The existing circumstances are probably as favorable as they are likely ever to be to India's intensive development of a major form of tangible national power. If the decision to do this and accept the necessary risks is not taken, that is, if India fails to develop strong support in Asia and is content with a gradual domestic military build-up, the major achievements of the nonalignment posture—and independent status in world politics—may be subverted.

CHAPTER 5

THE CHANGING UNITED NATIONS

HAROLD KARAN JACOBSON

The year 1960 not only marked the beginning of a new decade for the United Nations, but it was also a turning point in the U.N.'s development. Events occurred, or began, in that year that have had a significant impact on the organization, and as a consequence the United Nations of the 1960's is a considerably different institution from that of preceding periods.

I. THE EVENTS OF 1960

The first step in analyzing how the U.N. is different is to consider three events of 1960 and their significance. These events were: the swift expansion in the U.N.'s membership; the further evolution of Soviet strategy toward the organization; and the U.N.'s controversial and troublesome involvement in the Congo imbroglio.

Increased Membership

Seventeen new states became members of the United Nations in 1960. All but Cyprus were located in sub-Saharan Africa. This fundamentally altered the distribution of forces within the organization. To demonstrate this, the U.N.'s present membership can be divided into the following categories:

Africa-Asia: Afghanistan, Algeria, Burma, Burundi, Cambodia, Cameroon, Central African Republic, Ceylon, Chad, China, Congo (Brazzaville), Congo (Leopoldville), Cyprus, Dahomey,

---

HAROLD KARAN JACOBSON is associate professor of political science at the University of Michigan. He is the editor of *America's Foreign Policy* and the author of *The USSR and the UN's Economic and Social Activities.*

Ethiopia, Gabon, Ghana, Guinea, India, Indonesia, Iran, Iraq, Ivory Coast, Japan, Jordan, Kenya, Kuwait, Laos, Lebanon, Liberia, Libya, Madagascar, Malaysia, Mali, Mauritania, Mongolia, Morocco, Nepal, Niger, Nigeria, Pakistan, Philippines, Rwanda, Saudi Arabia, Senegal, Sierra Leone, Somalia, Sudan, Syria, Tanzania, Thailand, Togo, Tunisia, Uganda, United Arab Republic, Upper Volta, and Yemen.

Eastern Europe: Albania, Byelorussian S.S.R., Bulgaria, Czechoslovakia, Hungary, Poland, Romania, Ukrainian S.S.R., U.S.S.R., and Yugoslavia.

Latin America: Argentina, Bolivia, Brazil, Chile, Colombia, Costa Rica, Cuba, Dominican Republic, Ecuador, El Salvador, Guatemala, Haiti, Honduras, Jamaica, Mexico, Nicaragua, Panama, Paraguay, Peru, Trinidad and Tobago, Uruguay, and Venezuela.

West: Australia, Austria, Belgium, Canada, Denmark, Finland, France, Greece, Iceland, Ireland, Israel, Italy, Luxembourg, Netherlands, New Zealand, Norway, Portugal, South Africa, Spain, Sweden, Turkey, United Kingdom, and United States.

The first three groups, despite their obvious differences, also have certain similarities. They comprise what Vera Dean has termed the non-Western world. Admittedly, all of the categories are crude, but they do group states geographically and to a lesser extent culturally, and in most instances a state would have more characteristics in common with others within its category than with those in another. Moreover, the categories bear some resemblance to the major caucusing and voting groups within the United Nations,[1] and thus can be used to show certain gross relationships. To do this, these categories must be set against the pattern of the growth in the U.N.'s membership. In 1946, when the first session of the General Assembly opened, the U.N. had fifty-one member states. By 1950, the total membership had grown to sixty. After that year no additional states were admitted until 1955, when sixteen gained membership. Then came a period of relatively slow growth until the record year of 1960.

[1] See Thomas Hovet, Jr., *Bloc Voting in the United Nations* (Cambridge, Mass., 1960), and Thomas Hovet, Jr., *Africa in the United Nations* (Evanston, Ill., 1963).

How the balance of geographic and cultural forces within the United Nations has changed since 1945 can be seen in Table 1. The growth in

Table 1. Composition of the United Nations

	Africa-Asia	Eastern Europe	Latin America	Total non-West	West	Total Membership
1946	11 (22%)	6 (12%)	20 (39%)	37 (73%)	14 (27%)	51
1950	17 (28%)	6 (10%)	20 (33%)	43 (72%)	17 (28%)	60
1955	23 (30%)	10 (13%)	20 (26%)	53 (70%)	23 (30%)	76
1959	29 (35%)	10 (12%)	20 (24%)	59 (72%)	23 (28%)	82
1960	46 (46%)	10 (10%)	20 (20%)	76 (77%)	23 (23%)	99
1964	57 (51%)	10 (9%)	22 (20%)	89 (79%)	23 (21%)	112

the proportion of African and Asian states is the most striking phenomenon. They have increased from 22 per cent of the U.N.'s total membership in 1946 to 51 per cent in 1964. The declining relative significance of the Latin American states is almost as glaring. They have fallen from 39 per cent of the U.N.'s total membership to a mere 20 per cent. What is not as obvious, though, is that from 1946 through 1959 the relative strength of non-Western and Western states remained basically constant. Indeed, the Western states were in a stronger position by one percentage point at the close of the period than they were in the beginning. The real decline in the relative position of the Western states began in 1960. This is also true of the Eastern European states, the position of which had similarly been relatively constant prior to that point. This is much less important for several reasons, however, including the fact that of the four categories the Eastern European states have always comprised the smallest proportion of the U.N.'s total membership.

The increments to the organization's roster have not altered it so that at one point underdeveloped or non-Western states became the preponderant category for, as can be seen, this has always been the case. Nor is it true that smallness is a property found exclusively among the states which have joined the United Nations in recent years. The smallest U.N. member state, both in terms of area and population, is Luxembourg, a state which signed the Charter at San Francisco in 1945. Five of the original twenty Latin American states now have populations of less than two million, and a dozen, less than five million. Thus the real meaning of the expansion in the U.N.'s membership is to be found in the changing relationships among the various geographic, cultural, ideological and political groups.

These changes obviously have greatest significance in the General

Assembly, where each state has one vote and decisions require only a simple or two-thirds majority. Some of the effects of the changes can be seen in Tables 2 and 3. In both tables a two-thirds majority is calculated on the basis of the U.N.'s total membership. In actual practice, only those states voting for or against a resolution are counted in computing the necessary majority; states abstaining or absent are not counted. Therefore, in most instances the number of votes required to pass or block a resolution would be less than that shown in the two tables.

Table 2 shows how the task of mustering a majority in the Assembly has altered over the years. At the outset, the Western and Latin American states constituted a two-thirds majority by themselves. As the U.N.'s membership grew, it became necessary to add more and more African and Asian states to this basic combination. In these terms 1955 is

Table 2. Mustering a Two-Thirds Majority in
the General Assembly

Year	Total membership	Majority required	Combinations equaling a two-thirds majority	
1946	51	34	W + LA	or AA + EE + 17 (85%) LA
1950	60	40	W + LA + 3 (18%) AA	or AA + EE + 17 (85%) LA
1955	76	51	W + LA + 8 (35%) AA	or AA + EE + 18 (90%) LA
1959	82	55	W + LA + 12 (41%) AA	or AA + EE + 16 (80%) LA
1960	99	66	W + LA + 23 (50%) AA	or AA + EE + 10 (50%) LA
1964	112	75	W + LA + 30 (53%) AA	or AA + EE + 8 (36%) LA

AA—Africa-Asia   EE—Eastern Europe   LA—Latin America   W—West

probably a dividing point, for the task of winning over 35 per cent or more of the African and Asian states is certainly more difficult than that of convincing 20 per cent or less. Looking at the problem from a different perspective, from 1946 through 1959 a two-thirds majority could be constituted by combining the African and Asian and Eastern European states, and from 80 per cent to 90 per cent of the Latin American states. In 1960, if the African and Asian and Eastern European states voted together, only half of the Latin American states were needed in addition to constitute a two-thirds majority, and that proportion has declined since then. In sum, the task of mustering a majority became considerably more difficult for the West starting in 1955, and that for the African and Asian states, considerably easier, starting in 1960.

The ability to block the adoption of a resolution in the Assembly can often be as important as being able to muster a two-thirds majority. Table 3 portrays changing relationships with respect to this matter. In 1946 the Western states and 20 per cent of the Latin American states acting jointly could prevent the adoption of a resolution. A combination along these lines continued to hold a veto in the Assembly through 1959. In that year a combination of the Western and five Latin American states could exercise a blocking vote. The following year, however, the number of Latin American states needed in addition to the Western states increased to eleven, or from 25 per cent to 55 per cent of the Latin American group. Thus in 1960 the difficulty which the West faced in putting together a blocking vote increased sharply. The African and Asian states, on the other hand, have gone from a situation in which they had to work with all of the Eastern European states and one Latin American state to block the adoption of a resolution to one in which only two-thirds of the African and Asian group needs to act jointly. In this case the transformation has followed a somewhat more linear progression.

Table 3. Obtaining a Blocking Vote in the General Assembly

Year	Total membership	One-third plus one	Combinations equaling a blocking vote
1946	51	18	W + 4 (20%) LA or AA + EE + 1 (5%) LA
1950	60	21	W + 4 (20%) LA or AA + 4 (67%) EE
1955	76	26	W + 3 (15%) LA or AA + 3 (30%) EE
1959	82	28	W + 5 (25%) LA or 28 (97%) AA
1960	99	34	W + 11 (55%) LA or 34 (74%) AA
1964	112	38	W + 15 (68%) LA or 38 (67%) AA

AA—Africa-Asia   EE—Eastern Europe   LA—Latin America   W—West

In terms of these crude quantitative relationships the course of the U.N.'s development can be broken into three main periods. The first, lasting from 1946 through December 13, 1955, when sixteen states were admitted to membership, was one in which the Western and the Latin American states constituted the core and the largest portion of a two-thirds majority in the General Assembly. The second period lasted from December 14, 1955, until the opening of the fifteenth General Assembly in September, 1960. In this period the West had to appeal to ever increasing numbers of African and Asian states to muster a two-thirds majority. At the same time the West's ability to block Assembly action remained roughly equal to what it had been during the first period. The fifteenth Assembly inaugurated a new period—one in which the African and Asian states would find it significantly easier to muster a two-thirds majority, and the Western states much more difficult to obtain a blocking vote.

Whether or not any of these generalizations has validity, of course, depends upon the way in which states behave in the United Nations, not upon the numerical relationship of arbitrarily contrived categories. We shall turn to that later. For the moment, all that is important is to demonstrate the gross quantitative changes in the distribution of forces within the United Nations, and the importance of 1960 as a turning point.

Changing Soviet Strategy

It is not so easy to pin point the second element that contributed to making the United Nations of the 1960's a considerably different institution from that of the preceding periods. Soviet strategy toward the U.N., particularly its economic and social aspects, had been in the process of change since the early 1950's.[2] Some analysts have attributed this primarily to the changes in Soviet leadership resulting from the death of Stalin. Others have emphasized impersonal factors as well, such as the growing isolation of the Soviet Union within the U.N. during the late 1940's and early '50's and the changing relationships during the same period among the U.S.S.R., the West, and the underdeveloped countries. In any case, starting about in 1953 Soviet policy within the U.N. (as elsewhere) underwent a significant transformation. The U.S.S.R. joined specialized agencies which it had previously boycotted, for example, the International Labor Organization and the United Nations Educational, Scientific, Cultural Organization. It began to make voluntary financial contributions to the Expanded Program of Technical Assistance (E.P.T.A.) and the United Nations Children's Fund (UNICEF). Neither had previously received any Soviet funds, and both had at times been subjected to scathing attacks by the U.S.S.R. In December, 1953, the Soviet Union agreed to the creation of a new U.N. forum for disarmament negotiations, and in the subsequent talks it reversed its position and accepted several Western proposals that it had previously denounced.

In all U.N. organs the demeanor of the U.S.S.R. changed. Cooperativeness became the touchstone of Soviet actions. Where Soviet proposals previously would have had to be rejected time and again, the U.S.S.R.

---

[2] See Alexander Dallin, *The Soviet Union at the United Nations: An Inquiry into Soviet Motives and Objectives* (New York, 1962); Harold Karan Jacobson, *The USSR and the UN's Economic and Social Activities* (Notre Dame, Ind., 1963); and Alvin Z. Rubinstein, *The Soviets in International Organizations: Changing Policy Toward Developing Countries, 1953–1963* (Princeton, N.J., 1964).

came to be content with one defeat, often in a relatively unpublicized committee session. While in the past the rejection of its proposals would have led to Soviet opposition or abstention, the U.S.S.R. increasingly voted for resolutions "in the interest of unanimity," despite the defeat of its own proposals. Commentary within the U.S.S.R. dealing with the U.N. suddenly became much more favorable. By the end of 1955 it was clear that Soviet strategy, perhaps for the first time, explicitly aimed at exploiting the potential of the United Nations.

The new Soviet campaign placed principal emphasis on the issues of trade and development and disarmament. In addition, it stressed such themes as the detrimental effects of colonialism and the necessity of observing the principal of nonintervention in the internal affairs of states. Often Soviet verbal behavior differed only in tone from that of preceding years. The more important difference was that starting in 1953 the words of the U.S.S.R. came to be accompanied by concrete actions, which gave the former more substance and greater appeal.

Some observers saw opportunities in the new Soviet course for increased cooperation within the United Nations between Communist and non-Communist states. Others, however, believed that the U.S.S.R. had merely adopted more effective tactics for exploiting conflicts within the West and between the West and the developing nations. Whatever its motivation, by the end of 1959, the new Soviet policy could only claim limited achievements. The isolation of the U.S.S.R. within the U.N. had ended, but beyond that, there were few gains. Few Soviet proposals had been adopted, and the U.S.S.R. mostly joined, rather than mustered, majorities.

Apparently Soviet leaders expected that this situation would change with the demise of colonialism and the expansion of the United Nations membership. They obviously felt that 1960 would be a watershed in this respect because Soviet policies, which had been evolving since the early 1950's, underwent further changes then. As early as July, 1960, the U.S.S.R. announced that it would be willing to increase its contribution to the Expanded Program of Technical Assistance, and that fall, at the U.N.'s pledging conference, it pledged two million dollars to E.P.T.A. for 1961. This was twice the amount that it had contributed annually since its first contribution in 1954. The U.S.S.R. also increased its contribution to UNICEF at this time. Like that to E.P.T.A., the Soviet Union's first contribution of $500,000 made in 1955 had been repeated annually.

On July 31, 1960, the U.S.S.R. proposed that the flagging disarmament negotiations be discussed at the fifteenth session of the General

Assembly and that the U.N.'s member states should be represented by
their heads of government.[3] It soon became apparent that Khrushchev
was determined to act in this capacity in any event. Attending the General Assembly for a prolonged period as head of the Soviet delegation
would place his prestige at stake much more deeply and openly than had
been the case during his brief visit the year before. Obviously Khrushchev did not expect a hostile reception. On the contrary, he must have
expected that the Assembly—its ranks swelled with new states and new
members—would be a favorable arena for Soviet efforts. Whether or not
his expectation would prove correct is another matter. The present point
is to demonstrate the considerable evidence in 1960 of increased Soviet
interest in the United Nations.

The Congo Crisis

The third event in 1960 that had a profound impact on the United
Nations was the Congo crisis. When the Security Council voted early in
the morning of July 14, 1960, to authorize the Secretary General to
provide the government of the Republic of the Congo with military
assistance, it appeared on the surface that the United Nations was facing
a repetition of the Suez crisis of 1956, and that its actions could and
should follow the pattern established with relative success by the United
Nations Emergency Force. Assisting the Congo, it seemed, would
merely involve applying again Dag Hammarskjold's concept of preventive diplomacy. The U.N. would intervene in a situation in which the
super powers had not yet become engaged and would thereby forestall
their involvement. There would be no need for the U.N. troops to use
force except in self-defense. The U.N.'s effort would obviously have to
be on a larger scale than ever before, but beyond this few differences
were immediately foreseen. The affirmative votes of the U.S.S.R. and
the United States on the initial Security Council resolution overshadowed the abstentions of China, France, and the United Kingdom, and
seemed to augur well for the operation.

As the Congo crisis developed and as the U.N.'s involvement deep-
ened, many of these early surface appearances proved illusory. In
retrospect it is clear that the crisis was quite different from, and in
several respects more complicated than, any which the United Nations
had previously faced. There was, it was true, foreign intervention in the
form of the Belgian troops which had been dispatched in the wake of the
mutiny of the *Force publique*. In this sense the problem was similar to
that caused by the attack of Israel, France, and the United Kingdom

---

[3] United Nations, DC/158, Aug. 1, 1960.

against Egypt in 1956. However, unlike the earlier instance, there was an almost complete collapse of the administrative, economic, and governmental machinery within the Congo. In addition, two days before the Security Council met to consider the situation, Katanga, the Congo's richest province, declared its secession.

The lengthy and complicated details of the U.N.'s involvement in the Congo crisis have been amply covered elsewhere.[4] For present purposes we need only note that as early as mid-September, 1960, several facts about the U.N. involvement were already clear. First, it was obvious that the U.N.'s operation in the Congo was going to be much more expensive than any activity which the organization had previously undertaken. Secondly, it was apparent that the U.N. could not avoid becoming significantly involved in the internal affairs of the Congo, and that this would have serious implications both within the Congo and in world politics generally. Even at that point the Secretary General was estranged from Prime Minister Lumumba and at loggerheads with the U.S.S.R. and other states. Finally, questions were being raised concerning whether or not the U.N. could accomplish its purposes in the Congo without using force except in self-defense.

II. EMERGING PATTERNS IN THE UNITED NATIONS

The Fifteenth General Assembly

The forces generated by all three events converged at the fifteenth session of the General Assembly in the fall of 1960. The Assembly opened on September 20. That same day fourteen of the seventeen new states that joined the U.N. in 1960 were admitted to membership. On September 23, Khrushchev addressed the Assembly.[5]

His long and discursive speech touched on several of the events of the year as well as themes traditionally emphasized by Soviet delegates in the U.N. The subject which received the most attention in the latter category was disarmament, and following the course which he had set out the previous year, Chairman Khrushchev tabled a document embodying "Basic Provisions of a Treaty on General and Complete Dis-

[4] See chapter 9, also King Gordon, UN in the Congo: A Quest for Peace (New York, 1962); Arthur Lee Burns and Nina Heathcote, Peace-Keeping by U.N. Forces: From Suez to the Congo (New York, 1963); and Harold Karan Jacobson, "ONUC's Civilian Operations: State-Preserving and State-Building," World Politics, XVII, No. 1 (Oct., 1964), pp. 75–107.

[5] United Nations, General Assembly, Plenary Meetings, Official Records, 15th Sess., Part I, pp. 68–84.

armament." [6] In addition, Khrushchev's speech concentrated on two rather new elements. The first of these was an attack on the Secretary General's direction of the U.N.'s activities in the Congo, and a proposal that the executive authority of the United Nations should be reconstituted so that it would represent "the Western Powers, the socialist States, and the neutralist States." This was the noted troika proposal. The second new element in the speech was a lengthy attack on colonialism, which Khrushchev concluded by suggesting that the U.N. should spearhead the drive to abolish colonialism finally and forever. Specifically, he proposed that the United Nations should adopt a declaration on granting independence to colonial countries and peoples. [7]

The Soviet Union was obviously embittered by the fall of Lumumba, which was then in process, and the fact that Soviet ambitions in the Congo had been thwarted, at least partially through the activities of the U.N. At the same time, it apparently saw an opportunity in the changing composition of the United Nations to gain a new position within the organization. An attack against colonialism would be the chief vehicle for this campaign. Hopefully, the U.S.S.R.'s leadership, established on this issue, would enable it to achieve its purposes in other areas, and to mold the organization to its taste, including perhaps even reconstituting a principal organ, the office of the Secretary General.

When the fifteenth session of the General Assembly finally adjourned on April 21, 1961, the U.S.S.R. had made some progress toward its objectives, but had fallen far short of completely achieving them, and the record raised doubts that it ever could. The Assembly had adopted a resolution on the ending of colonialism, but not precisely the one which the U.S.S.R had suggested. While the Soviet Union's role was not as important in these, the Assembly had also adopted certain resolutions on economic matters which the U.S.S.R. had supported and several major Western states had opposed. On the other hand, the Assembly had failed to take any action on Soviet suggestions concerning disarmament. And while Khrushchev's troika proposal had never been put to vote, it had been rejected implicitly on several occasions. The most notable instance occurred on April 15, 1961, when the Assembly, by a vote of 83 to 11, with 5 abstentions, refused to delete the words, "by the Secretary General," from an operative paragraph authorizing further action in the Congo. [8] Despite the U.S.S.R.'s strong opposition, the Assembly had also adopted various resolutions concerning the financing of

---

[6] United Nations Document A/4505.

[7] United Nations Document A/4502 and Corr. 1.

[8] United Nations, General Assembly, Plenary Meetings, *Official Records,* 15th Sess., Part II, p. 325.

the   Congo, which among other things would
make   sory for all U.N. member states. In sum,
riding th   nial sentiment in the Assembly was a tactic
which wou   .R. only so far. It would not catapult it into a
position of ge   ip.

Nevertheless,   1 its entirety, the outcome at the fifteenth session of the Gener.   sembly was significantly different from that of
preceding sessions. The ingredients, including increased membership,
changed Soviet strategy, and an unprecedented crisis, were different
and consequently so were the results. New patterns were established
in the U.N. which have prevailed since then.

Anti-Colonialism

The most marked difference between activities of the United Nations
in the sixties and in the preceding years is in the realm of colonialism.
At the fifteenth session of the General Assembly, as an alternative to
Khrushchev's proposal, forty-three African and Asian delegations
offered their own draft resolution on the ending of colonialism.[9] In
some ways the African-Asian draft was even stronger than that sponsored by the U.S.S.R.; it was certainly broader. In introducing their
proposal, several of the sponsors of the African-Asian draft stated that
they felt that former colonized states should lead the movement for
decolonization, and that they did not want the issue to become involved
in, or appear to be an aspect of, the cold war. Eighty-nine states voted
for the African and Asian proposal and none voted against it; but nine
abstained, including Australia, Belgium, the Dominican Republic, France,
Portugal, Spain, the Union of South Africa, the United Kingdom, and
the United States.[10]

The preamble of the resolution, eventually numbered 1514 (XV),
expresses the belief ". . . that the process of liberation is irresistible
and irreversible and that, in order to avoid serious crises, an end must
be put to colonialism and all practices of segregation and discrimination
associated therewith." The call to battle could hardly be clearer. The
linking of racial discrimination with colonialism was obviously aimed at
South Africa and its apartheid policies. In the operative part of the
resolution the "subjection of peoples to alien subjugation, domination

[9] United Nations Document A/L. 323 and add. 1–6.
[10] According to one member of the American delegation, the United States vote
"was the direct result of pressure by the United Kingdom," and, "President Eisenhower himself made the decision to abstain." (Wayne Morse, *The United States in
the United Nations: 1960—A Turning Point, Supplementary Report to the Committee on Foreign Relations* [Washington, D. C., 1961], p. 20.)

and exploitation," was declared to constitute "a denial of human rights," to be "contrary to the Charter of the United Nations," and to be "an impediment to the promotion of world peace and co-operation." Another paragraph proclaimed the right of self-determination for all peoples, and included within it the right of peoples to determine their own course with respect to their cultural, economic, political, and social development. Even though the resolution was adopted in December, 1960, when the chaos in the Congo was painfully visible, a third operative paragraph asserted that "inadequacy of political, economic, social or educational preparedness should never serve as a pretext for delaying independence." Other operative paragraphs called for the cessation of armed action against dependent peoples, urged that immediate steps should be taken to transfer all powers to the peoples of territories that had not yet attained independence, and enjoined against attempts to disrupt the national unity or territorial integrity of countries. Obviously the last injunction was framed with the Katanga problem in mind.

The head of Ghana's permanent mission to the United Nations, Ambassador Alex Quaison-Sackey, has written that there is no doubt in his mind that General Assembly Resolution 1514 (XV) "is as important to Africa as the Charter of the United Nations and the Universal Declaration of Human Rights." [11] Although many might not go this far, no one can doubt that the adoption of resolution 1514 (XV) marked a new era in the United Nations. It set the tone for the U.N.'s activities with respect to colonialism in the 1960's. For example, in 1959 it had proved impossible to muster the necessary two-thirds majority to secure the adoption of a resolution urging *"pourparlers"* among the parties to the Algerian dispute to determine the conditions necessary for exercising the right of self-determination, a principle that both sides had publicly accepted. In 1960 the Assembly adopted, by a vote of 63 to 8, with 27 abstentions, a resolution recognizing "the right of the Algerian people to self-determination and *independence"* (my italics).

In 1961, at its sixteenth session, the General Assembly voted, 97 to 0, with 4 abstentions (France, South Africa, Spain, and the United Kingdom), to establish a special committee to check on the implementation of Resolution 1514 (XV). Again the resolution that was adopted was one submitted by several African and Asian states as an alternative to one proposed by the U.S.S.R. And again the Assembly refused to accept the Soviet proposal that an immediate time limit should be set for the final termination of colonialism.

Since its establishment, the Special Committee on the Situation with

<hr>

[11] Alex Quaison-Sackey, *Africa Unbound: Reflections of an African Statesman* (New York, 1963), p. 139.

Regard to the Implementation of the Declaration on the Granting of Independence to Colonial Countries and Peoples has replaced the pallid Committee on Information from Non-Self-Governing Territories, and it has been given and has assumed powers, involving the right to receive petitions and visit areas, hitherto reserved to the Trusteeship Council.

The committee has begun a far-reaching examination of every remaining dependent territory. In each case, at the conclusion of its consideration, it has recommended a resolution for adoption by the General Assembly. The Assembly has adopted all of these, except those which had been made obsolete by changed conditions. So far these resolutions have been hortatory in nature. Nonetheless, of the eleven such resolutions adopted at the seventeenth and eighteenth sessions of the Assembly, only three were adopted unanimously. Several of the major Western states voted against three of the resolutions and abstained on the remaining five.

In the U.N.'s anti-colonial drive, Southern Rhodesia, the Portuguese territories, and South Africa have been singled out for special attention. In the last two instances the Assembly has attempted to go beyond hortatory actions. In 1962, at the seventeenth session of the Assembly, it voted to request member states to impose an arms embargo against Portugal and limited sanctions against South Africa.[12] It did this despite the opposition of the major Western states, whose compliance would be necessary for the measures to be effective. Thus far the resolutions appear to have had little effect.

There can be no question that the African and Asian states will continue to make maximum use of the United Nations in their campaign against colonialism. Indeed, many of them see this as the organization's primary purpose.[13]

Economic Issues

Although the change in the nature of the U.N.'s activities with respect to economic issues is not marked, it is still significant. Perhaps it can be seen most clearly in two areas. The first concerns the financing of economic development, the second, international trade policy.

In the early 1950's a movement began to establish within the framework of the United Nations itself a fund which would make grants or long term loans at low rates of interest for purposes of economic devel-

[12] United Nations, General Assembly Resolutions 1819 (XVII) and 1761 (XVII).
[13] For a clear statement of this position see Ali A. Mazrui, "The United Nations and Some African Political Attitudes," *International Organization*, XVIII, No. 3 (Summer, 1964), 499–520.

opment.[14] The original scheme was to create a Special United Nations Fund for Economic Development (SUNFED). After 1957, this title was dropped, but the concept remained the same. The reason that the underdeveloped states sought to establish SUNFED within the framework of the United Nations, rather than that of a specialized agency such as the International Bank for Reconstruction and Development, is that they wished to avoid the decision making structure of the latter, in which votes are allocated on the basis of financial contributions and where consequently the Western powers have predominant influence.

The United States, the United Kingdom, and several other Western countries have consistently opposed the creation of SUNFED or any similar institution. However, over the years the Western powers have taken several steps which have had the effect of making more financial assistance available to the underdeveloped countries and some of it on easier terms. For instance, they sponsored the creation of the International Development Association (I.D.A.) which makes so-called soft loans. I.D.A. was established, however, as an affiliate of the International Bank, and the same decision making structure applies. In this situation, until 1960, the General Assembly annually ultimately deferred to the Western opposition.

In 1960, in contrast, the General Assembly decided "in principle that a United Nations Capital Development Fund shall be established." [15] The vote was 71 to 4, with 10 abstentions. Australia, South Africa, the United Kingdom, and the United States voted against the resolution. Belgium, Canada, France, Japan, New Zealand, and Sweden, all important potential contributors, abstained. Although the U.S.S.R. and other Communist countries voted for the resolution, it was clear that the bulk of their contribution to a Capital Development Fund would be in nonconvertible currencies, as it had been to the Expanded Program of Technical Assistance. If the E.P.T.A. experience were a precedent, there would be difficulties concerning the utilization of such contributions.[16] Since 1960, the Assembly has continued to adopt resolutions on a United Nations Capital Development Fund, but it has been unable to make real progress, because of the continued opposition of the major Western states.

The second area where the difference in the nature of the U.N.'s activities is notable concerns international trade policy. As a part of the

[14] John G. Hadwen and Johan Kaufman provide an excellent account of the negotiations on this issue through 1960 in their book *How United Nations Decisions Are Made* (Leyden, The Netherlands, 1962).

[15] United Nations, General Assembly Resolution 1521 (XV).

[16] See Jacobson, *The USSR and the UN's Economic and Social Activities,* pp. 239–44.

changes in its policies toward the U.N. in the mid-1950's, the U.S.S.R. began to press for a number of things concerning international economic relationships. Specifically, it sought to have the U.N. (1) prepare a declaration on the principles which should govern international economic intercourse, (2) convene a world conference on trade, and (3) create a new international organization in this field. Several of the Western states tended to view these proposals as being principally subtle attacks on their programs of controlling trade with Communist countries. Until 1960 all of the Soviet proposals were rebuffed.

With the change in the composition of the United Nations, however, these proposals found a more favorable reception. A Draft Declaration on International Economic Cooperation which the U.S.S.R. submitted to the fifteenth session of the General Assembly,[17] was referred to the Economic and Social Council (ECOSOC) for its consideration. In 1961 ECOSOC decided to solicit the views of governments on the issue, and the following year, after some prodding by the General Assembly, it appointed an *ad hoc* committee "to prepare a formulation on this subject." [18] As of mid-1964, the *ad hoc* committee was still at work and the outcome was not clear. Early indications were, however, that the controversies in the committee were more between developed and underdeveloped countries than between the East and West, and that it was the underdeveloped rather than the Communist countries that would succeed in using the declaration as a vehicle for achieving their purposes.

In August, 1962, at its thirty-fourth session, the Economic and Social Council decided to convene a United Nations Conference on Trade and Development (U.N.C.T.A.D.). In this action, the Council finally acceded to a long-standing Soviet objective. As recently as May, 1962, Khrushchev had vigorously renewed the Soviet call for a world trade conference. However, the resolution which the Council adopted was based on a draft proposed by Brazil, Ethiopia, India, Senegal, and Yugoslavia. Moreover, the action was more in response to the endorsement of the idea of such a gathering by the Cairo Conference on the Problems of Economic Development, which was held in July, 1962, and attended by states from Africa, Asia, and Latin America, than it was to Khrushchev's call two months earlier.

During the United Nations Conference on Trade and Development, which was held from March through June, 1964, the U.S.S.R. continued to press for its long-standing goals. The dominant feature of the conference, however, was the unity of the seventy-seven self-styled "develop-

[17] United Nations Document A/C. 2/L. 466.
[18] United Nations, ECOSOC Resolution 875 (XXXIII).

ing countries." They clearly controlled the proceedings, and the Final Act represented their concepts, with relatively few concessions to other points of view.[19]

The fact that the Soviet Union usually voted with the majority could not obscure the equally important fact that it was not able to lead this majority. Indeed, there was a tendency among the developing countries to classify the U.S.S.R. with the principal states of the West, as the developed or rich countries. This tendency caused Soviet polemicists considerable alarm, and they went to some lengths to argue that the Soviet Union's relationship with the underdeveloped countries was not marred by a past record of colonial domination and thus its aid was "friendly help," not repayment of a debt incurred through past exploitation.[20]

The Soviet Union's difficulties, though, were small comfort to the West, and particularly to the United States. Of the fifteen General Principles adopted by the conference, the United States voted against nine, and of the twelve Special Principles, it voted against four. The United States abstained on two of the remaining General Principles, and on five of the remaining Special Principles.

U.N.C.T.A.D. called for a number of additional studies. Beyond this its recommendations were largely exhortations concerning international and national economic policies. In addition, it recommended that the General Assembly consider the establishment of a specialized agency for industrial development. It also recommended that the United Nations Conference on Trade and Development should be established as a permanent organ of the Assembly, and that it should meet at intervals of not less than three years. Although unanimity was eventually achieved on this recommendation, it went farther than the Western powers desired in terms of creating a new international institution in the field of international trade, but at the same time not as far as the Soviet Union wished.

Political and Security Matters

The activities of the United Nations with respect to political and security matters have always been and continue to be considerably broader and more diverse than those in other areas. They range from resolutions by U.N. organs, through the mediatory efforts of the Secretary General, to the deployment of observer teams and military forces in

---

[19] See United Nations Document E/Conf. 46/L. 28.
[20] See S. Mikoyan, "Economic Forum in Geneva," *International Affairs* (Moscow), X, No. 5 (May, 1964), pp. 46–50.

troubled areas. For this reason alone, it is more difficult to ascertain and characterize the changes in this area.

In some respects, resolutions by U.N. organs on political and security matters have been marked by increasing militancy. This is especially true of those which have concerned nuclear weapons. The majority of the states of Africa, Asia, and Latin America have always been very sensitive about nuclear weapons. For them, nuclear weapons have been an all too evident symbol of the overwhelming strength of the super-powers. Moreover, they know that the effects of nuclear war would not be confined to the states directly involved. Similarly, fallout caused by testing nuclear weapons has spread throughout the world. Because of this, many of the states of Africa, Asia, and Latin America have felt that the super-powers have shown a flagrant disregard for the sovereign rights of other states in their testing programs. Since 1960, Assembly resolutions urging a cessation of testing, with or without a test ban treaty, have become more fôrceful. At various times, depending on the situation at the moment, both East and West, sometimes singly and sometimes together, have been the target of such resolutions. On balance, the West appears to have been in the better position. The United States voted for four of the seven resolutions which the Assembly adopted on this subject during its fifteenth, sixteenth, and seventeenth sessions (that is, prior to the signature of the partial test ban treaty in Moscow in August, 1963), opposed one, and abstained from voting on the other two.[21] In contrast, the U.S.S.R. voted for only two of these resolutions, both of which were adopted in 1960, opposed four, and abstained from voting on one.

On the other hand, despite the strong opposition of the United States and other Western powers, in 1961 the Assembly voted to declare that, "The use of nuclear and thermo-nuclear weapons is contrary to the spirit, letter and aims of the United Nations and, as such, a direct violation of the Charter of the United Nations." [22] The proposal was sponsored by Ceylon, Indonesia, and ten African states. It was adopted by a vote of 55 to 20, with 26 abstentions. The U.S.S.R. and the other Communist states voted for the resolution. It was in accord with the long-standing Soviet cry to ban the bomb, though perhaps not with the U.S.S.R.'s current military strategy. Since 1961, again despite the opposition of the principal Western states, the Assembly has continued to promote the convocation of a conference which would have as its purpose the signing of a convention prohibiting the use of nuclear and

---

[21] United Nations, General Assembly Resolutions: 1577 (XV); 1578 (XV); 1632 (XVI); 1648 (XVI); 1649 (XVI); 1762 A (XVII); and 1762 B (XVII).

[22] United Nations, General Assembly Resolution 1653 (XV).

thermonuclear weapons, a proposal introduced in the first resolution which the Assembly adopted on this subject.[23]

Even at the fifteenth session of the General Assembly it was evident that the Soviet attack on the office of the Secretary General would fail. As if to acknowledge this, in the fall of 1961 instead of exploiting the opportunity provided by the death of Dag Hammarskjold to press its troika proposal, the U.S.S.R. acquiesced in the appointment of U Thant as Acting Secretary General, and the following year it agreed that he should have a four-year term in his own right.

Not only has the office of the Secretary General been preserved intact; the mediatory functions performed by the Secretary General have declined little if at all from the peak achieved during Hammarskjold's tenure. During the Cuban missile crisis of 1962 both the United States and the U.S.S.R. welcomed the services of U Thant, and he has performed useful roles in several lesser confrontations. The need for a relatively impartial authority in today's divided world has not disappeared, and all U.N. member states appear to have recognized, explicitly or implicitly, that on certain occasions the Secretary General can easily and usefully perform such a role. Whatever else happens in the U.N., this is unlikely to change.

Formally, the Soviet Union's attack against the U.N.'s peacekeeping activities also appears to have been rebuffed. The International Court of Justice (I.C.J.) has given its opinion that the expenses incurred through the U.N.'s operations in the Middle East and the Congo are "expenses of the Organization" within the meaning of paragraph 2 of Article 17 of the Charter, and thus in its view member states must pay their obligations or, under the terms of Article 19, jeopardize their vote in the General Assembly. At its seventeenth session, the Assembly voted 75 to 17, with 14 abstentions, to accept this opinion.[24] The I.C.J. opinion and the Assembly resolution represented a clear and sharp rejection of the Soviet contention that Assembly assessments for such activities were not obligatory. The fact that in 1963–64 the United Nations engaged in peacekeeping operations in the Middle East, the Congo, Cyprus, West Irian, and Yemen—a record number—also seemed to indicate that the organization's capability in this respect had not been impaired.

However, surface signs can be deceptive. It was less than certain that the sanction envisaged under Article 19, loss of voting privileges in the General Assembly, would actually be imposed against those states such as the Soviet Union and France that refused to contribute to the U.N.'s

---

[23] See United Nations, General Assembly Resolutions 1801 (XVII) and 1909 (XVIII).

[24] United Nations, General Assembly Resolution 1854 A (XVIII).

peacekeeping operations. Moreover, the U.N.'s operations in Yemen, West Irian, and Cyprus were financed by *ad hoc* arrangements that did not involve obligatory assessments on all U.N. member states. It is therefore conceivable that the principle of obligatory contributions to peacekeeping activities by the U.N. may be won on the condition that it never be applied again.

It is perhaps also significant that when military forces mutinied in East Africa in early 1964, the countries involved chose first to call on the former metropole and then on the Organization of African Unity for assistance, rather than the United Nations. The leaders of Tanganyika, Kenya, and Uganda all saw the U.N.'s operations in the Congo as providing significant opportunities for external interference in the internal affairs of that state. Moreover, they were all impressed with the difficulty that the U.N. had in deciding to authorize its agents in the Congo to employ military force for purposes other than self-defense and were impatient with the time that it took to execute this decision. It was November, 1961, before such a decision was actually taken, and the winter of 1962–63 before the secession of Katanga was effectively ended. In their own crises in 1964, the East African states preferred to deal first with a known quantity, the British, and then with a smaller organization, the Organization of African Unity, in which their own role and voice were larger.

Finally, the fact that the United Nations Yemen Observer Mission was withdrawn in September, 1964, without having accomplished its mission of overseeing the fulfillment of a disengagement agreement between Saudi Arabia and the United Arab Republic might be just as significant as its establishment. Nor was the U.N. force in Cyprus making rapid progress toward the accomplishment of its pacification objectives. In sum, there were reasons for arguing that the U.N.'s peacekeeping activities would be curtailed, as well as for arguing that they would be expanded.

III. FUTURE PATTERNS: AN EXTENSION OF THE PRESENT OR A RETURN TO AN UNFULFILLED PAST?

Ernst B. Haas has observed that the phase of the United Nations' history that began in 1955 was earmarked by an interregional and interfunctional balancing process in which increasing economic assistance and support for decolonization efforts were demanded in return for support on questions relating to political and security issues.[25] Until 1960 conditions within the General Assembly, which had become the U.N.'s most prominent organ, facilitated this process. In highly over-simplified terms, the Latin American states were the key to the creation of any two-thirds majority in the Assembly, and they served as a con-necting link between the African and Asian states on the one side and the Western states on the other. The subjects of prime concern to the African and Asian states were economic development and decoloniza-tion, while the Western states were much more concerned with political and security issues. For a variety of reasons, the Latin American states were interested in all three substantive areas. In practice neither the African and Asian states nor the Western states could achieve their objectives in the United Nations without the collaboration of most Latin American states and some members of the other group. To obtain the necessary two-thirds majority, trade-offs among the three substantive areas had to be made and demands had to be moderated.

The role of the Soviet Union and other Communist states in this balancing process was minimal. They were often the explicit or implicit object of the U.N.'s political and security actions. Although they would vote with the African and Asian states on colonial and economic issues, since they neither had colonies nor were willing or able to become the chief contributors to the U.N.'s development programs and since their votes would not guarantee a two-thirds majority, this support was not vitally significant in the politics of the Assembly.

Starting in 1960 the conditions which facilitated the interregional and interfunctional balancing process began to change. The same groups existed and their objectives were basically the same, though as cold war tensions subsided, Western political and security needs became less pressing. What changed was the numerical strength of the African and Asian states and the position of the Communist countries. In the Assem-bly, the African and Asian states became less dependent on the Latin American states for the constitution of two-thirds majorities. In this context Communist support became more important to the African and Asian states, because with it little more was needed. This occurred at the same time that Soviet policy within the United Nations became more active. On the other hand, the Western states continued to have physical possession of the colonies and to be the most important financial con-tributors to the U.N.'s development and peacekeeping activities. They held the keys to action. The result has been that in several areas a

---

[25] "Dynamic Environment and Static System: Revolutionary Regimes in the United Nations," in *The Revolution in World Politics,* ed. Morton A. Kaplan (New York, 1962), p. 295.

significant gap has developed between the U.N.'s declaratory and its operational activities. The demands expressed in the U.N.'s hortatory resolutions, especially those concerning decolonization and development, have risen sharply, but the U.N.'s operational activities have not kept pace.

This is not to say that the interregional and interfunctional balancing process no longer operates, for it obviously does. The Western powers have continued to make concessions on decolonization and development, and some of the African and Asian states have continued to support the West on political and security issues. A crucial difference, however, is that Assembly resolutions dealing with decolonization and development are now more often instruments in the struggle rather than expressions of the outcome. And the operation of the balancing process has become much less smooth.

The fact that the United States, the most important single source of financial support for the United Nations, has not generally felt that its own interests were threatened by the U.N.'s activities with respect to decolonization, has been a vital factor in the continued operation of the interregional and interfunctional balancing process. Indeed, the United States has felt that its own interests would be served by the peaceful and orderly liquidation of colonialism and that the U.N.'s activities facilitated attaining this objective. Often the United States' reluctance concerning the U.N.'s activities with respect to colonial issues has been more a concession to allied unity than an expression of disapproval. It is the willingness of the United States to go along with the African and Asian states that has kept the gap between the U.N.'s declaratory and operational activities concerning decolonization from growing even larger than it is.[26] Many of the Western European metropolitan countries obviously do not share the American view in these matters. On the other hand, several of them have been more sympathetic than the United States to the demands of the African and Asian states concerning development. Here as elsewhere, though, the United States holds the most important purse strings.

What the future will bring is difficult to foretell. Dean Rusk has obliquely predicted that the old balancing process would be restored. In the Dag Hammarskjold Memorial Lecture on January 10, 1964, he said that he was convinced that all, or most, of the smaller members of the U.N. know:

[26] Conor Cruise O'Brien has gone even further and has argued that all U.N. action depends on mobilizing a coalition consisting of the United States and some African and Asian states. See *Conflicting Concepts of the United Nations* (Leeds, Eng., 1964), pp. 4–7.

"—that the U.N. can be effective only if it has the backing of those who have the means to make it effective;

"—that the U.N. is made less, not more, effective by ritualistic passage of symbolic resolutions with no practical influence on the real world." [27] Presumably his remarks would imply either a shifting of power from the Assembly to smaller organs such as the Economic and Social Council and the Security Council, where Western influence was greater, or the exercise by the African and Asian states of voluntary restraint in pressing their voting strength in the Assembly. Both contingencies are possible. However, if African and Asian states view the United Nations as a means of redressing the distribution of physical power,[28] it is also plausible that the present situation could continue, and for the immediate future it probably will. As an instrument for hortatory activities, the United Nations is without parallel in the contemporary international system. U.N. resolutions can count on receiving a favorable hearing by at least some segments in most of the Western countries. They are thus an effective means for bringing pressure to bear on governments. One result of continued use of the U.N. in this manner might be that its peacekeeping functions would atrophy, for lack of Western support, but the African and Asian states might not consider this a significant cost.

Soviet behavior is also an important variable in predicting the future in the United Nations. As long as colonialism remains an issue, it seems unlikely that the U.S.S.R. would forego the opportunity that the U.N. provides for embarrassing and twitting the Western metropolitan countries. On the contrary the U.S.S.R. will most likely continue to fan the flames of anti-colonialism within the U.N. However, colonialism will eventually pass, though perhaps not as rapidly as some have speculated that it would. If development then became the dominant issue in the U.N., the U.S.S.R. conceivably could find itself linked with the principal states of the West in a rich state-poor state division. If the present East-West détente and the Sino-Soviet dispute continue, the Soviet Union might well decide that its best option within the U.N. was collaboration with the principal Western states. Obviously the latter would have to foreswear using the U.N. against Soviet wishes and interests, but they might feel that this was no longer necessary or possible. Or they might feel that the sacrifice was a price worth paying to gain an ally in North-South controversies. It is conceivable that when colonialism ends, the United States attitude toward the United Nations might also change. In

[27] "The First Twenty-Five Years of the United Nations—From San Francisco to the 1970's," *The Department of State Bulletin*, L, No. 1283 (Jan. 27, 1964), 112–19.

[28] Some of them clearly take this view; see Mazrui, "The United Nations and Some African Political Attitudes," pp. 511–13.

such circumstances the U.N. might operate on the basis of great power supremacy as was planned in 1945. The U.S.S.R. has already hinted at such a possibility.[29]

Many scholars and statesmen have noted that in the first fifteen years of the United Nations the principal problem was that of discovering and developing techniques so that the organization could function in the absence of great power unanimity. There can be no question that in its second fifteen years the U.N.'s principal problem will be that of adjusting to the numerical dominance of African and Asian states. It would indeed be ironic if in the process and as a result, great power unanimity within the U.N. were restored.

[29] See the "Memorandum of the Government of the USSR regarding certain measures to strengthen the effectiveness of the United Nations in the safeguarding of international peace and security," United Nations Document S/5811.

PART II

The Instrumentalities of Foreign Policy

CHAPTER 6

THE FOREIGN AID INSTRUMENT:
SEARCH FOR REALITY

LUCIAN W. PYE

Neither defenders nor critics of foreign aid have been anxious to settle for the realities inherent in this novel addition to foreign affairs.[1] Idealistic champions of the program have never emotionally accepted the idea that foreign aid is merely another instrument in America's foreign policy arsenal, and in trying to deny the policy restraints on aid they have wishfully hoped for a world in which vigorous attacks on economic stagnation and backwardness might in themselves solve most of the vexing and frightening problems of contemporary international politics. The enemies of foreign aid have been equally energetic in describing another artificial world in which all efforts at aid have been futile and even self-defeating, and in which all programs are staffed with rogues, nincompoops, and spendthrifts.

With the protagonists committed to such extreme views, public debate on our foreign aid program has been singularly unenlightened. This instrument of foreign policy, which was uniquely the product of the American imagination, has been buffeted about by the most volatile of our moods about foreign relations. Realistic reasoning and refined policy calculations, the accepted guides for all the other tools of foreign

---

LUCIAN W. PYE is professor of political science and senior staff member of the Center for International Studies at the Massachusetts Institute of Technology. He is the author of *Guerrilla Communism in Malaya* and *Politics, Personality, and Nation Building;* co-author of *The Politics of the Developing Areas* and *The Emerging Nations;* and editor of *Communications and Political Development.*

[1] This chapter relies heavily on two of my articles, "Soviet and American Styles in Foreign Aid," *Orbis* (the quarterly journal of world affairs, published by the Foreign Policy Research Institute of the University of Pennsylvania), IV, No. 2 (Summer, 1960), 159–73; and "The Political Impulses and Fantasies Behind Foreign Aid," *Proceedings of the Academy of Political Science,* XXVII, No. 2 (Jan., 1962) (published by Columbia University, New York). The publishers have granted permission to include these materials here.

policy, tend to be obscured in foreign aid by the scope given to fantasy and emotions.

Economic aid and technical assistance are essentially American innovations in the realm of foreign affairs. In the classical nation-state system, allies did on occasion assist each other with credits, and wealthier states frequently used economic means to influence poorer and weaker nations. Foreign aid in the modern sense, however, is clearly the product of American decisions. Indeed, some might say that foreign aid reflects accurately the peculiar genius of the American people, for it combines an opportunity for expressing idealism and generosity with an eminently practical device for advancing our enlightened self-interest. Be this as it may, the fact remains that during the immediate post-war period we had a monopoly in this field that was only slightly less complete than our monopoly of atomic weapons.

American inventiveness in conceiving foreign aid has not been matched by an American political process capable of giving its creation positive and sustained support. Indeed, foreign aid seems uniquely able to expose our most vulnerable weakness in conducting foreign affairs, our inability at times to coordinate our division of powers. Annually the foreign aid program triggers such a clash between Congress and the administration that at times Washington seems to forget who our real enemies are. Much has been made over the idea that foreign aid has no "constituencies," but this is not entirely true. Others have suggested that the inevitable tension arises from the fact that Congress is closer to the American people while the administration must be more sensitive to foreign opinion and foreign developments. But independent measurements of American opinion, particularly the Gallup Poll, show that foreign aid is not particularly unpopular. On the other hand, there is evidence that foreign opinion, at least in some countries, does not unanimously approve of American aid.

Others have suggested that in American politics foreign aid has become the hapless victim of the legislature's frustration over not having a larger voice in the making and implementing of foreign policy. The power of the purse strings, of course, makes foreign aid peculiarly vulnerable to the moods and sentiments of Congress. But this is equally true of most of the other arms of government and hardly explains the peculiarly intense feelings Congress frequently displays toward foreign aid. Although it is easy to discern particular lawmakers who seem to have a personal distrust of foreign aid, it would grossly exaggerate their power to suggest that their idiosyncratic feelings can sway all of Congress. Clearly there are deeper reasons for the difficulties of foreign aid in American politics.

It is not our purpose here to examine the basis of congressional feelings about foreign aid. It is sufficient to say that much of the difficulty is that congressmen, like both citizen and administrative official, must rely heavily upon subjective considerations because of the impossibilities of determining objectively the prospects of underdeveloped societies. The truth is that we do not have sound knowledge as to the precise nature of social, economic, and political development. As a nation we do not know how to explain to the world why some countries are rich and powerful and others are poor and backward. Instead of being guided by tested theories in explaining the nature of underdeveloped countries, we have had to depend upon a strange and unaccountable mixture of faith and hope, hunch and prejudice, charity and goodwill, and questionable extrapolations from our knowledge of domestic American politics.

I. SOURCES OF AMERICAN SENTIMENTS ABOUT FOREIGN AID

In the last few years, through the work of the mass media and of the advocates of a greatly expanded foreign aid program, we have built up an American image of the underdeveloped areas. We have ascribed to them many common qualities, some of which are grounded more in our own preconceptions and fantasies than in reality. This generalized picture reflects such basic American predispositions as our belief that the physically weak, particularly if they are being courted by the strong, should represent morality. We expect even societies which are undergoing profound and confusing change—which have lost their traditional moral standards and can only opportunistically grope for new standards—to become somehow a moral force in international politics.

Another element of our official illusion is the belief that the underdeveloped countries are enthusiastically committed to rapid and thoroughgoing economic and political change. Americans have been the ones who talk most about the "revolution of rising expectations" and the need to accomplish in "one generation what the West took centuries to do." We are the ones who will not admit publicly that the great problem in many underdeveloped countries has really been an appalling apathy, which at times explodes in the form of undisciplined and blindly aggressive emotionalism only to subside back into public purposelessness.

Increasingly, in recent years, Americans have tended to recognize that perhaps we have been using somewhat distorted and romanticized pictures of the newly emergent countries. Nevertheless, instead of seeking to alter our general approach, we seem merely to have fallen into the cynical and unhealthy practice of employing different images in different connections. We continue to use the old one in public discussions; a far less complimentary image, however, is the basis of much of our private and unprinted discussion. Indeed, it seems almost as if we compensate for our unwillingness to call a spade a spade in public by adding bitter and emotionally aggressive overtones to our private characterization of the underdeveloped areas. Disillusionment and frustration can lead to the belief that change is impossible, that some peoples are hopelessly doomed to their present circumstances, and that the effort to transform chaotic societies into modern nations is beyond the power of our resources. The basic American spirit of optimism, however, prevents this gloomy view from becoming our national outlook. Instead, disillusionment has tended only to increase criticisms of our own foreign aid efforts. The result is not necessarily a greater sense of reality about transitional societies.

There are many reasons for our conflicting and unstable sentiments about foreign aid. By surveying the emotional associations and historic antecedents of foreign aid we can gain a better appreciation of why it has been so difficult to achieve a straightforward and complete commitment to this new instrument of foreign policy. Even a brief summary of the roots of our unstable and ambivalent feelings about relations with underdeveloped countries may help explain some of our problems in designing strategies and tactics for the rational utilization of this particular instrument of national policy.

The Missionary Tradition and Doctrines of Cultural Relativism

American sentiments about foreign aid seem to be heavily influenced by two somewhat conflicting traditions: that of the missionary endeavor and the spirit of helping less fortunate peoples, and that of cultural relativism and the need to respect the values of others. Not only in the American public mind do there seem to be elements of continuity between foreign aid and the earlier missionary movement. A close observation of American aid missions at work reveals a remarkable continuation of traditions: the emphasis upon techniques; the friendly, open, and yet brusquely down-to-earth approach; the desire for team work; the urge to be self-liquidating in favor of a native leadership; and the belief that doctrine and ideology can best be served by not relating them too directly to practical matters of technical assistance—these are all characteristics common to the missionary movement of the late nineteen-thirties and our foreign aid missions of the late forties and fifties.

Thus we still find in our thinking about foreign aid the belief that enthusiasm is to be valued and, indeed, that the contagious nature of enthusiasm is the prime vehicle for transmitting skills and transforming peoples and societies. We also continue to believe that a high degree of personal self-sacrifice, physical fitness, and hardiness of mind are appropriate in our relations with people who have less advanced technologies. In addition, we seem to expect that such relations be wrapped in a cloud of idealism—despite our acknowledgment of the dangers of idealism in other situations.

Another American tradition which has colored our relations with less advanced societies is that of cultural relativism. It has long had its practitioners but not until the forties did its ideologists appear, in the persons of Ruth Benedict, Margaret Mead, and the other anthropological exponents of "national character."

From this tradition we have derived a strong sense of uneasiness about the idea of even wanting to change the ways of other peoples, for every culture is supposed to be valued on its own terms and no one is supposed to be able to say who is "superior" and who is "inferior." Tied to the rise in the respectability of cultural relativism has also been a decline in our traditional faith in "progress" and our old belief that every material advance guarantees a better tomorrow. In the light of these changes we seem uncomfortable with almost any vocabulary for labeling the foreign societies we have in mind when we speak of aid: first, it became taboo in American circles to use such terms as "backward," "uncivilized," and "poor"; then we became uneasy with "less advanced," "underdeveloped," and "non-Western"; and, now we are careful to use "developing" and "emerging." [2]

The mixture of these two traditions of the missionary and the cultural relativist seems to produce a strange ambivalence in our approach to foreign aid. At one moment we seem to feel that we must rouse ourselves to a high state of moral and idealistic enthusiasm to make great sacrifices for the underdeveloped peoples of the world. But simultaneously we wonder whether we should be trying to change their ways. This feeling, on the one hand, that we should launch a great crusade and this questioning, on the other hand, of the very propriety of the activity leaves us vulnerable to criticism from every side.

All this means that in the staunchest "missionary" for foreign aid there is a bit of the cultural relativist, and thus there is always an element of qualification, some room for doubt, less than complete commitment. At the same time, in most ardent "cultural relativists" there is enough of the missionary to suggest that those of widely different back-

---

[2] Recently I had the experience of having a Pakistani apologize profusely to me for having said to my face that his country was "backward," for as he said, "I keep forgetting how sensitive you Americans are."

grounds should still be helped to find a "better life." We can neither give ourselves fully to the spirit of foreign aid nor can we deny completely the spirit of working to improve others.

The Illusion of Democracy and Incomplete Fraternal Commitments

In recent years we have sought to escape the dilemma caused by the "missionary" and the "cultural relativist" in us by proclaiming that in our foreign aid we only want to help others to attain what they themselves desire. Although in our own minds we may feel that the dilemma can thus be side-stepped and that we can act in the spirit of the missionary because we are also respecting the individual aspirations of others, in actual practice this has not proved to be true. The problem is that transitional societies are almost by definition societies in turmoil. They lack a coherent political process and both leaders and people are generally deeply unsure of precisely what they want. It is thus clearly impossible for us to discover with any confidence what they in fact are seeking as their national goals. Above all, we cannot be sure whom we should consider as the appropriate representatives and spokesmen of what these countries would like to become. The problem becomes peculiarly awkward when the government of an underdeveloped country indicates it wants to conduct its affairs in ways we cannot approve. In practice we find it extremely difficult to follow the policy of only helping others to do what they want—except, of course, when they want what we think they should want.

We have generally sought to remove such difficulties by professing our faith in a peculiar brand of democracy: we declare we should deal with people and not with governments. We cannot here go into the fascinating reasons why Americans appear to believe that there is virtue and little impropriety in displaying contempt for the formal governments of underdeveloped countries and why we persist in believing that the common people in such societies must have views consistent with ours. For our purposes it is only important to observe that this bias is so strong that we find it nearly impossible to avoid a deep distrust of officialdom in most underdeveloped countries. Consequently, we tend to the view that most of these governments need reforming; in spite of our cultural relativism we are easily convinced that American policy demands too seldom that the governments of small and weak countries mend their ways and adhere to our sense of values.

Here we come to another American ambivalence which seems to compromise the effectiveness of our foreign aid instrument. On the one hand we often declare strongly that other governments should reform in order to qualify for our aid; yet, on the other hand, we find it nearly impossible to hold in respect any government which would yield to outside pressures and demands, even if these be our own. It is, of course, a natural human tendency to despise authority that is weak, ineffectual, and easily influenced. Our repugnance with impotence, especially when combined with our distaste for less than democratic rule, makes us inherently uncomfortable in our dealings with government after government in the new states. The result is that we find it difficult to achieve, in our relations with the basically insecure and frustrated officials common to underdeveloped countries, the kind of easy working partnership which is essential in cross-cultural enterprises.

The Appeal of the Exotic and the Urge to Escape from the Cold War

We have clearly become involved in foreign aid as a direct response to the Communist challenge. Yet, oddly, we often look upon the problems of the new countries as an escape hatch from precisely the frustrations of the cold war. Concern with questions of development can take us away from the haunting anxieties which arise in modern industrial life and in a thermonuclear age. For many individual Americans the idea of aiding underdeveloped countries is closely associated with personal adventure and the romance of faraway places. Many of the people attracted to such programs are individuals who fail to find satisfaction in contemporary American urban society.

Ideologically, there is also the appeal of the underdeveloped areas as representing less intense and brutally dangerous political problems than those arising from direct confrontation with the Soviet Union and Communist China. For many Americans the problems of the new countries have seemed to be more tractable, more compatible with a moralistic view of politics than the problems associated with military strategy and nuclear armaments. For some Americans this urge takes the form of believing that they would rather deal with constructive than with destructive instruments.

This hope that we can find in the underdeveloped countries a less dangerous, a more positive and more idealistic way of being internationally involved clashes with our feeling of competition with the Soviets for the allegiance of the "uncommitted" peoples. As a result we seem at times not entirely sure of the extent to which we should be influenced by the threat of communism in our policies toward underdeveloped areas. The African and Asian insistence that cold war considerations should be kept out of all questions relating to their national development tends to accord with our basic sentiments. Yet we also recognize that the intensity of our concern in any particular country is heavily colored by the degree of the Communist challenge. Here again we find the strange American wish that our foreign aid instrument could be untainted by policy considerations and that we could live in an apolitical world.

From this brief survey it has become apparent that our entire foreign aid effort thus rests upon a very unstable foundation of sentiment and emotion, the consequence of which we shall return to shortly.

II. Moods Underlying the Soviet Approach to Foreign Aid

It is appropriate to ask now about the moods which underlie Soviet involvement in the underdeveloped areas. Our purpose in making comparisons with Soviet sentiments and practices is not to suggest in a veiled fashion that we can or should learn from the Russian example, but rather to provide a heuristic device to help us better appreciate the essence of the American approach. Philosophically, we of course differ greatly from the Russians and we wish to preserve our distinct approach; and technically we stand far ahead of the Russians in our practical skills in administering foreign aid programs.

Indeed, contrary to the popular notion that the Russians have been extremely ingenious and diabolically clever in responding to the realities in the underdeveloped areas, all the evidence suggests that the Russians have generally adopted a direct and uncomplicated approach to them. Uninhibited by any sensitivity for the perplexing complexities of transitional societies, the Russians follow their normal political and administrative procedures. Whenever the situation seems excessively confusing they appear to gain a sense of clarity by arbitrarily imposing upon reality their doctrines about the political nature of "colonial and semicolonial" societies. The fact that their doctrines do not correspond with reality does not disturb them greatly for they are committed to the task of mastering and changing reality.

Observation of Soviet behavior in Asian and African countries suggests that the traditional isolation of Russia from the tropics has left its people little prepared for work in the underdeveloped areas. Lack of experience and simple ignorance have apparently forced the Russians to fall back upon two devices: first, that of simply doing things just as they would at home, and second, that of relying heavily upon their formal ideology.

We cannot dwell on all the various images and sentiments about the underdeveloped areas which appear in the massive body of Communist literature on the "colonies and semi-colonies." Two features are, however, particularly significant for understanding the Russian approach toward foreign aid. First, there is the basic bias of expecting positive and friendly relations with the peoples of the underdeveloped areas, and the firm expectation that any hostile and unfriendly reception of the Soviet Union can only be a manifestation of bourgeois or feudal sentiments which will shortly be swept away by the forces of history. The Russian mood is thus one of very simply applying the calculus of friend and foe and relating it to a positive view of historical trends. The Russians never show any signs of the complicated and compromising qualms which seem to trouble us as we wonder whether those who are friendly to us are really deserving or at all representative of their peoples. Instead of our expectation that possibly it is "natural" for backward peoples to be against us, which leaves us not quite sure what our posture should be, the Russians are quite prepared to accept the unfriendly governments of underdeveloped countries as enemies who in time will have to be dealt with. For the Russians, friends are to be supported, enemies threatened, and vacillating neutrals kept off balance until they can be won over.

Another marked tendency of the Soviet approach is to view the underdeveloped areas within a larger context encompassing the industrialized parts of the world, for they have learned to think of the underdeveloped areas in terms of their relationship to the imperialist system. Instead of seeing the underdeveloped regions as separate and more or less autonomous societies striving to develop themselves, as Americans often do, the Russians see the relationship between the industrialized and the backward societies as being always the crucial consideration.

This perspective gives the Russians a constant sense of proportion. They seldom seem to be disturbed over the question of priorities between Europe and the Afro-Asian world. By themselves the underdeveloped countries have little significance for the Russians; they have importance only if they can in some way affect developments at the center of world affairs. On this score again the Russian approach seems to be far less complicated than the American one, which contains within it no easy way of clarifying questions about the relative significance of the underdeveloped areas.

III. Comparison of American and Soviet Foreign Aid Doctrines

The same contrast revealed by an analysis of the ethos underlying American and Russian foreign aid appears again in the more formal doctrines, the intellectual underpinnings, as it were, of the two approaches. On our side, we find contradictions and a basic ambivalence;

on the Russian side, a strongly partisan political approach becomes even more evident.

Many American economists concerned with foreign aid hold a rather strange belief in the non-political character of economic manipulation. This American view presupposes a dichotomy between "technical" and "political" considerations. The former are thought to be guided by sound knowledge uncolored by values, while the latter are assumed to involve essentially emotional and irrational conflicts always distracting men from a universally desired goal of efficiency.

The currently influential generation of American economic technicians was educated at a time of great excitement over the prospect that a whole society could be changed by governmental manipulations of the economy. Its members were trained to think that the miracle of government was its capacity to act along technical rather than political lines. They believed that great political changes would be made in an apolitical spirit and according to the logic of a supposedly value-free body of technical knowledge. This misconception—that it was possible to be apolitical while really being deeply involved politically—did not originate with American economists, but appears to have come from the traditional American aversion to direct manipulation of human affairs. Only with modern economists, however, has it been possible to believe that subtle manipulations of a technical economic nature can have profound effects on an entire society.

From this faith we have derived much of our doctrine on foreign aid. It has left us with the belief that there is virtue in characterizing our aid programs as essentially apolitical. Unfortunately, it has also left us without a clear idea of how to handle the relationship between our aid programs and current political issues. For example, we find it almost impossible to say how far we should go in differentiating between our friends and those who are unfriendly "neutrals."

Our unwillingness to accept explicitly the political dimensions of economic manipulations makes it difficult to explain to ourselves and to others the fundamental purpose of our aid programs. This is why we first insist that we are providing foreign aid not out of charity and friendship but as a hard act of enlightened self-interest, and then become bitter toward any recipient government that agrees with this explanation.

Proceeding with our analysis, we find that there is a significant difference between American and Russian feelings about the management of social change, which affects our respective approaches toward foreign aid. American thinking seems to be very optimistic about the possibilities of rapid and significant change in the new countries. We seem to think that it can come from marginal investments, that small inputs can yield large outputs. This is partly because of our appreciation of the "multiplier effect" in any economy. Even more important possibly is our belief that change is progress and that it must be popular for this reason. We are convinced that people will "naturally" work for self-improvement.

In contrast the Russians, believing that significant change can occur only through revolution, tend to see social change as extremely costly and are convinced that great efforts are likely to produce only small changes. They agree with us that change is likely to be progress, but their expectation is that people usually resist rather than welcome change, and that people will "naturally" slip back into lazy and tradition-bound ways.

A second distinction between American and Soviet thinking consistent with this first set of assumptions, is related to the question of the popularity of social change. In the American picture of the underdeveloped regions, the people are anxious for change and impatient with any deterrent to progress. In the American view, it is not inconsistent to depict the people of the underdeveloped countries as engrossed in a "revolution of rising expectations" and yet to spend considerable sums on techniques and programs to stimulate, prod, and encourage these very same people into giving up their old ways and taking greater interest in the prospects for change. People may be ignorant of the possibilities for self-improvement, but once shown new ways they are certain to accept them eagerly and to reject their old and inefficient ways. It is this assumption which gives us such confidence in the demonstration effects of pilot projects. A few well-run model enterprises should have incalculable influence on all who can see or hear about them.

Also, since we have little appreciation for why people may not be consistently enthusiastic for change, we tend to be discouraged by examples of back-sliding. In our thinking there is very little room for the notion that traditional modes of life can be comfortable while change and progress are painful. We are too much the products of acculturation ourselves to hold such views; we know the value of becoming Americanized, but not the costs.

The Soviets, to the contrary, assume that people stubbornly resist all forms of change. The problem of stimulating change is to overcome more than just the firm grip of tradition, for people, even when presented with the opportunity to improve their lot, are generally too lazy and slovenly to alter their habits. If the masses are not constantly prodded they are certain to slip back into their old practices. Such students of Bolshevik behavior as Nathan Leites and Merle Fainsod have noted the anxieties of Russian Communists about relaxing, for the alternative to determined effort is disintegration and the aimless ways of the peasant. The theme that ran through the entire early history of the radical movement among Russian intellectuals was that of frustration and exasperation at the Russian peasant for not showing greater interest in improving his lot. In the Soviet view today, any attempt at modernizing is certain to be only a superficial effort if it is not driven on by the select few who understand the problems of revolution. Thus in spite of reference to "revolutionary tides," and "intensified contradictions" that bring about "popular demands," the basic Soviet feeling is that ceaseless struggle is necessary to create the new in a world in which people tend to resist change tenaciously.

If we turn next to the problem of planning social development, we find that Americans and Soviets differ on time perspectives and the relationship of the short run and the long run. Our feeling is clearly that the long run is all important, and considerations of the short run are a constant source of danger that threaten the realization of our ultimate objectives. We are firmly convinced that a great hazard is that administrators will be overpowered by the demands of their day-to-day problems and lose sight of their long-run objectives. The demands of the immediate world are frustrating and exasperating and can absorb all of one's energies and time. (At the same time we tend to feel that while the long run is all important it should be relatively easy to "solve" long-term problems if only we could escape from the day-to-day pressures.) Our suspicion is always that others, and particularly our enemies, are somehow able to avoid the demands of the present and follow more long-run considerations.

The Soviet tradition, in contrast, is that the long run is predetermined by the "laws of history" and all attention and energies should be directed to the problems immediately at hand. A basic Bolshevik attitude is that people are all too likely to idle their time away with heated but futile discussions of the distant future. Some students of Russian affairs see the Bolsheviks as standing in sharp opposition to the propensities of earlier Russian intellectuals for engaging in endless speculation and agonizing soul searching about ultimate questions. For the new Russian man nothing can come of such activities, and progress can only follow from a complete commitment to the pressing problems of the moment. Effective action is, in fact, short run action. The true revolutionary takes pride in not wasting time or energy in thinking about the long term; instead he throws himself completely into day-to-day problems.

The Soviets thus see danger in the seductive appeal of philosophical reflection and safety in the concrete and the immediate. Their suspicions are exactly the opposite of ours. They tend to believe that their enemies are better able to focus their energies on immediate issues while they fear that those who profess to champion revolution will have their eyes fixed too much on the long run and will thus be ineffectual.

At a deeper level American doctrine on foreign aid rests on an extremely sophisticated and complex image of the nature of human society. Although the Soviets proclaim their ideology to be founded upon the most advanced "scientific" theories of human society, in practice Americans work with far more subtle notions about social relationships. In our thinking nearly all aspects of society are in some way interrelated; this means that in terms of policy it should be possible to deduce the secondary and tertiary effects of any particular action. In a sense we are inclined to think of a society as being analogous to a complex machine with interconnecting parts so that any movement or development in one part will be readily transmitted into movements in the other parts.

Thus with respect to social change, we are prepared to intiate activities in one sphere with the expectation that we will be able to calculate and predict their effects in other spheres of life. In our view the interrelated nature of the social system convinces us, as we have seen, that changes in the economic sphere will have predictable consequences in the political realm. We even take at times the position that very delicate and fine adjustments can be made through indirect manipulations of facets of the society, for we readily appreciate the importance of such control mechanisms as we have in our monetary and fiscal policies.

The Russians, in contrast, tend to feel that since only revolutionary changes will produce significant effects in a society, there is little point in calculating the more subtle consequences of any policy action. The Russians therefore act as though it were impossible to predict the indirect effects of any action and they tend to assume that it is absolutely essential to gain complete and direct control of events. In their approach all effort must be directed toward controlling and commanding immediate developments. There is thus a necessity for a frontal assault in achieving all objectives.

These differences in the American and Russian assumptions about the interrelatedness of the different parts of human society, the possibility of predicting the consequences of action, and the need for direct controls are basic explanations of the differences between American and Russian doctrines of foreign aid. In contrast to the American doctrine, which suggests that indirect effects of policies are predictable and hence direct controls are not always necessary, the Russians tend to feel there is a constant need for control because it is impossible to predict any indirect effects on policy.

This brings us to a final distinction in the American and Soviet approaches toward foreign aid, namely attitudes toward the autonomy and interrelatedness of specialized bodies of knowledge about human society. It seems that in spite of our mental image of the interrelatedness of all facets of society, we generally act as though each of the spheres into which we arbitrarily divide society has its own "laws," which should be acknowledged and respected. We accept the idea that there are different perspectives for viewing human behavior, which generally correspond to the separate academic disciplines. Thus we have the economic and the sociological, the psychological and the political approaches, each one of which is assumed to have its own body of "laws." Consequently, we assume that programs can be guided by economic, technical, or administrative principles and hence they can be essentially apolitical in character. Once again we return to the American doctrine which views our foreign aid efforts as inherently non-political; moreover we fully expect other countries to recognize this to be the case.

At the same time, we believe that our economic policies will have an indirect impact in the political realm. We seem to push the possibility of contradiction out of mind by assuming that in the final analysis there must be a basic harmony among the various bodies of knowledge and perspectives for viewing society. What is good sense according to economic theory must also be good politically. It is inconceivable to us that there can be fundamental conflicts in the outcomes of the various approaches or disciplines. We also seem to believe that if we act according to the best knowledge of any particular field we will also be acting in the best interest of the United States. There is not only a basic harmony of the spheres of knowledge, but this harmony extends to the American national interest.

We sometimes acknowledge, at least in theory, that the specialized knowledge of any technician can be the servant of any political master, and thus the specialist must be given guidance in matters of values, and he must accept the direction of the "broker" in values, the politician. Thus the economist, like the soldier and all other specialists, will acknowledge that the ultimate choices in policy must come from the political authorities. In practice, however, all specialists tend to feel that they are qualified experts in the realm of values and are capable of judging the national interest. Indeed, most of the various experts tend to see their specialties as being peculiarly important to the national interest. Although the conflict of specialists is endemic in our system of government, we still preserve our faith in the inherent harmony of all knowledge by attributing such conflicts to faults in personality, to ambition, and to the evils of "playing politics."

The Soviets seem to avoid these problems by assuming all specialized bodies of knowledge to be subservient to political considerations, for any form of knowledge can be used to political advantage. The unity of society is, for the Soviets, the all-pervasive character of politics. There are no such things as apolitical acts in international affairs. Therefore, there is no point in pretending that foreign aid is not influenced by political ambitions.

The Soviets generally act as though explicit political considerations provide the only basis for ensuring the harmony of the various special fields of knowledge. Indeed, in the Soviet mind, knowledge cannot be neutral; instead there are, for example, "bourgeois" economic theories and Communist theories. All must bow to the logic of politics.

It may be helpful to summarize the differences we have been noting by presenting them in the form of a paradigm.

American	Soviet
1. Great social change can come from marginal investments. A small input may result in a large output because of the "multiplier effect."	1. Social change is extremely costly; big investments of effort yield slight changes.
2. Change is progress and it is popular.	2. Change is progress but people resist it.
3. People will "naturally" work for self-improvement.	3. People will "naturally" slip back into lazy ways.
4. The long run is all important, but short-run considerations tend to absorb all one's time and energies.	4. The long run is predetermined, but people tend to waste their time and energies in idle speculations about the distant future. The need is for people to channel their energies into the short run.
5. One's enemies and competitors have the advantage of being able to reflect on the long run.	5. One's enemies and competitors have the advantage of being able to direct effectively all their attention to immediate problems.
6. All aspects of society are interrelated; secondary and tertiary effects are important because	6. Secondary and tertiary effects are unimportant; there is a necessity for a frontal assault in

American (*Cont.*)	Soviet (*Cont.*)
of our mechanistic vision of society.	achieving all objectives because indirect manipulations are ineffectual.
7. The indirect effects of policy are predictable and hence direct controls not necessary.	7. There is only a limited possibility for predicting the immediate effects of policies, and hence a need for constant control.
8. Different bodies of knowledge have their own laws and hence it is possible to have apolitical policies.	8. All specialized knowledge is the servant of political considerations and hence no action can be apolitical.

IV. Comparative Basis for Policy Action

To summarize our analysis to this point, the American foreign aid efforts rest upon some very diffuse, unstable, and ambivalent sentiments, but are guided by an extremely sophisticated and subtle view of the nature of social change and the organization of societies. Our basic sentiments prevent us from making unequivocal commitments to any particular course of policy, and we are prone to have a feeling of uneasiness and doubt about foreign aid which we can only suppress by calling for a crusading and self-sacrificing effort. Yet, on the other hand, our doctrine of foreign aid is profoundly optimistic and we create in our minds the possibility of performing some remarkably ingenious manipulations in directing change in foreign societies.

In seeking to resolve the tensions between our sentiments and our calculations about foreign aid, we are prone to alternate between complete doubt of the value of aid and the expectation that aid should solve all our foreign policy problems, between feeling that others should bear the responsibility for their backwardness and believing that we ourselves are to blame for the slow rate of progress in the countries we would help. Since our general moods about the underdeveloped areas are so grossly out of line with our expectations of what is possible in the realm of subtle social change, we are unable to be in any sense satisfied with foreign aid as an instrument of national policy.

The basic Russian orientation toward the underdeveloped areas is generally from this point of view much more optimistic than ours. They see the peoples of the backward societies as inevitably their eventual friends and collaborators in building a new world. At the level of immediate calculations the Russians are, however, far more pessimistic for they do not seem to expect any dramatic changes in the structure of the societies which are recipients of aid from either West or East. Above all, their approach is more blunt, less complicated, and more directly political.

The Soviets seem to expect their economic aid to create associations which will in time provide the basis for direct political influence. In their thinking such a direct link between the economic and political spheres has always seemed most "natural." At present they seem to treat foreign aid as a device for gaining respectability for communism and for neutralizing Western influences. Thus, in the last analysis, the Soviets are quite frank in stating that they are willing to use their aid to win friends and to strengthen "fraternal bonds"; nowhere in Soviet propaganda is there a counterpart to the American disclaimer of willingness to use foreign aid for "merely" winning friends.

In the American case, we find that in spite of our hosts of reasons for feeling involved in the problems of the underdeveloped areas we have not as yet been able to devise a coherent way of mobilizing and directing our energies. It would seem that this is largely the case because we have been so reluctant to make explicit in our own minds the political function of our aid program. Our uneasiness even about discussing the politics of foreign aid has made it hard to bring together all the diverse sentiments that might have been mobilized in this activity. Consistency in the Soviet approach to foreign aid is due to the extraordinary degree to which they have been willing to be uninhibitedly political in their approach. Out of the logic of politics they have been able to realize the coherence between ends and means, between goals and techniques. We built up our doctrine as though little explicit attention needs to be given to the possible relationships between our practices and the goals we seek.

V. Foreign Aid and the Evolution of a World Order

In implying that the American approach has been deficient in recognizing the value of explicit political considerations, we do not have in mind a narrow and partisan-based concept of politics. Rather we are speaking of politics in a more fundamental sense as the method by which people can order their social relations so that power can be directed to realizing human values, and social change becomes possible without destroying an over-all sense of community. In all our uneasiness about speaking across the gap in technology and in standards of living between us and the underdeveloped areas, we have shied away from open discussion of questions about values and about the appropriate purposes of our actions.

We must repeat again that we have no intention of suggesting that the Russians are about to excel in the use of foreign aid. There is still a tremendous gap between ourselves and the Russians with respect to the volume of aid and skill in administering it, and in basic knowledge of the nature of transitional societies. The Russians at this time offer little that is worth emulating.

In looking to the future, the disturbing question is not our competition with the Russians in the foreign aid field but whether we will be able to realize the full potential of this aid in building a stable world order. From an historical perspective the problems of foreign aid merge into the far broader problem of trying to create a stable and just world order. In coping with the daily problems of foreign aid we, the Russians, and the leaders of the new countries are all participating in a very fundamental historical process, that of breaking down static, traditional social orders and building in their place modern nation-states. As the chief defenders of an international order based upon sovereign states we have a special responsibility for seeing that this process of social upheaval takes place without unduly disrupting the world scene.

For over three hundred years a world culture has been evolving out of Europe. This culture is based upon creative science and technology, a rational and secular view of government, a respect for fundamental justice, an expectation of expanding possibilities for human welfare, and the acceptance of the nation-state as the prime unit of political organization for the advancement of public policies and thus for the satisfaction of the need for community identity. As this culture has been diffused throughout the world, traditional orders have been weakened and the processes of change have been set in motion. For a long time the international system which grew up in the wake of this cultural diffusion has been confronted with the dual problem of facilitating the continued diffusion of this culture as it steadily weakens the remaining traditionalist societies, and of preventing the ensuing tensions and uncertainties from disrupting the security of the international order. For the last two hundred years colonialism was a prime mechanism in this process.

In the postcolonial era we still find it necessary to search for ways to facilitate the diffusion of the world culture while at the same time preserving the stability of the international order. The great difficulty in this process is that it seems to produce some extremely profound psychological reactions which are likely to manifest themselves in various forms of disruptive political behavior. We cannot here attempt even to outline the host of reactions which transitional peoples tend to manifest as a consequence of being driven out of their traditional ways and forced to face the demands of modern life. Our concern here is only with the disturbing fact that although colonialism was in many respects remarkably effective in initiating these basic processes of social change, in the end it also stimulated some profoundly negative reactions. These were not just reactions against the colonial authorities. They have also included far deeper psychological reactions which seem to have left those touched by the process without the basic competencies, the will for action, and the capacities for effective decision-making, which are all essential for the stable modernization of their societies.

The crucial question now is whether in the management of foreign aid we shall be able to prevent the same kind of serious reactions. It seems to me that in all our urging for larger sums of aid and for more enthusiastically conceived programs we may be running away from the truly difficult question of policy. This is the question of whether we have as yet found the most effective ways for facilitating the transition of people from their traditional societies into the modern world with the least amount of psychic damage. Much further research is necessary if we are to be confident that the diffusion of the world culture under our auspices is not going to produce eventually the same reactions as have been turned against colonialism. These would include not only resentment and hostility toward the United States but also the same kinds of psychological anxieties which have been the basis of so many of the tensions, apathies, and inefficiencies of the postcolonial governments.

Faced with this massive and yet psychologically delicate task it is particularly disturbing to reflect on how easily the moods which underlie our efforts can drive us into doing the wrong things. The point is not just that we reduce our own capacity for effective action by vacillating between a narrow-minded economic approach and a diffuse desire for uncritical and "friendly" relations with the underdeveloped areas. The point is that in alternating between the false ideal of allowing our aid to be allocated by rigid economic criteria and the equally false ideal of relating it to specific, partisan political considerations, we have tended to miss the prime objective, which is to facilitate the diffusion of the world culture and nation-building process in ways that will contribute to the development of a stable international community of states.

We have tended to lose sight of the fundamental fact that behind all the competing considerations that influence our policy actions there is one fundamental, overriding issue. This is the question of what kind of a world order we hope to create to replace the classical international system of the colonial era. The clear and present dangers of the cold war tend to obscure the fact that in addition to our political struggle with communism we also have the fundamental responsibility to help shape a satisfying new world order, one in which people at different levels of technology and with differing systems of values can realize satisfying relationships. In our concern with "winning the game" we often forget that we must also help establish the agreed "rules of the game" and thus build the constitutional basis of the new world order.

Unquestionably the new international order will eventually emerge out of a host of contemporary political issues and processes, ranging from the struggle between democracy and communism to ways in which the world culture is spread throughout the transitional countries. It would, however, be helpful if we had a clearer vision of the structure and dynamics of the international order we are seeking. The attempt to make more explicit our idea of a satisfying democratic world order may not greatly accelerate the realization of that order, but it might give more coherence to our day-to-day policy actions. The effort would assist us and others to separate more clearly in our minds those policies that reflect our partisan political commitments as a nation from those that reflect our commitment to a larger international community. We could then make it unmistakably clear to the people involved in the nation-building process that we at least do not confuse modernization with Americanization. By learning to distinguish more sharply between policies to support a viable international order and those to support our particular interests as a nation within that order, we should also be able to clarify the distinction that we feel exists between those neutralists who seek to avoid deep involvement in the cold war and those who are opposed to the creation of a system of responsible international relations. We would likewise be able to distinguish between forms of anti-Americanism which are annoying to our national pride and those which are veiled attacks upon the very concept of an orderly and cooperative international system.

Beyond all these considerations is the prospect of achieving a far more secure and viable basis for our relations with the new countries if we can offer them the vision of a new international system that will enable them to realize their national honor and dignity. If we can give substance to the fundamental idea that we are joined with them in a constitutional endeavor to create a world order in which all peoples can find their separate identities, it should be possible for us to achieve that degree of integrity in our relations which will make it possible to avoid hypocrisy and to disagree at times without malice. Acculturation need no longer appear as a process in which some people take on the ways of others, but instead as one in which everyone is seeking to change and develop in order to build a better world community.

CHAPTER 7

POLITICAL DEVELOPMENT: VARIETIES OF POLITICAL CHANGE AND U.S. POLICY

W. HOWARD WRIGGINS

Never before have so many entities called themselves states and claimed the rights of sovereignty.[1] Yet never before have so many bearing that name been so ill-equipped to exercise these rights. A host of new states now crowding the world stage grapple with nearly overwhelming problems of rapid change and political weakness.

United States policy toward the newer states has sought to develop governments capable of maintaining their independence, their political integrity and effectiveness while absorbing inevitable social and other changes, and ultimately capable of achieving sustained economic growth at least commensurate with their rapidly growing populations. At the height of the cold war, we sought to shore up faltering regimes all along the periphery of the Sino-Soviet realm with large security inputs of both military and financial assistance. More recently, except in extreme cases such as Vietnam, we have been placing greater stress on economic development assistance to those regimes most capable of using it to promote their own economic growth. Underlying these general strategies has been the assumption that sound politics could grow behind the security shield we helped to develop or within an environment of expanding economic activity. Political integrity, effectiveness, and resiliency too often have been thought of as derivative of either military security or economic growth.

W. HOWARD WRIGGINS is a member of the Policy Planning Council of the Department of State. His publications include *Ceylon, Dilemmas of a New Nation*.

[1] This essay is a revision of material first published by Prentice-Hall, Inc., in *Self Government in Modernizing Nations,* ed. by J. Roland Pennock, © 1964, and used with their kind permission.

Yet desirable political conditions are also the result of the peculiar political circumstances in each emerging country, a blend of personalities, ideas, political practices, and the relationships between diverse and often conflicting political forces. Successful economic development depends as much upon the political art of a country's leadership and the climate for economic endeavor they create as the actual level of resources they accumulate at home or attract from abroad. Modern weapons in the hands of well-trained troops are no guarantee of security against foreign enemies or internal subversion unless there are the political skills to enlist a modicum of popular acquiescence and to ensure the loyalty of the officers and men. Sound politics, then, emerge not merely as derivatives of successful economic development or the organization of effective security forces. They result from essentially political creation by men concerned for the arts of mastering and manipulating political power in ways likely not only to enhance their own personal power but to improve the institutional framework of sound governance.

Accordingly, it may be that only by a more conscious effort to influence the course of political development and change in emerging countries will we be able truly to assist them to consolidate more effective and responsive governments.

With such an end in view, this essay briefly considers outstanding political weaknesses of many emerging countries, the advantages of these weaknesses to Communist policy, and the principal functions governments generally must perform to be successful. It then sketches seven typical political situations of change or circumstance which political leaders must grapple with if they are to maintain their polities in satisfactory working order.

Political inadequacies are of many kinds. Some governments are unable to ensure that their writ runs throughout their territory; others are riven by regional, religious, or ethnic antagonisms. Others cannot absorb new groups rising in influence until, in their frustration, these groups seize power by force. Some have cohesion and considerable flexibility, but no adequate means for deciding policies. There are others with tolerable means for determining what should be done, but they lack the political will or executive means for effective action. Too many others function under the aegis of one paternal figure, but have no accepted means for transferring power to other hands.

Government weakness or government rigidity in new countries are relevant to the Communist countries and the United States, but in opposite ways. To the Soviet Union and to China, weakness means opportunity to infiltrate with the aim of creating independent centers of power as a prelude to later political take-over. Rigidity, on the other hand, opens the way to growing impatience, sometimes to despair and a grasping at extreme measures from which either Communist power can benefit.

For our part, we stand to gain if emerging countries are able to develop their political ideas, institutions and skills so as to combine effective with responsive rule, continuity with change. The more the new nations are able to develop resilient polities commanding the loyalties of their people, the more they will be immune to Communist intrusion and can contribute to the cumulative variety and richness of the non-Communist world.

Political development is the process by which the frame and process of governance is improved. Political reality is too diverse to follow a unilinear transition from such abstractions as feudalism to democracy. But there is a series of identifiable political functions that a tolerable operating polity must perform if it is to be sustained.

Governments must accumulate enough power to give thrust and direction to their activities while they achieve sufficient political support to ensure effective government that requires only a minimum of coercion. While thus concentrating power and generating a base of support, a political system must also be able to accommodate major social, political, and economic changes. Institutions and practices must grow which allow a political system to attack its fundamental problems with greater effectiveness for the short run while working toward responsiveness of the regime to popular demands in the longer run.

It is in combining effectiveness with responsiveness that the real problem of political development can be seen, for effective government is not merely a matter of good administration. It is fundamentally the political art of enlisting popular support, giving the populace and administrators a sense of direction, inducing at least their acquiescence and, at best, their ready cooperation. This demands the gift of leadership, the growth of institutions to define objectives, to resolve differences over public policy, and to project a vision of public purpose, as well as a sensitivity to the needs of those outside the ruling entourage if coercion is to be held to a minimum. Durable political institutions require a readiness on the part of the ruling elite to draw new groups into participation, turning the machine of government in new directions when domestic and foreign political circumstances require. They also call for recognized ways of transferring power to new hands.

It is easy to state in such abstract terms the major imperatives of governance. More difficult is the art of bringing these generalities into effective relationship with the ambiguous and often mercurial realities of political life. The seven typical political situations discussed below encapsulate in many ways the major challenges facing emerging countries. Each is a prototype of a characteristic political change or circumstance that imposes its own imperatives on political leaders. It is hoped that turning the kaleidoscope of politics in this way will highlight at least some of the major elements of each type's present or recent experience.

I. GUERRILLA INSURGENCY SUPPORTED FROM ABROAD

Guerrilla activity may be virtually entirely indigenous: a home-grown effort to overthrow a tyrant. Alternatively, guerrilla forces may receive support and training from the territory of a neighbor, and there find sanctuary for rest and regroupment. In either instance, there is a combination of grievances against the government, and the use of terror and force. The Anglo-American tradition leads many of us to underestimate the role that terror and force can be made to play if insurgents are ruthless enough and well supported. Conversely, we are likely to overestimate the decisiveness of "doing something about real grievances." Proper policy requires a measured combination of steps designed to deal both with genuine grievances and with terror and force consciously organized by the guerrillas.

Every counter-guerrilla endeavor is long and costly. It is so much easier to disrupt the fragile growth of social order than to create it, that the advantages seem to be all on the side of the disrupters. Our experience in Greece, Magsaysay's strategy in the Philippines, and General Templer's experience in Malaya represent successful instances where Communist-organized and inspired guerrillas were dealt with.

In each instance, the task seemed nearly hopeless at the outset, grievances were real enough, and one skilled guerrilla could pin down perhaps fifteen times his number of regular troops. Major military and police activities of a specialized sort, designed to bring security to isolated villages and improve the precision of civilian intelligence against the guerrillas, were necessary steps. Often, the military and police had to change their traditional role, acting no longer merely as an arm of the central government but becoming instead friends of the people against the privileged and corrupt. Governmental reforms, popularly desired administrative changes, redress of grievances, and efforts to meet economic want together played their part.

If foreigners are to assist, they must be wary of becoming the enemy of the populace. Experience in Greece and in Malaya, however, demonstrates that it can be done. The end of guerrilla activities may come only long after a beginning has been made in developing tolerable political and administrative institutions. The second cannot wait until the first is accomplished.

Perhaps in no other type of political situation does the nexus between military, political, and economic actions emerge in such clear light as in the heat of a hard fought counter-guerrilla campaign. It is therefore worth noting that only recently has American literature begun seriously to explore these interrelations. The bookshelf on guerrilla warfare has greatly expanded in the past three years. Much has been learned. There is even a tolerable body of doctrine emerging. But much more remains to be done, particularly in the tricky area where foreign nationals participate in an active or close-in advisory role in situations of growing nationalism and incipient xenophobia. Vietnam provides a continuing reminder, too, of the complex and urgent problems of implementation where sustained external assistance to guerrillas meets chronic internal rigidity or weakness.

As for U.S. policy, we may be able to assist a threatened country to bring to bear the lessons of insurgency elsewhere. The optimum U.S. involvement is a delicate matter, since where there is insurgency there is often rising nationalism, if not xenophobia. Hostility to the local government may grow if it too obviously depends on foreign help, and if the outsider makes his presence unduly prominent. There is, therefore, a narrow path in counter-guerrilla activity between leaving a friend in the lurch and overwhelming him with attention.

Moreover, the matter is not simply one of improving firepower, troop mobility, and improved intelligence, although these are important. Much must be done in the realm of the political arts, inspiring popular support on behalf of a government, improving two-way communication between government and people, improving the skill and ability of civilian authorities to respond to grievances and to govern on behalf of the governed. Without an improvement in the political abilities of a government, the military effort can be only a holding operation, if that.

II. Overthrow of Long-standing Dictatorship and Creation of Democratic Governments

We have had some experience in dealing with this situation following the defeat of Nazi Germany and Imperial Japan and the liberation of Korea. More recently, in the Dominican Republic we have witnessed a classic case of the opportunities and difficulties facing a broadly representative civilian regime following protracted one-man rule. The following sketch is by no means authoritative, but it may suggest some of the major issues.

After the elder Trujillo was assassinated and his son agreed to step down, several political groupings appeared, including (a) a variety of exile organizations which promptly returned to the island, (b) a broad but inchoate civilian front, (c) a tightly organized conspiratorial extremist group, in addition to (d) the remainders of Trujillo's machine, the Dominican Party. As in many analogous situations in Latin America, the military forces held the only effective power.

The island people were ready for a major change, the linch-pin of the old regime had been removed by assassination, the community of American states was virtually united in its determination to give the democratic forces a chance, and the island was unusually susceptible to concerted influence from the Americas. A truly free election was shortly held and the new reform regime of Juan Bosch sought to free the Dominican Republic from the Trujillo thrall and consolidate its hold. But the new regime was short-lived.

Despite his overwhelming popular victory at the polls, Bosch did not have full support or confidence of important sectors of Dominican society, including the armed forces. The new president had been a political exile for many years. Not surprisingly, the exiles and those who had remained behind tended to regard one another with distrust. Businessmen and property owners were suspicious of Bosch's appeals to class sentiment and to the desire for social reform, feeling that these appeals were sometimes marked by demagoguery. Hostility arose on the part of opposition political groups because of the activities of Bosch's party, which seemed at times intent on building an all-powerful political machine. Gradually, communication between Bosch and the opposition, as well as between Bosch and the property owning classes, broke down. The armed forces became progressively more uneasy over the situation. Finally, the military leaders became convinced that there must be some truth in charges that Bosch was an extreme Leftist with Communist sympathies. Lacking support of the most influential political elements, he was then easily overthrown by the armed forces when they determined the time had come.[2]

The creation of democratic government after a long-standing tyranny is more difficult than overthrowing the tyrant. And the play of indigenous political forces sets narrow limits to what outsiders can do, unless they undertake full responsibility, as we did in defeated Germany and

[2] Donald A. Allan, "Santo Domingo: The Empty Showcase," *The Reporter*, Dec. 5, 1963, pp. 28–31.

Japan. Even then, of course, the end result is much more a German and Japanese achievement than our own creation.

As for U.S. policy, it may be possible by prompt and generous economic assistance to tide a new regime over its most difficult period—when the old network of economic and political relationships lies scattered and a new one must be laboriously constructed. If the new men have had little experience in governing, there may be advisors who can help to bring the voice of wider experience to their assistance. The service attachés and the men engaged in military assistance programs, if there be any, can urge caution on their uniformed counterparts and make clear that if they yearn to take the reins before the new men have a chance to prove themselves, they will find their military pipeline rapidly drying up. One should be alert to the ways in which critical civilian institutions can be reinforced during the early period by technical assistance advisors and well-directed assistance of other types. Much, too, depends on the celerity of aid, since a new regime may not be given much time. Again, however, a new regime can be made repugnant to its people by too much attention from abroad.

III. Long-standing Oligarchy Challenged by Rising Claimants to Power

This case is more common. In many emerging countries, the leadership is relatively conservative, and its power is based on land, often in alliance with the upper levels of the army and the senior bureaucracy. During recent decades, there has been a remarkable movement of individuals from the country into rapidly growing cities; educational facilities have been extended and more modern economic and administrative functions have given increasing opportunity to an urban middle class. Educated younger people in the bureaucracy, in the rapidly growing but underpaid communications media, younger, often foreign-trained military officers, share a growing frustration. They believe the ruling groups are over-privileged, lacking in zeal and competence to manage affairs, and standing in the way of the rising generation. Those with influence in the traditional society find it hard to share responsibility, but hang onto their prerogatives as elders.

The new contenders for power are often more adept at criticism than they are skilled at responsibility. Often highly individualistic, they find it difficult to organize themselves for sustained and considered political activity. By contrast, it is the men of the conservative Right, long habituated to power and still retaining many positions of influence through their wealth, or the men of the extreme Left, organized within disciplined and "hard" agitational parties with consciously developed organizational skills, who tend to sap the will and weaken the capability of these broad reformist center groups seeking to succeed the ruling oligarchs.

Accordingly, the policy problem is often a genuine dilemma. On the one hand, it seems likely that these oligarchic regimes cannot long survive. Yet the experienced know that only in retrospect does history seem inevitable. There is often a hope that perhaps reforms can come in time without a major change. There is doubt that a capable, effective coalition of center forces can be organized to take the place of the present, narrowly based traditionalist regime. The organized, extreme Left may be ready and waiting. Accordingly, although we suspect that if the lid is held on too tight the whole system will blow up, it sometimes still seems prudent policy not to disturb a regime's precarious political hold.

There are other instances where it is more prudent to press the pace of change and place one's hope upon the new contenders. These may be much more moderate if they come to power soon than if they stay out of power for ten more years; and they may be much more ready to believe that cooperation with us is in their best interests if we do not now attempt to stand in their way. We may even be able to strengthen their competence and their ability to use power responsibly by policies we adopt now.

The Alliance for Progress has been seeking to implement such a policy. It has two special diplomatic problems. How much diplomatic friction with the government in power are we—or they—prepared to tolerate as we attempt to persuade them to adopt reforms we think necessary; and how far is it legitimate to press a government to risk its own political future, if it believes the adoption of reforms or other measures we urge will dissipate indispensable political support at home?

As to U.S. policy, the circumstances are rare indeed where we can induce an oligarchy to relinquish power before it is thrown down. On the other hand, there have been examples in history, notably Great Britain, Switzerland, and Scandinavia, when oligarchies have artfully shared power before they lost it, and remained with a major share themselves for decades. Armed with these examples, there may be some historical lessons to be shared. There may be economic steps we could take to make reform and a sharing of power worthwhile to the oligarchy in other ways. If careful analysis suggests there is little we can do to help them adjust to the forces of history, we should at least make clear to the probable successors that we are not, by our policies, standing in their way. This always risks the stigma of being declared *persona non grata,* but that is better than going down with the oligarchy when their day has come.

IV. Precarious Post-oligarchic Coalition

In the previous case, the historical problem appears to be the broadening of the political base of a regime by encouraging it to adopt reforms. In the case of the precarious coalition, on the other hand, the oligarchy has already been displaced and the key political problem is that of accumulating sufficient political power for effective government.

New men have arisen. They are less familiar with the problems of governing, though sometimes they have technical knowledge superior to their predecessors'. There is a readiness to innovate; often there is a doctrinaire, theoretical approach to problems. The traditional ways of organizing power no longer succeed and there is a search for new ways to structure the processes of politics. Trade unions and professional groups already are developed to an important degree. Rural movements may organize peasant demands.

But these organizations are relatively new; they are not yet aware of the necessity for compromise and working collaboration toward ends they share. Very often the coalition is so balanced that economically sound and decisive policies are hard to adopt. Sometimes the balance between forces leads to the type of immobilism that so weakened the third and fourth French republics. If it persists, younger military or Communist-influenced groups are likely to attempt a coup. An important element of the government's energies has to be devoted merely to staying in power. The leader must employ great political skill to continue the balancing act.

On the positive side of the ledger, however, such precarious coalitions are often more responsive to popular needs than their oligarchic predecessors. Mass organizations, like trade unions, grow rapidly, providing for urban workers and the lower middle class a new type of social group with which to associate themselves in efforts to protect their own interests from the harshness of early industrialization. If leadership is skilled, new energies may be released and turned to constructive tasks of internal development and a sensible approach to long-standing international quarrels.

If the precarious coalition is willing to have the U.S. active within its country, there are a variety of ways we may contribute to that government's success while helping it avoid the risks of immobilism. If we are able to make economic resources available, many political difficulties can be eased by additional transfers of food, capital goods, or temporary foreign exchange support. When leaders are able to go to other countries on exchange or other programs, they may perceive the art of compromise as others practice it and return with a broader perspective on their own internal quarrels and ambitions. They may become more pragmatic, less committed to early ideological attachments. There may also be ways in which we can influence opinion leaders and others to be more responsible in their criticisms, more positive in their interpretations, and more constructive in the ways they approach the problems of development.

V. Protracted Military Rule

In this instance, military leaders may have taken power to bring more effective governance, to press reforms, or assert their traditional prerogatives. Excluded from consideration here are those short-lived military regimes which have seized power from dictators or political incompetents and held the ring while civilian politicians negotiated with one another and formed new governments. The more long-lived military rule is here in question.

Military regimes possess the short-run advantage of being based on an existing structure of power, hierarchically organized to get certain things done. At the outset, they are usually able to avoid the annoying compromises, the polemics, the petty or dramatic corruption, and the public quarrelsomeness that has done so much to lower the repute of democratic practice in many emerging countries. Services dependent upon the public administration usually improve—the trains run on time, the streets are relatively clean, marketing is supervised, and profiteers may be properly dealt with. In many instances, the military institutions are among the most modern and provide the best opportunities for the technically trained modern young men. Where the nation is beset with communal or regional differences, the army may be the most important single institution working toward molding the society into one nation.

But few polities can persist for long on the basis of command alone. The military leaders, like their civilian predecessors, must deal with subsidiary centers of power, whether they derive from traditional sources of influence, such as regional, tribal, or familial attachments or the more modern ways of mobilizing influence through mass organizations or through indispensable economic enterprises. These leaders must persuade if they cannot coerce. Where corruption and favors are part of the tradition of office, the army rarely remains immune. We should not

exaggerate the capability of a coercive system to accumulate the resources necessary for development. It may easily turn out that the state's
growing budget for coercion and the tendency of a military regime to
intimidate important sectors of the population will inhibit economic
growth more than the relatively disorderly and helter-skelter civilian
ways before the take-over. Nevertheless, it is possible that a puritanical
military regime, capable of inspiring support, can develop a higher rate
of savings for investment than its predecessor, and there are notable
examples of economic progress achieved under military leadership.

All such regimes face a major difficulty. How can they keep in sufficient touch with popular desire to minimize the inevitable tensions between rulers and ruled? If the military regime persists, by what steps can
public office be gradually returned to civilian hands? How do they
loosen their hold without inviting political disintegration? Some such
regimes have consciously adopted programs designed to provide channels for the expression of grass roots opinion and to release the energies
of the rural populace in the direction of development.

United States representatives may counsel moderation in the use of
coercion against the populace. We can avoid demonstrative approval of
a harshly authoritarian leader. We should direct our aid programs to
strengthening organizational and productive skills among civilians,
particularly improving the civilian bureaucracy and professional organizations as possible long-run alternatives to military rule. We should
work with the military rulers to encourage their efforts toward civic
action programs of use to the civilian economy. Military training
programs can include emphasis on the adverse effects on most armies of
protracted involvement in the political arena.

VI. Activist Authoritarian Rule

Government in this case is overshadowed by the dynamic personality
who rises to power with the support of the modernist bourgeois elite,
and who uses religious or other evocative symbolism to consolidate his
position. Efforts to develop an inclusive political movement to transcend
the traditionalist tribal or ethnic differences have some success at the
outset. He seeks to free the society from the traditionally influential. By
a series of excitements directed at internal or external enemies, he
gradually downgrades or purges others in the elite who also helped to
bring independence and reaches down in the society for support of the
less well educated urban youth, who are more amenable to his inspiration. These become a corps of irregulars, who help maintain him in

power. The entourage becomes narrower and narrower, with increasingly difficult access for anyone who is not a full-time political activist in the leader's organization. Economic innovations result in reducing the country's heavy dependence upon agriculture, increasing state control, and restricting, if not eliminating entirely, types of business which might provide a source of independent support for opposition elements.

The leader's efforts to override the traditional power structure, to eliminate other leaders, and to control intellectual life while using economic resources derived from the rual sector for industrial and urban-centered investments arouse many specific opposition groups. These, however, remain divided, finding it difficult to combine effectively. Increasingly restrictive policies designed to control these multiple sources of opposition generate still further antagonism. Temporarily, these repress the expression of opposition, although the life of the leader is continually in jeopardy.

The leader may be able to generate enough enthusiasm and mobilize the moderately educated youth sufficiently to substain himself in power for a number of years, and much constructive economic innovation may take place. The pace and direction of the economic program and the increasingly narrow political base of such a regime, however, makes prognosis uncertain.

Since such regimes are unlikely to want close working relations with the United States, there is little that we can do to encourage the development of a broader institutional base which may provide greater political resiliency.

VII. POLITICAL POWER CONCENTRATED IN ONE RELATIVELY STABLE PARTY

Political systems of this type, characterized by Mexico and India, are notable for their single ruling party, which dominates the political landscape. The party is a rather loose but nevertheless inclusive affair, nationwide, with a rural base, claiming some descent from the social revolution or national independence movement. Internal power is sufficiently dispersed so that most tendencies in the country have an opportunity to express their demands and press their claims within the party's capacious and competitive interior. New groups do not need to form new parties to have their voices heard; most critical national political issues are fought out within the party, thus avoiding the acute fragmentation which appears to mark countries where the European multiparty system becomes established. These inclusive parties in India and

Mexico have shown they can generate sufficient political power to direct significant resources into development, and both have been strongly nationalist in their insistence on maintaining as independent a foreign policy as possible. They have recognized means for dealing with internal factional quarrels; each consciously seeks to draw in younger people, at least at the lower levels. In India, there have been remarkably few changes in top personnel. In Mexico, by contrast, there has been a regular succession of leading personalities, each of whom has stepped down without complaint at the end of his elected term.

While such polities have many virtues, there may develop liabilities. The lack of genuine political competition at the national level may make for party lethargy, for an unreadiness to respond to the winds of change in their own countries. In some instances, there may be a growing tendency toward corruption as patronage becomes an increasingly important source of the party's cohesion. Indeed, as the party machine becomes better established, patronage may at times appear to overshadow many other functions of the party.

Nevertheless, such inclusive yet loosely organized and open single parties are important political innovations in traditional societies in transition. They represent major forward steps toward tolerable government in areas hitherto lacking either national cohesion, a tradition of personal responsibility in public affairs or effective and responsive government. At an early stage, they represent a substitute for the as yet unfound national community. Later on, they may prove to be the forerunners of more familiar modes of two-party competitive politics.

From the point of view of U.S. policy, political pressures may be reduced if economic resources are readily available or the terms of trade improve. Technical assistance and systematic personnel exchanges can help to improve skills and develop non-ideological approaches to organizational and productive problems. Unless international threats require, relatively few resources need to be used for purposes of coercion, and effort can be focused on education, industry, or agriculture.

These observations do not provide a blueprint for U.S. policy toward political development and change in different situations. They are in the nature of reflections on different aspects of our problem. They suggest that as we consider policy toward emerging countries it is not sufficient to assist in strengthening their security position or in promoting their economic development in cases where they are willing and able to press their own economic growth. These are important and deserve as much thought and effort as we can devote to them. But assisting the growth of sound polities through such indirect means is not enough. We should direct more systematic thought and imaginative action to strengthening political practices more likely to lead, over the longer run, to effective and responsive regimes.

The examples cited above suggest the variety of situations we have to deal with. The comments on U.S. policy in each instance suggest how narrow are the margins of our influence under most circumstances. A world of sovereign independent states, as well as many other factors, sets limits to our rights and to our ability to affect the political affairs of others. It is presumptuous to expect that we, as Americans, can lay down a line of approach to one-half the world's people, each seeking the sinews of nationhood within its own peculiar situation.

Nevertheless, we should seek a sufficiently clear understanding of political change in diverse situations and have greater confidence in our judgment. This confidence would enable us, when confronted with a range of choice, to more often choose knowingly those steps likely to favor the purpose we share with many others—movement toward a community of free nations increasingly capable of coping with their own problems by means that ensure continued internal order, a growing effectiveness of government, and an increasing ability to be responsive to broadly based popular wants.

CHAPTER 8

THE INTELLIGENCE ARM:
THE CUBAN MISSILE CRISIS

FRED GREENE

We are all aware, after two decades of cold war, that foreign policy poses difficult problems for the democratic process of government. Traditional concerns about the need for secrecy, speed of action, special information, and sensitivities of foreign governments place foreign policy in a special category of governmental affairs under any circumstances. These concerns apply with even greater emphasis to intelligence, which has become a special arm within the realm of American foreign policy in recent decades. This development has further magnified the problems of exercising responsible controls over the policy process, and bringing to bear adequate judgments concerning operational effectiveness.

Even the most straightforward categories of military intelligence, those that affect the national security directly and immediately, including estimates of an opponent's preparations for a surprise attack or a dangerous shift in the disposition of his strategic forces, raise issues that are far from simple and clearcut. We can all agree, for example, that information regarding Soviet missile deployments is of the highest importance. But verification usually takes considerable time, especially if previous information had been proven incorrect after painstaking review. Or the political price of collection might be very high, as was the case in the U-2 crisis of 1960. Someone must measure at the outset the relative costs of "not knowing" as against the price of finding out, all *before* an incident has occurred or a particular fear is confirmed. Similarly, it takes great wisdom to decide what degree of verification, short of certainty, can justify a grave retaliatory or preventive measure.

FRED GREENE is professor of political science at Williams College. He is the author of *The Far East* and *Dynamics of International Relations*.

Still more complex and elusive is the field of political intelligence involving answers to such questions as: What policies and objectives are other states pursuing? Under given circumstances which of the particular options apparently open to them will they choose? And what would their reactions be to the specific policies or proposals put forward by the United States?

I

The Cuban missile crisis lends itself to detailed study of the complex intelligence craft because the crisis was of limited duration, the major events of the drama were sharply etched in detail, and intelligence played a central role in the formation of policy before and after the discovery of the Soviet strategic missiles in Cuba. From this incident, many general principles of the intelligence function may be derived; from it too we may see how intelligence serves (effectively or otherwise) as an instrument of foreign policy. For this confrontation required of intelligence a general estimate of a basic political situation: that of the Soviet-American power equation and of fundamental Soviet security policy. Intelligence also had to look for specific signals that would indicate important changes in Russian behavior patterns. The policy stakes involved in effective collection and accurate evaluation of evidence were high, but so were later decisions on how to use and disseminate this hard-won information. Throughout the crisis, intelligence provided the decision makers greater leeway than otherwise would have been the case, in such crucial choices as the timing of their reaction, the diplomatic method and arena of response, and even the substance of the policy adopted.

The political roots of the missile crisis lay in the decision of the Castro government to throw Cuba into a deep socio-economic revolution along what its leaders held to be Marxist lines. This was combined with a diplomatic alignment with the Soviet Union, source of much aid and favorable trade agreements during 1960–61. Among the more important American reactions following the Bay of Pigs incident of April, 1961, was the determination to remove Cuba as a participant in the inter-American system, an effort that bore fruit after considerable debate at Punta del Este in January, 1962. There, by a bare two-thirds majority, the O.A.S. went beyond its 1960 condemnation of Communist intervention in hemispheric affairs to exclude, but not expel, Cuba from its system.

During the months that followed, the Cubans apparently sought the protection of a Russian alliance and treaty of guarantee but instead received the Soviet offer to place surface-to-surface missiles (S.S.Ms.) on their soil. A treaty between the two states, announced on September 1, 1962, promised Cuba arms and technicians "to resist the imperialists' threats."

American intelligence operations by the beginning of September had already discovered the presence of various defensive dispositions, the most significant of which were anti-aircraft or surface-to-air missiles (S.A.Ms.), and the presence of at least 3,500 Russians in Cuba. During the first half of September, President Kennedy and other high officials reported in detail on defensive weapons entering Cuba, said that no offensive weapons (especially S.S.Ms. and bombers) had arrived, and repeatedly warned Moscow against placing such weapons in Cuba. The Soviet Union stated somewhat ambiguously on September 11 that all dispositions were defensive in purpose, stressing, that is, intent rather than type of weapon. In retrospect, it appears that after the mid-summer decision to place S.S.Ms. in Cuba, the Russians began to ship supportive materials there in early September and the missiles began to arrive in the middle or latter part of that month.

American responses in late September included a congressional authorization on September 24 for the President to call up 150,000 reservists and an effort by the U.S. Air Force to have its Tactical Command combat ready in one month.[1] Air reconnaissance was intensified though bad weather and the elaborate nature of the effort delayed total coverage for a while. However a U-2 flight on October 14 revealed the construction of S.S.M. sites and later photographs enabled intelligence officers to estimate the full scope of the Soviet effort. The week of October 16–22 was devoted to reaching a decision as to the basic American response and the following period, October 22–28, brought on the famous confrontation. The President revealed the crisis in a speech on October 22; the naval quarantine on missile shipments to Cuba took effect on October 24; Mr. Khrushchev's first letter arrived October 26; an American U-2 was destroyed October 27 in the only military engagement of the incident; and the Soviet Union agreed to a withdrawal of its strategic weapons on October 28.

Although a brilliant success in the end, the Cuban missile crisis of 1962 also brought in its train many disagreeable surprises. The Russians did manage to ship strategic weapons across the ocean in secrecy. They also apparently operated with unexpected speed and efficiency. Compar-

[1] Henry M. Pachter, *Collision Course* (New York, 1963), p. 7.

isons with Pearl Harbor come to mind immediately: misreading the opponent's intentions, misjudging his technical capacity, not crediting him with sufficient audacity, and analyzing how he would act by imagining how we would act in such a situation. Still we succeeded in 1962 in contrast to the disaster of 1941, and end results still count importantly in evaluating an intelligence effort.

Nonetheless, within the United States, the aftermath brought considerable criticism of the intelligence community. This criticism, which placed in sharp relief many of the issues and lessons of the crisis, fell into two main categories—those regarding basic concepts and those dealing with particulars. Among the former or more philosophical issues is the problem of weighing theory and fact as guides to an analytical effort. This involves the eternal need to develop some working hypothesis that enables an analyst to place masses of information in some meaningful pattern; against this is the requirement to guard incessantly against jumping prematurely to conclusions, by letting the facts speak for themselves, at least to a certain extent. A second conceptual issue concerns the intelligence official's approach—should he emphasize the worst or most dangerous interpretation of the facts or possible evolution of a situation, if only to protect the harassed policy maker from experiencing unpleasant and critical surprises? And what stress should intelligence place upon intentions as against the capabilities of a given antagonist?

The second category of criticism underlines the specific inadequacies of intelligence as a given situation unfolds. This involves an ability to make accurate deductions from known facts—in this case, for example, whether the presence of air defense missiles signified the presence of other, strategic missiles. In other words, were the analysts too optimistic in their interpretation of the facts on hand? Then there is the matter of timing: did intelligence officers overlook critical evidence regarding the presence of strategic missiles in the crucial twenty-four days between September 21 and October 14, 1962? On a point not squarely within the intelligence framework, can we distinguish between defensive and offensive weapons in this instance; or does the effort to do so mislead an opponent with regard to the nature of America's planned response? How can one estimate whether, and to what degree, an opponent was aware of the depth of America's emotional involvement in the Cuban issue? [2] In addition to this range of problems, we must also consider the effect of the existing bureaucratic structure upon the ability of the intelligence community to function properly.

---

[2] Klaus Knorr places special emphasis on this point in "Failures in National Intelligence Estimates: The Case of the Cuban Missiles," *World Politics,* XVI (April, 1964), 464–65.

II

I believe that our intelligence effort came out well with regard to those issues raised by such critics as Senators Keating and Stennis (in his Preparedness Subcommittee report) and Mr. Hanson Baldwin. A major point in the entire controversy centers upon the fact that the United States intelligence community, because of its *theoretical orientation,* was surprised by the Soviet effort to put strategic missiles so far from its homeland. The Stennis Preparedness Subcommittee pointed out that there was a certain philosophical conviction in the intelligence community "that it would be incompatible with Soviet policy to introduce strategic missiles into Cuba." [3] This fundamental assumption rested on the belief that the Soviet Union would not risk placing vulnerable and important weapons outside of the area in which it exercised direct physical control. It had never done this before and, save for the error of the Korean War—a mistake that Khrushchev had acknowledged indirectly many times—the Soviet Union cautiously refrained from risking a major and direct confrontation with the United States. Building on this analysis, both Mr. Baldwin and the Senate report came to the unwarranted conclusion that the intelligence community tried to make the facts fit its preconceptions and pet theories, and so failed to allow empirical evidence to call the tune.[4]

Actually, as of September, 1962, the intelligence analysis of Soviet behavior patterns rested squarely on the then available facts gathered with painstaking care. To assume a Russian strategic missile effort in Cuba as late as mid-September would have been the theoretical flight of fancy that the critics rightly consider so dangerous. The issue, then, does not center upon a misguided effort to force reality to comply with predetermined views. Rather, it is far more complex and agonizing, especially because the analysts based their reasoning on the solid foundation of prudence and experience. Since we know that nothing continues on the same course forever, the question emerges: when does a situation change and when do all precedents or existing patterns become dangerously out of date? That is, when must an intelligence officer decide that a foe is about

[3] U.S., Congress, Senate, Armed Services Committee, Preparedness Investigation Subcommittee, *Investigation of Preparedness Program,* 88th Cong., 1st Sess., 1963, S.R. 75. See the *New York Times,* May 10, 1963, for the report's "Summary of Major Findings."

[4] Hanson Baldwin, "The Growing Risks of Bureaucratic Intelligence," *The Reporter,* Aug. 15, 1963, pp. 48–52. Mr. Baldwin quotes approvingly the Senate report on this and other matters.

to do something rash and novel, something that is quite dangerous, and something for which hard evidence is lacking? This problem more accurately reflects the issues that emerged in 1962 and deserves further consideration and research. Past experiences involving both strategic surprise and anticipations that never became reality (possibly because of preventive measures) require careful investigation. This involves an examination of the estimates made, their degree of accuracy, and the significant patterns, if any, that emerged in those situations marked by drastic and unexpected actions.

A related problem is whether an intelligence officer should *emphasize the worst situation* that might develop in light of available evidence. The Stennis report holds that "there seems to have been a disinclination on the part of the intelligence community to accept and believe the ominous portent of the information which had been gathered. In addition the intelligence people apparently invariably adopted the most optimistic estimate possible with respect to the information available. This is in sharp contrast to the customary military practice of emphasizing the worst situation which might be established by the accumulation of evidence." As we shall soon note, there was absolutely no hard evidence before September 21, 1962, concerning strategic missiles, so that before that date it would have taken a clairvoyant to "accept and believe" anything of the sort. (One almost gets the impression from studying criticisms that evidence is of a secondary nature, almost a mere verification of overwhelming intuitive knowledge that the missiles were already there.)

When a situation is not clear-cut, and various interpretations are possible, it is indeed the duty and tradition of intelligence to point out the worst possibility. Yet this act does not suffice to guarantee security in a given situation, since officials responsible for actual plans and operations will discount a Cassandra who consistently emphasizes the greatest danger. Their own experience tells them that less dangerous and more likely developments in a spectrum of possibilities frequently come to pass. They will discount new and dire intelligence warnings in ambiguous situations if they have already had their fill of them. There is, at the same time, an opposite danger that those who wish to alter an existing policy radically will seize upon any anticipation of great danger, no matter how carefully qualified in an intelligence analysis, to argue for the adoption of their position as the only escape from impending disaster.

A third conceptual problem, one repeatedly stressed by Mr. Baldwin, is that we must go by *capabilities* rather than by *intentions*. These words connote a sharp contrast between reliance on the facts (capabilities) as against trying to guess what is in the enemy's mind (intentions). To stress intentions, Mr. Baldwin feels, is to give intelligence control over policy makers, by compelling the latter to follow the single line of action that best reflects the analysis of intentions. This is an unfair criticism, if only because the alleged difference between capabilities (inference: facts) and intentions (inference: guesses) is a myth. Nor do calculations based on intentions necessarily put a nation's security on more dangerous grounds than when we base estimates only on capabilities. For example, we assumed that the Russians had the capability of manufacturing X number of missiles in the late 1950's, based on our knowledge of their physical plant and their technical capacity. Is this a meaningful, hard fact if other information, a point argued vehemently by Secretary of Defense Thomas Gates, leads us to conclude that they intend to produce, say only $\frac{X}{Y}$ missiles? [5] Is one not derelict in his duty to stress only the larger sum if the other figure looks correct? If we always went by capabilities, how would we ever keep our own arms below our own maximum capability?

More fundamentally, evidence of an intention must rest on hard facts to a degree sufficient to make capability—another set of hard facts—an unsure basis of analysis. Otherwise the uncertainty would not appear in the first place. In short, we usually have two sets of competing hard facts, making an estimate in either direction somewhat of a guess. Analysts therefore follow the more convincing evidence or the more frequent or meaningful experience. Otherwise, to chain oneself to capabilities— for example, the Russians can invade Iran or they can overturn the Finnish government—could lead to a harmful diplomatic and military posture at a given moment, if other evidence regarding intentions indicates that these are unlikely events. Would not an exclusive stress on capability also mean control over policy makers by intelligence? Clearly, the problem of capabilities and intentions is too subtle to resolve simply by identifying either one with "the facts."

III

The intelligence community has also been subjected to the criticism that its thinking was influenced by *wishful and optimistic interpretations* of the facts, thereby making its evaluations and estimates far too san-

---

[5] See for example the Testimony of Secretary Gates in *Department of Defense Appropriations for 1961,* Part 1, esp. p. 23. Hearings, Subcommittee of the Committee on Appropriations, 86th Cong., 2nd Sess., 1960.

guine. Thus, the Preparedness Subcommittee held that the intelligence community was inclined to accept only those things which bolstered an optimistic interpretation. Yet in the late summer of 1962 the intelligence community was considerably disturbed, even though it had patiently screened a tremendous amount of information without finding evidence that the Soviets had placed strategic missiles on the island.[6] Because they were worried, intelligence officials increased their efforts to make certain that nothing was amiss. The critics themselves, in different contexts, have reported the considerable variety of efforts at intelligence collection undertaken that September. No one held that a strategic missile base on the island lay outside the realm of possibility; indeed, because of the dangers involved, intensive efforts were made, leading to the alert and rapid discovery of the missile emplacements.

Before September 21, as Mr. Baldwin has noted, there was no evidence that the Russians had strategic missiles in Cuba. Yet Mr. John McCone, Director of the Central Intelligence Agency, felt that the Russians would install missiles of a strategic sort and he proved to be correct. He based his view on a deduction that the emplacements of S.A.Ms. indicated an intent to install S.S.Ms. on the island. Mr. McCone was proven correct in the Cuban case. However, the Russians have put S.A.Ms. in Indonesia; Iraq had them before the 1963 coup; the U.A.R. was reported in the press to have them in 1964; and India has been promised a sizable number of S.A.Ms. It is quite possible that the Soviet Union will give or promise surface to air missiles to other states, since they bring large political dividends at little economic cost. Some states will reject these weapons as unnecessary or too expensive to maintain; others might find the offer attractive, for prestige and security reasons.

This is not to say that the establishment of S.A.M. sites in Cuba in mid-1962 was not of itself a politically and militarily serious development. But though significant, this did not allow a firm conclusion that S.S.Ms. were also present, without substantiating evidence. The existence of S.A.Ms. did arouse suspicions, thereby adding to the intelligence community's determination to intensify its surveillance. To go beyond such prudent responses and to argue that the presence of S.A.Ms. equals the presence of S.S.Ms. does not afford a reliable basis for analyzing the significance of S.A.M. emplacements in other parts of the world.

---

[6] See the letter by Congressman Samuel Stratton in *The Reporter*, Oct. 10, 1963, defending the intelligence officials, and the editor's response, quoting the Senate report, supporting the criticism made in the report and by Mr. Baldwin, pp. 8, 10.

IV

There is also the question of *timing*. When was the evidence physically there? When did we learn about it? When did we actually believe it? Here we are dealing with what ultimately proved to be America's greatest triumph. Mr. Baldwin has noted that "irrefutable evidence becomes available, commencing about September 21." [7] This statement contains an inference, albeit vague, that there was some degree of certainty in the evidence during the twenty-four days between September 21 and October 14. Senator Keating has stated that he was told early in October of evidence from sources other than aerial reconnaissance; the latter, he observed, did not "fully record the presence of strategic missile sites until October 14." [8]

Was irrefutable evidence obtained—and overlooked—in those twenty-four days? Was it new and strikingly different from the vast number of false alarms, such as those reported in the press, of the previous two years? Or are we again dealing with the clarity of 20-20 hindsight, which made the evidence both irrefutable and clearcut after the aircraft had done their job? Senator Keating himself has noted that via aviation we received "fully recorded" evidence on October 14. That date was about the earliest on which evidence of actual construction could have been perceived through this medium. This remarkable achievement does not mean that other evidence was not required or sought. But it does indicate that we learned through air photography what the Russians were doing just as they mounted a significant effort to build their missile delivery structure in Cuba.

Was the evidence that came in earlier through different sources sufficient to make a convincing case within the United States? Would it have enabled the government to take the diplomatic and strategic offensive? And how pressed were we for time? To take the last question first, we should note that even after October 14, the President wanted eight more days in which to prepare his program and his arguments, and then it took five additional days to settle the issue. Hence we still had time— almost two weeks—after the Russian missile construction effort reached a sufficiently advanced state on October 14 to be photographed.

Even more important was the relationship between the type of evidence available and the diplomatic strategy that the President selected. Having decided on open diplomacy and a direct confrontation rather

---

[7] Baldwin, "The Growing Risks of Bureaucratic Intelligence."
[8] Letter by Senator Kenneth Keating in *The Reporter*, Sept. 12, 1963, p. 6.

than a covert effort to force the Russians out, conclusive evidence presentable in an open forum became pivotal to his endeavor. With this as national policy, decided upon by the responsible officials (in accordance with the requirement that intelligence should not control or direct policy), it seems only reasonable to conclude that the evidence gathered by aerial reconnaissance was both essential and timely. It admirably suited the President's basic objective of getting the missiles out of Cuba.

To be valuable, intelligence cannot operate in a vacuum; rather it must help broaden the choices available to the prudent leader and make these options more meaningful. It is of greatest service when it enhances national policy in the diplomatic context within which it is employed. In the effort to convince the diplomatic and public opinion of the world, any evidence accumulated by the United States government by means other than aerial photography during the last week in September and the first two weeks in October, however important, would not have done this job. Nor, as we have seen, did the time span in this situation have a significant negative effect on our ability to respond. What does emerge is that other types of firm information are difficult to acquire, take time to verify, require the most careful evaluation, and present formidable problems as instruments of diplomacy. These handicaps will continue to beset intelligence as an arm of foreign policy in the foreseeable future.

V

There remains the issue of whether a distinction can be made between *offensive and defensive weapons*. The administration carefully distinguished between them in September, stressing that only the former were unacceptable. But did the administration's attitude, in accepting one type of missile, lead the Soviet Union to feel that the United States would take a less determined stand against the presence of strategic missiles? Mr. Baldwin avers that the distinction is impossible because defensive weapons (for example, S.A.Ms.) can protect offensive ones, thus making the context of employment rather than physical properties the key factors. Yet the administration did not appear confused on this score in 1962; nor did it believe as Senator Keating argues, that it had blurred the issue by drawing such a distinction. It was in fact issuing a last warning to the Russians against going beyond their significant defensive build-up in Cuba. During the first half of September, the President in his press conference on September 13 and Under Secretary Ball in his testimony before the Congress on October 3 both stressed the difference between offensive and defensive weapons in this vein.[9] Mr. Ball's testimony, detailing the presence of defensive weapons, was published in full. Mr. Walter Lippmann in a long follow-up analysis carefully went over this presentation, pointing out the distinctions between defensive and offensive weapons and warning about the consequences of the latter.[10] The effect of these public statements and writings was to clarify the differences between the two types of weapons and to underline the danger that would follow if the Russians placed strategic missiles or bombers in Cuba. It is difficult to see how any of this could have left the Russians confused, because, unlike other situations in the past, these signals from Washington came through quite distinctly.

The evidence thus reveals a fairly clear picture. The Russians simply chose to disbelieve what was said, or concluded that Washington did not mean what it said. Perhaps they felt that the United States would not act before the missiles were in position and then would be afraid to act, so that it did not matter what statements were made in September. Since their calculations were made long before September, it seems only fair to conclude that the Russians in their gamble were insensitive to all American statements, rather than encouraged or confused by them. If such is the case, then we should properly concentrate on how such a dangerous condition came to pass.[11] On the other hand, the Russians may well have acted rationally in recognizing the large risk involved but felt that it was worth taking because of the great benefits that success would bring. Once launched on this course, they may have convinced themselves that the risks were not so high, and so disregarded American warnings.

In the end, it was Russian thinking and analysis that was seriously mistaken and the Soviet Union had to pay a very high price as a consequence. We should recall that American intelligence credited Moscow with a desire, based on the record of the past, to operate in a prudent, non-provocative way. The intelligence community considered actions in violation of such precepts to be out of character and foolish, and in the end it was proven correct. Perhaps the critics who overlook this fail to recognize that many actions on the part of foreign governments are

[9] The *Washington Post and Times-Herald*, Sept. 5 and 14, 1962.

[10] *Ibid.*, Oct 9, 1962.

[11] Knorr, in "Failures in National Intelligence Estimates," argues that the Soviet leaders failed to grasp the depth of American feeling against Cuba and so underestimated the risks their action incurred. However, in light of the audacity of the move, it is difficult to assume that the Russians did not realize that this was a most risky enterprise. Moreover, it was not emotionalism over Cuba but concentration on the danger posed by Soviet power that sparked the American reaction, which emphasized the bipolar nature of the confrontation.

beyond our capacity to influence. Is this another variation of the "illusion of American omnipotence"?

Each side apparently made the mistake of identifying its opponent's mode of calculation with its own. Thus Russian estimates of American reactions to Russian initiatives were quite possibly colored by Moscow's knowledge of how it itself would react. After all, the Kremlin stood by while the United States ringed it with air and missile bases during the 1950's. Thus each side "plays all the roles"—but calculates the other's initiatives or responses from its own perspective. Overcoming this inclination is a formidable task—worthy of the most patient effort. Certainly, at the time, the argument that our acceptance of defensive weapons and our warnings against offensive ones blurred the issue would not have been credible. We need only remember the shocked response of the American public when the President spoke on October 22 in order to realize how sharply the country distinguished between the two.

VI

In addition to considering philosophic precepts, the question of timing and type of intelligence, and the nature of the weapons involved, we must also examine some comments made about the organizational setting of the intelligence operation in Washington. Mr. Baldwin has noted that it suffers from excessive bureaucratic centralization and from a predisposition to follow administration policy objectives in a way that prejudices its interpretation of data. Actually the component agencies that comprise the intelligence community are independent and autonomous bodies, somewhat removed from the policy effort. They come to their own conclusions based on their own efforts. The rise of the Defense Intelligence Agency (D.I.A.) as a centralizing body within the Defense Department may reduce the voices of the three services, but it is also possible that the Department of Defense will speak with four independent voices rather than three as in the past. Not only do the existence of D.I.A. and C.I.A. as potential rivals make it clear that we are a long way from centralized, monolithic control, but the other intelligence groups in Washington retain their independence because they are component parts of still other branches of the government involved in national security matters.

These different bodies have their own sources of intelligence and their own requirements, and each stresses differing aspects of this broad field. This means that richness of sources is not necessarily mere duplication, for different requirements elicit significantly different kinds of information. One great marginal advantage is the wide scope this allows for cross-checking. In any event, we must overcome the notion that duplication in government is the same "bad thing" as duplication in business. The question of profit-through-efficiency and singleness-of-effort are not necessarily the criteria by which one can judge success in an enterprise so dangerous and tricky as national security. We find considerable autonomy even within the defense establishment and C.I.A., let alone in the relations between these two components or between one of them and other intelligence bodies. As in other forms of political and social organization, there are recurrent conflicts of view within an agency, and serious disagreements often produce alignments that cut across formal bureaucratic lines. All too often a finished product will suffer from compromises among the interested parties, who water down its content excessively. This is a far cry from the imposition of a single viewpoint from a higher political or administrative authority.

This raises the question of how to balance vigorous autonomous efforts in the research and evaluation field with a substantial final version that gains community-wide acceptance. All one can arrange institutionally is a framework that allows for diversity and some method of objective appraisal and judgment. Even so, those in opposition to an adopted position have every right and duty to take exception and they are quite willing to do so when issues of national security are involved. Thus intelligence is not made to fit a finished product or to coincide with presidential viewpoints or statements. To argue that intelligence officials dare not disagree once the President says there is a certain number of troops in Cuba is to ignore the fact that the statement is based on the findings of the intelligence community. If a minority of the intelligence officials holds a different view on this or any other point, what is the President to do? Is he simply to base his statement on the minority position, because it is more ominous or more reassuring? All this should not inhibit those in the minority from adhering to their position or trying to prove themselves correct.

Finally the power of outside forces to investigate and police the intelligence community is highly underrated. The Congress has great powers in this field and if it does not exercise them, it is not because the machinery of government prevents it from doing so. It may reflect an unwillingness to bear the burden of dealing with vast amounts of sensitive information. Yet when one looks at the performance of the Joint Congressional Committee on Atomic Energy, involving the most serious and horrendous matters, as concerns both security sensitivity and destructive capacity, it seems that the Congress could logically play as effective and constructive a role in the intelligence field as well. A joint committee on intelligence would doubtless have a salutary effect in both policy and administrative matters.

VII

In conclusion, the Cuban missile crisis indicates that, though the intelligence community was surprised at the start, it handled the situation fairly well. The careful nature of its effort in late summer and early fall, and the manner and speed with which it uncovered evidence indicate that it was not entirely napping. At the same time, the critics, by raising issues in public perform a valuable service in requiring officials to re-examine and re-study their activities and calculations during a crisis. Much has been done to clarify the facts and illuminate problems in the public realm. All this is to the good. In the course of this intellectual encounter we have seen how certain basic principles of intelligence affect the formulation and conduct of foreign policy. We have also seen how an elemental objective of intelligence, to provide for a nation's strategic security, encounters numerous and unexpected difficulties. Research into earlier crises, evaluation of the impact of intelligence upon events for good and for bad, and explanations of unanticipated developments—all admittedly with the aid of hindsight—are essential for a broader understanding of the achievements and limitations of intelligence as an instrument of foreign policy.

CHAPTER 9

THE U.N. AS A FOREIGN POLICY INSTRUMENT: THE CONGO CRISIS

ERNEST W. LEFEVER

The United Nations enterprise [in the Congo] *is the most advanced and most sophisticated experiment in international cooperation ever attempted.*—Walter Lippmann, July 21, 1960

On July 1, 1960, the former Belgian Congo became the world's most dramatic example of independence by panic. After a half century of paternalistic rule, the Congolese were cut loose on six months' notice, chiefly because some high officials in Brussels feared that the Congo might become a "Belgian Algeria."

When the externally imposed instruments of order and cohesion were abruptly withdrawn, the endemic centrifugal forces of tribalism, geographical diversity, and political ambition asserted themselves. Chaos and violence followed. The wealthy and strategically located Congo quickly became an arena of cold war rivalry. It was to discipline this rivalry, to restore law and order, and to guarantee the abruptly given independence that a United Nations peacekeeping force was sent to the Congo. This vast tropical expanse, the size of Western Europe, became the first severe testing ground for the international organization as a peacekeeping instrument.

In evaluating an operation as complex and controversial as the U.N. peacekeeping mission in the Congo, three questions might be asked.

ERNEST W. LEFEVER is on the senior staff of the Foreign Policy Studies Division of the Brookings Institution. He is the editor of *Arms and Arms Control* and the author of *Ethics and United States Foreign Policy*. He teaches international politics at the American University in Washington.

The author gratefully acknowledges the helpful comments of Ruth B. Russell and Robert E. Osgood in the preparation of this chapter, which was written when he was on the staff of the Institute for Defense Analyses.

What impact did the mission have upon the Congo itself? Did it serve the larger interests of international peace and security? And did the U.N. serve as an effective instrument of United States interests? We are concerned here primarily with the last question.

The Congo crisis was rooted in two failures of Western imperial power—the failure of the metropolitan nations to prepare their colonies adequately for eventual statehood and the failure to develop a philosophy and strategy for relating their power and wealth to the emerging states in the inevitable "postcolonial" era. These failures can be attributed largely to two contradictory assumptions—the liberal assumption that the right of self-determination was tantamount to the capacity for self-government, and the conservative assumption that the post-independence relationship between a new state and its former master would be very much like the old relationship of dependence. This conservative view, widely shared in Belgian political and financial circles, was expressed in a simple equation by the last commander of the Belgain-run Congo Force Publique: "After Independence = Before Independence."

Rapidly unfolding events in July, 1960, proved both assumptions wrong. Independence neither endowed the Congolese with the capacity for self-government nor permitted them to re-establish their earlier dependence upon Brussels. The new political leaders and the Congo army, entirely officered by Belgians, were singularly unprepared for the responsibilities of statehood. It was assumed that the 1,100 Belgian officers would continue on indefinitely, gradually training Congolese to replace them. But six days after independence the Congolese soldiers, who had never been taught the meaning of loyalty to a state, started to throw out their officers. Prime Minister Lumumba and the other fledgling leaders in Leopoldville were confronted with a mutinous and irresponsible army whose self-appointed Congolese officers had stronger ties to tribe or faction than to the new republic. The Congo was a state in search of a nation.

The army mutiny was exacerbated by tribal strife and separatist political movements. Lumumba was encouraged and supported by the Soviet Union. Tshombe's declaration of independence for Katanga was stoutly upheld by the financial interests in the mineral-rich state and by influential sectors in the Brussels government. There were plots and counterplots. In short, internal weakness was being exploited by external economic interests to maintain a privileged position in the Congo and by external political interests to gain a foothold there.

I. After Four Years of Peacekeeping

It was into this steaming caldron that a U.N. peacekeeping force was promptly dispatched by the Security Council at the request of the new Congo government, with the strong support of the United States. Its chief task was to maintain law and order until the Congolese were able to do so themselves. Four years of peacekeeping came to an end on June 30, 1964. During this time a total of 93,000 men and officers from 34 countries had served in the force which had an average strength of 15,000. The United States has paid about 42 per cent, or $168 million of the total cost of $402 million.

What has been the impact of this "most advanced and most sophisticated experiment in international cooperation," as Walter Lippmann described it, on the Congo and its capacity to maintain internal security? News from the Congo in the latter half of 1964 bore a striking resemblance to the news four years before, suggesting that nothing fundamental had changed. The government was still faction-ridden and ineffective. The army was still weak and irresponsible. The government was assailed on all sides by externally supported rebels. European lives and Belgian investments, estimated to be more than $3 billion, were still in danger. And the United States was deeply concerned about stability in Central Africa.

In spite of its vague and often conflicting mandate, the novelty of the mission, inadequate legal authority or military capacity to fully achieve its assigned objectives, and the unwillingness of several great powers (notably Britain, France, and the U.S.S.R.) to support the operation, the U.N. force made a positive contribution to internal stability during its stay. It helped to maintain law and order and to deter tribal warfare. It performed humanitarian services for refugees and protected U.N. civilian operations designed to shore up the economic and administrative structure of the country. It succeeded in ending Katangan secession. The country did not erupt into civil war and its territorial integrity was preserved. But the U.N. did not succeed in transforming the weak and irresponsible Congolese army into a reliable instrument of internal security. As one observer said, the U.N. "may have lanced the Congo boil, but it failed to cure the infection." [1]

[1] Donald H. Louckheim, "New Rumbles in the Congo Are Really an Echo," *Washington Post and Times-Herald*, Sept. 13, 1964.

II. ESTABLISHING THE SUPPORTING COALITION

On the twelfth day of independence the Congo cabinet, with Lumumba and President Kasavubu absent, cabled Washington for American assistance to restore law and order. The immediate response of the State Department and President Eisenhower was to urge the Congo to request help through the U.N., with the assurance of U.S. help through that channel. Two days later the Security Council authorized "military assistance as may be necessary, until . . . the national security forces may be able, in the opinion of the Government, to meet fully their tasks." The resolution also called upon Belgium to withdraw its troops. The U.S.S.R., which had also received an unofficial plea for unilateral aid from Lumumba, voted for the resolution. Britain and France abstained.

The Security Council action was based on the "peaceful settlement" provisions of the Charter (Chapter VI), and not on the sanctions provisions of Chapter VII, though as the Congo drama unfolded elements of Chapter VII crept in. In strict legal terms the Congo mission was never an enforcement action. No state was declared an "aggressor" and the operation was based on the consent of all states directly involved.

Throughout the four years, the U.S. was the strongest and most consistent political supporter of the U.N. mission, providing substantial financial and logistical assistance. Washington was, in fact, the leader of a reasonably stable supporting coalition, including many neutralist and Latin American states, the Scandinavian lands, Canada, and several others. Without initial U.S. support the force would not have been authorized. Had U.S. support been subsequently withdrawn, the effort would have collapsed.

In the light of the infrequent and limited deployment of U.N. administered military personnel in the past, how can this rare degree of consensus on the Congo be accounted for? There have been scores of political crises and conflicts that have threatened the peace, including thirty-eight wars with an average duration of 5.8 years between 1945 and 1962.[2] As of 1960 the U.N. had intervened only ten times with a military

---

[2] These statistics have been derived from Evan Luard, *Peace and Opinion* (London, 1962) and L. F. Richardson, *Statistics of Deadly Quarrels* (Pittsburgh, Pa., 1960). See also Lt. Col. Fielding Lewis Greaves, U.S.A., " 'Peace' in Our Time," *The Military Review,* Dec., 1962, pp. 55–58.

presence, but never, with the exception of Korea, for other than observation or police functions.

The broad consensus supporting U.N. intervention was the product of mixed motivations which reflected two ways of looking at the Congo crisis. The Soviet Union and some neutralist states that supported Lumumba blamed the crisis on the "external aggression" and "colonialist machinations" of Belgium, to use the words of Lumumba's appeal to the U.N. The U.S. and other Western states emphasized the Congo's internal weakness and were concerned about unilateral Communist Bloc intervention. Though Moscow never succeeded in getting the Council to brand Brussels an "aggressor," virtually all states supported the repeated call for the withdrawal of Belgian forces.

III. Moscow's Initial Support and the Colonial Issue

Since the U.S.S.R. and many neutralist states had shown little interest in sending a U.N. Force to deal with "threats to the peace" before 1960, it may be assumed that their lively concern about the Congo crisis was closely related to their desire to expel Western colonialism.

The assumption on the part of some neutralist states that the Congo crisis would disappear once the Belgian military presence was exorcised was not sustained by subsequent events. By early September, 1960, all Belgian forces except 114 officers and 117 other ranks who had been seconded to the *gendarmerie* of Tshombe's secessionist Katanga. By the end of the following September all of these seconded officers had been withdrawn under an agreement between Prime Minister Spaak and the Secretary General, leaving behind only mercenaries from France, South Africa, and the Rhodesian Federation. But the Congo crisis continued.

The Soviet bloc had been cultivating Prime Minister Lumumba and regarded the Congo as a rich plum ripe for "national liberation." Moscow looked upon the U.N. military presence as a stratagem for expelling the Belgians, limiting U.S. influence, and thus providing an opportunity for the Russians to support and direct the Lumumba government. As things turned out, the net effect of the U.N. presence and an active American diplomacy was the downfall of Lumumba and the installation of a moderate pro-Western government in Leopoldville. The more ambitious Soviet designs were frustrated and the diplomatic representatives from Moscow were unceremoniously expelled from the country on two occasions.

IV. WHY THE U.S. SUPPORTED U.N. INTERVENTION

Two and a half years after President Eisenhower urged the Congolese to go to the Security Council, Assistant Secretary of State Harlan Cleveland recalled the choices confronting Washington with the first mutiny of the Congolese troops: "Should the Congo's chaos be attacked by a hastily assembled international peace force; or should we send in a division of U.S. Marines; or should we just sit on our hands and wait for our adversaries to exploit the situation?" We wisely decided, he added, "not to risk a confrontation of nuclear powers in the center of Africa"; we believed a U.N. force would serve "the national interest" of the U.S. and the great majority of U.N. members.[3] Earlier Adlai Stevenson had said that "the only way to keep the cold war out of the Congo is to keep the U.N. in the Congo." Stevenson's statement was more rhetorical than accurate, because U.N. intervention both reflected and assured big power interest in the local crisis. The U.S. was not seeking to back out of a contest with the Communist Bloc or blocs in the Congo, but it did want the contest to be fought by acceptable ground rules that excluded unilateral military intervention.

The fear of a "confrontation of nuclear powers," had President Eisenhower accepted the Congo's request for U.S. assistance in July, 1960, was hardly justified in light of earlier unfulfilled Soviet threats to intervene by direct military means in distant disputes. Logistically, any substantial military action by the U.S.S.R. would have been virtually impossible in the Congo. The real danger was Communist exploited instability rather than a direct clash between American and Russian soldiers. The danger of nuclear war, even by escalation of the conflict, was virtually nil.

In addition to achieving stability, the U.S. sought to keep on good terms with the new African states, to avoid a major military commitment in Africa, and to strengthen the peacekeeping capability of the U.N. These three motives, weighted differently among top officials, all pointed to U.S. involvement through the U.N. rather than through a bilateral program.

One former American ambassador to Leopoldville said the U.N., like a lightning rod, was expected to absorb charges of neo-colonialism that might otherwise be directed against the U.S. The lightning rod did not always work; U.N. troops were often referred to as "American mercenaries" by the opponents of U.S. support of the operation.

It would be difficult to prove that direct U.S. assistance in 1960

---

[3] Speech, Jan. 17, 1963, Department of State Press Release No. 34, p. 3.

would have seriously damaged America's credit with the new African states over the long haul, though it would have drawn a bitter attack from some quarters. The emotional outburst in December, 1964, against the American-Belgian rescue of foreign hostages held by the Congolese rebels indicates that an invitation for assistance from a legitimate African government does not protect the assisting government against charges of "aggression." In radically different circumstances, British prestige probably did not suffer in January, 1964, when Britain at the request of the three newly independent East African governments sent in troops to put down mutinous army units. A timely, effective, and restrained police action by the U.S. within the Congo and at the request of the government in 1960 could conceivably have resulted in enhancing American prestige in Africa.

Perhaps the situation was so confused that U.S. assistance would not have been effective. On the other hand, a quickly dispatched American force would not have been subject to the severe political restraints of the U.N. force and might well have been more effective in restoring order than the U.N. proved to be. After all, the military capacity of the mutinous Congolese soldiers was slight indeed. An effective show of force might have been sufficient. Further, the U.S. would probably have been able to deal with Brussels more effectively than the U.N. But in the light of Washington's desire to avoid substantial military involvement in Africa, and given the uncertainties of the situation, the option of bilateral assistance was quickly dismissed.

Moscow never made a moral or political distinction between direct U.S. military assistance to the Congo, which started quietly in October, 1962, and U.S. involvement through the U.N. If anything, America's alleged use of the U.N. as a cover for its "imperialistic ambitions" was more loudly condemned by the Russians than open bilateral aid.

If the U.S. strategy toward Africa in 1960 was to play a quiet supporting role to the former metropoles and to avoid major military involvement, the use of the U.N. as an instrument was a logical choice. But as the situation developed, the four-year, multilateral peacekeeping effort did not preclude direct American military involvement. Since its formal military aid mission was established in Leopoldville in late 1963, U.S. military assistance has included the provision of vehicles, aircraft, and communications equipment, as well as some small training missions in the Congo and the training of about a dozen Congolese officers at Fort Knox, Kentucky. In June, 1964, two or three C.I.A.-recruited Americans flew combat missions in Kivu Province against rebel positions until they were grounded by the State Department. United States military aid in fiscal 1964 totalled $6.6 million.

Within a ten-day period in August, 1964, following rebel advances including the capture of Stanleyville, the U.S. sent to the Congo four large transport planes (C-130 turboprops capable of carrying ninety-two fully equipped troops), three helicopters, and three B-26 planes to support the sagging Congolese army. The transport planes were accompanied by a hundred officers and men, including forty paratroopers. Previously the U.S. had provided six T-28 fighters and fifty servicemen to maintain them.

As of early 1965 no American troops or officers were scheduled for combat functions. Washington, however, was continuing to provide logistic support for Tshombe's mercenary-led campaign against the rebels.

Though the U.S. has been anxious to avoid a major military involvement in the Congo, a more substantial commitment cannot be ruled out if the situation deteriorates and if other outside assistance does not materialize. It is difficult to suppress the speculation that a modest bilateral commitment by the U.S. in July, 1960, might have prevented the subsequent erosion of civil order that has involved the U.N. in four years of peacekeeping and has necessitated direct military assistance from Belgium, Israel, and the United States. In terms of political cost, a small amount of effective help early is better than a large amount of help, even if effective, later.

A marginal factor which influenced the U.S. decision to enter the Congo through the U.N. was the desire of a number of State Department officials to enhance the peacekeeping capacity of the world organization. The U.S. had long advocated U.N. peacekeeping in principle and had been the most consistent supporter of U.N.E.F. and the nine other previous U.N. missions involving military personnel. Washington was satisfied with the performance of these missions and believed that they all operated in harmony with American interests. This positive view toward peacekeeping was sustained by the confidence that the U.N. was unlikely to authorize any significant peacekeeping force over the determined opposition of the U.S. despite the recent influx of neutralist states into the U.N. For practical, financial, and logistical reasons, as well as for substantial political reasons, U.S. officials have rightly felt that there were adequate safeguards for American interests.[4] This unique experience with multilateral peacekeeping reinforced a disposition to turn to

⁴ See Francis O. Wilcox, "The Nonaligned States and the United Nations," in *Neutralism and Nonalignment,* ed. Laurence W. Martin (New York, 1962), pp. 121–51. See also statement by Adlai Stevenson, "Review of U.S. participation in the U.N.," in *Hearings Before a Subcommittee of the Committee on Foreign Relations, U.S. Senate,* 88th Cong., 1st Sess., March 13, 1963, pp. 12–15.

the U.N. in certain types of crises where bilateral or alliance action are deemed unsuitable. In his Dag Hammarskjold Memorial Lecture, Dean Rusk expressed the hope that the peacekeeping capacity of the U.N. could "be seen realistically for what it is: an indispensable service potentially in the national interest of all members—in the common interest of even rival states." [5]

Without making a judgment on the wisdom of the American decision in July, 1960, the fact is that the U.S. chose U.N. intervention over noninvolvement or bilateral assistance. Since it made this choice, it is appropriate to assess the utility of the U.N. as an instrument of American purposes in Central Africa.

V. Constraints on the U.N. as an Instrument

From the first day of Congolese independence, the U.S. sought a unified nation with a stable, moderate, and pro-Western government in Leopoldville. Washington also sought the continuation of a prosperous economy and the protection of European investments throughout the Congo. The U.S. sought to frustrate Soviet subversion, to avoid civil war, and to integrate Katanga peacefully. All these specific goals were compatible with the larger objective of stability and peaceful change in Africa. The American policy in the Congo, unlike that of Belgium, had many facets; it had to take into account the views of Belgium, France, Britain, and other NATO states that were not enthusiastic about U.N. intervention in Katanga, as well as the views of the neutralists supporting the Congo operation.

Washington's interpretation of the Congo crisis was generally consistent with successive U.N. resolutions that called for the end of Katangan secession, a constitutional government acceptable to all major factions, and a peaceful solution to internal problems. The objectives of the U.N. mission—to maintain peace and order, prevent civil war, preserve territorial integrity, help retrain the Congo army, and help establish a government of national reconciliation—were beyond the capacity of any outside party, and especially of one circumscribed by the legal constraints and the military limitations of a "peaceful settlement" force. The U.N. was never given sufficient authority to achieve fully its assigned objectives, nor did the resolutions clearly distinguish the objectives that the U.N. Force could pursue on its own from those that would require the active or passive cooperation of the Leopoldville government, although most of them fell into the latter category.

[5] Jan. 10, 1964, Department of State pamphlet, Series s, No. 17, p. 8.

This imbalance between ends and permissible means confronted the U.N. with serious legal problems, but the exceeding of its authority was not one of them—with the possible exception of the use of force on September 13, 1961, the day Conor Cruise O'Brien announced to startled reporters in Elisabethville that the U.N. had ended the "secession of Katanga." No other U.N. official ever claimed authority to use force to end Katanga's secession. The real legal problems had to do with the impossibility of ascertaining precisely what authority the U.N. had, especially in relation to the authority of the Congo government, and the attempt to achieve broad objectives with limited means and unspecified authority.

The force was sent to the Congo at the invitation of the host state and it operated with the basic consent though not in accord with the whim of the government. At the outset U.N. troops were permitted to use force only in self-defense. Eighteen months later, on February 21, 1961, the Council extended the permissible use of force to the prevention of civil war, and on November 24, 1961, the Council extended it still further to the apprehension and detention, of "all foreign military and paramilitary personnel and political advisers" not under the U.N.

The force was never given explicit authority to expel Belgian troops, to end Katangan secession, or to train or reorganize the Congolese army. Yet each of these objectives was urged in one or more resolutions. The U.N. was never authorized to use force to restore law and order, its primary mission, unless it were acting in self-defense or to prevent civil war. Incidentally, the U.N. never justified any of its operations by invoking its authority to use force to prevent civil war. The U.N. was not even given the authority of ordinary border police to inspect incoming traffic to identify prohibited persons or war matériel.

With so little explicit authority, and with the requirement of consent from the Congolese government and from the governments contributing troops, the force was severely limited. It was further handicapped by the failure of certain states to fulfill their legal obligations to support the U.N. operation they had authorized. These difficult circumstances called forth the unusual political and legal skills of Dag Hammarskjold and his chief aides. Hammarskjold's acute political sense enabled him to identify and move ahead on a working consensus of the governments most directly concerned. U Thant has attempted to follow his example.

In terms of legal authority, Hammarskjold insisted on "freedom of movement" for the force. This ground rule was based on the U.N.E.F. experience. It was never challenged by the Council or Assembly and was written into several agreements with Leopoldville. Freedom of movement was understood by him simply as a right essential to any police or military force in the pursuit of its legitimate objectives. This right in theory conferred upon the U.N. command a very broad authority. In practice, however, it was exercised selectively and with restraint, not only because of the fidelity of Hammarskjold and Thant to the resolutions as they understood them, but because of the inherent military limitations of the force and the necessity for the U.N. to secure the consent of the host government for any significant operation. The U.N., for example, never insisted upon freedom of movement to disarm the Congolese army, an essential first step in any serious retraining effort. The goal of retraining and reorganization of the Army was repeated in several resolutions and strongly endorsed by the Secretariat and the United States. The U.N. exercised restraint in this case partly because of General Mobutu's persistent opposition to any U.N. assistance for training his Army and his apparent preference for bilateral aid, especially from Belgium.

VI. U.N. Action in Katanga

The utility of the U.N. as an instrument of American purposes can perhaps best be assessed by focusing on the Katanga problem which proved to be the most knotty legal and political question faced by the U.N. and the governments supporting the Congo operation.

On July 11, 1960, President Moise Tshombe of Katanga proclaimed his province an independent state because, he said, Lumumba was following a Communist line. He appealed for and received Belgian military aid. At no time was secession an authentic expression of indigenous "nationalist" sentiment. The people of the province were never really consulted on the matter. Though a politically significant portion of the population in South Katanga supported Tshombe's policies, the Balubas of North Katanga were always violently opposed to his regime.

With only 10 per cent of the Congo's population, Katanga in 1960 provided about 50 per cent of the Congo's revenue. It produced about 8 per cent of the world's copper, 60 per cent of its cobalt, and important quantities of radium, uranium, zinc, and other minerals.

From the beginning, secession was a political stratagem designed to serve the interests of Tshombe and his political associates, the Belgian residents in the province, and the foreign investors in Union Minière and other economic enterprises in Katanga. The giant mining firm was the single most important and consistent supporter of the regime and of autonomy for Katanga. This does not mean that Tshombe was simply a puppet of external economic interests or his Belgian constituents. There was a symbiotic relation between the Tshombe regime and Union Minière, each using the other to advance its own interests.

The widely held assumption that foreign mercenaries were the back-bone of the regime is not the full story. Probably more important was the financial and administrative support of Union Minière and the political cooperation of the Rhodesian Federation, the Congo Republic (Brazzaville), the Portuguese in Angola, and, in the earlier period, influential segments of the British and Belgian governments. Incidentally, no government, not even those encouraging Tshombe, ever recognized Katanga as a sovereign state.

Repeated U.N. resolutions called for the end of secession and urged member states to refrain from assisting Katanga directly or indirectly. Katangan secession was considered the most serious challenge to the "territorial integrity" of the Congo by Leopoldville and by the states supporting the peacekeeping mission. The entry of the U.N. force into Katanga was regarded as "necessary for the full implementation" of the first three Council resolutions. In its efforts to arrest mercenaries in Katanga and to establish freedom of movement in the break-away province, the U.N. force had three small clashes with Tshombe's mercenary-led *gendarmerie*. It is not clear who actually fired the first shot in the controversial September, 1961, action. The clashes of December, 1961, and of December, 1962, were started by Katangan gendarmes, and the U.N. force replied initially in self-defense. The third clash ended the secession of Katanga.

After the first clash in September, 1961, Tshombe fell increasingly under the influence of his fanatical French mercenary officers. These men felt they had been betrayed in Algeria by the de Gaulle government and were dedicated to the defense of white economic interests against the "black tide" of Africanization. Ironically, the departure in September, 1961, of the Belgian officers, who had a certain respect for law and civilian authority, though not committed to a united Congo, virtually assured the triumph of the "ultras" in the *gendarmerie* and in the government. When Tshombe in late 1962 began talking about launching Algerian-type guerrilla warfare against the U.N. and of a scorched earth policy, his Union Minière supporters started to have sober second thoughts and showed some disposition to listen to Belgian Foreign Minister Spaak, who was urging Elisabethville to come to terms with Leopoldville along the lines of the U Thant plan of national reconciliation promulgated the summer before. This change of heart was motivated in part by the build-up of U.N. military strength in Elisabethville which preceded the third clash.

The three rounds in Katanga were modest police actions, carried out with great restraint by the U.N. and in the face of considerable provocation. Though accurate casualty figures on the Katanga side are not available, probably fewer than 300 gendarmes and 50 civilians, including perhaps a dozen Europeans, were killed in the three operations. On the U.N. side forty-two men and officers died. In contrast, estimates of the Congolese killed during these four years by tribal fighting or starvation connected with tribal conflict run into the tens of thousands. In Katanga there were some atrocities on both sides, but the number committed by the U.N. appears to be less than "normal" for police actions of the same scale in that part of the world. A portion of the public press, fed by Katanga propagandists, greatly exaggerated misdeeds by U.N. troops.

The Secretary General based U.N. military action in Katanga on the force's rights of self-defense and freedom of movement. In terms of the Council resolutions, the U.N. legal case stands up well. There is no clear evidence that the force exceeded its authority, but there is a great deal of evidence that it did not exercise the full authority it did have. Because of limited military capacity and the lack of consent from the host and donor governments, the U.N. force did not insist upon freedom of movement to restore law and order in many areas outside Katanga, or to disarm or reorganize the Congolese army, as vigorously as it finally insisted upon freedom of movement in secessionist Katanga.

Because the U.N. focused on the Katanga problem and neglected some other problems, it has been accused of taking sides in the internal conflict. The U.N. has also been charged with taking orders from Leopoldville, especially after the advent of the Adoula government in August, 1961, rather than strictly following the Council resolutions. With limited means the U.N. had to establish priorities for the deployment of the force. The U.N. mission obviously had a profound effect upon internal political developments in the Congo, whether so intended or not, but it is not correct to conclude that the Secretariat deliberately sided with one political faction against another.

In a series of interpretations, challenged by a few governments, but not challenged by the Council or Assembly, the Secretary General defined the policy of "non-intervention" in the Congo as one designed to secure a peaceful and constitutional solution to a turbulent and seriously divided state. Seen in this light, Thant's claim that the U.N. had "scrupulously avoided any support for or opposition to any Congolese official or candidate" is true to the spirit of "non-intervention" as interpreted by the developing mandate of the operation. The U.N. was committed to help preserve the territorial integrity of the state and to help establish, hopefully by constitutional means, a united government acceptable to all major factions. It cooperated with all Congolese political leaders who accepted these objectives and ground rules and found itself in opposition to those, chiefly Lumumba and Tshombe, who did not. The U.N. action can be characterized as legally authorized intervention, but not as capricious or politically interested interference.[6]

The ending of Katangan secession was the most politically sensitive and controversial accomplishment of the U.N. force. With the possible exception of the O'Brien incident, the U.N. pursued only authorized objectives and only by permissible means, exercising great restraint in the use of military force. The U.N. troops did not fire until fired upon, and then only in self-defense, or to establish freedom of movement.

In terms of the American interest in a territorially united Congo, the U.N. served as an effective, if somewhat cumbersome, instrument for achieving this objective. Territorial integrity should not be confused with political unity, much less with national cohesion. Some observers believe that the U.N. force could have ended secession a year earlier than it did, if the military strength of Tshombe's *gendarmerie* had not been over-estimated. Even if the U.N. clearly had had sufficient military capacity to do this, it probably would have been politically impossible because Britain, France, and other governments resolutely opposed the coercive solutions of "internal conflicts" by the U.N. Washington itself under-went considerable internal debate before it was willing to support the use of coercion to end secession.

At one point in the fall of 1962 direct U.S. military assistance to integrate Katanga was contemplated, but the President decided to pursue this objective through the U.N. for many of the same reasons which motivated Washington to opt for U.N. intervention in the first place. Direct U.S. intervention in late 1962 may well have met with the general approval of the neutralist states who were fed up with what they regarded as Tshombe's stalling tactics, but it might have raised a temporary tempest in NATO. Again, it is difficult to predict what the political costs of U.S., as opposed to U.N., intervention might have been, but Washington was simply not prepared to take the risk.

VII. OBSERVATIONS AND CONCLUSIONS

1) In spite of the vague, ambiguous, and sometimes conflicting U.N. mandate, and the fact that the permissible means were not adequate to

---

[6] Ruth B. Russell also concludes that the U.N. force operated within the legal constraints of the resolutions. See her *United Nations Experience with Military Forces: Political and Legal Aspects,* Brookings Institution Staff Report (July, 1964), pp. 86–126. This study originally appeared under the same title as Research Paper, P-27, of the Institute for Defense Analyses (May, 1963).

the authorized objectives, the U.N. force carried out its mission without exceeding or otherwise misusing its legal authority. This under-use of authority was due to the limited military capability of the force and the necessity for the consent of the Leopoldville government. The U.N. was also circumscribed by the necessity for the consent of the governments contributing troops and by the constraints of successive Security Council and General Assembly resolutions.

2) Given the political, legal, and military constraints of the force and considering that it was the instrument, not of a single political will, but of a coalition of states operating under a vague mandate, it performed its essential task well. Compared to the efficiency of the United States Army, it could be rated as fair to poor. But the U.N. mission must be judged primarily in terms of its political mandate, and only secondarily in terms of efficiency. While its operational efficiency might have been considerably improved by a modest degree of prior planning, the significant barriers to effectiveness were political in character, not military or financial.

3) The failure of the Council resolutions to define the relationship between the U.N. force and other indigenous or foreign military personnel within the Congo was a fundamental problem. During the first three months of the mission there were three separate and independent military establishments on Congolese soil without a clear understanding of the relationship or primacy among them. The mutinous Congolese army of 25,000 men was in the process of throwing out its 1,100 Belgian officers. By mid-July, 1960, Belgian forces numbered perhaps 10,000. The quickly improvised, multinational U.N. force had grown to 16,000 by the end of August.

In a sense, the U.N. force was intended to replace both the Belgians and the Congolese army, but it lacked any explicit authority to expel the former or disarm the latter. The Belgian military presence was speedily withdrawn, except for the small number of seconded officers who remained in Katanga.

The tense and undefined relationship between the U.N. and the Congo army was the most perplexing and persistent problem of the operation. The U.N. was not able to disarm, retrain, reorganize, or utilize the services of any units of the Congo army with the exception of the integration of a Congolese battalion of about 700 men into the U.N. force for eighteen months. Throughout the entire period the weakness and lack of discipline of the Congolese troops continued to be a major source of disorder.

For understandable political reasons the new and proud Congo government was reluctant to sign a status of forces agreement with the

Secretary General which would have placed its troops, however unruly, in a subordinate position to the U.N. force. But if the government was desperate enough to require substantial outside assistance, it might have been persuaded to accept a carefully defined and temporary limitation on the role of its military establishment. This problem, which has also risen in acute form in the U.N. operation in Cyprus, deserves careful study.

4) The precarious internal security situation in the Congo in early 1965 does not mean that the U.N. as an instrument had failed, though it clearly means that it was insufficient for the task. The U.N. military presence was only one of many factors impinging on the chaotic situation. Powerful internal forces such as tribalism, political rivalry, illiteracy, witchcraft, a weak and corrupt government, an unreliable army, and economic realities together had a far greater impact on the Congo's destiny than the U.N. force. There were also influential external forces at work in the Congo, ranging from Belgian financial interests and American diplomacy to Red Chinese subversion. Insofar as the force and the U.N. presence as a whole did influence developments, it was clearly on the side of greater law and order, a united Congo, and a moderate government in Leopoldville.

5) The U.N. proved to be a reasonably effective instrument of American objectives and of the larger interests of peace. It contributed to stability in Central Africa, helped to impose ground rules that made it difficult for the Soviet Union to capture the Lumumba government, and served as a thin buffer against some charges of American neo-imperialism. The U.N. did not and could not reasonably be expected to achieve other American supported objectives, such as the creation of a responsible Congo army or a strong government. Nor did it prevent the Communist exploitation of endemic disorder.

6) The fact that the U.N. did serve as a useful instrument of U.S. interests does not mean that the U.N. was a tool of Washington. Nor does it necessarily mean that these interests might not have been equally or even better served by American bilateral assistance, an alternative which can now be retrospectively examined. The mood in Washington in mid-1960 included an imprecisely articulated fear of Soviet military intervention in the Congo and an oversensitivity to neutralist criticism of U.S. policies. To be sure, Moscow regarded the Congo, with its background of paternalistic Belgian rule and its wealth, as a classic candidate for "national liberation," and it could be expected to employ all plausible political, diplomatic, economic, and subversive means in its arsenal to capture the Lumumba government. But the sending of a significant military presence to the heart of Africa was hardly plausible. And the

giving of U.S. military aid would scarcely have changed either the political or logistical constraints on the U.S.S.R.

Regarding neutralist criticism, the State Department is rightly concerned with attempting to get along with the newly independent states. Obviously the U.S. did not want to become a substitute target for hostile passions directed against the "Belgian colonialists." But it does not necessarily follow that bilateral U.S. assistance to Leopoldville would have suddenly changed the cherished anti-colonial image of Washington into that of colonialist exploiter, except in the twisted slogans of the Communist propagandist. Washington has a host of responsibilities around the world—deterring nuclear war, maintaining the NATO alliance, containing brushfires, and fostering stability in underdeveloped areas, to name a few—and sometimes inadequately examined inhibitions against the use of a little coercion in a politically sensitive situation tend to take precedence over what, in the larger prospective, are really more substantial considerations. The U.S. did not hesitate to use invited but unilateral coercion in Lebanon in 1958. But Washington is reluctant to use coercion in a newly independent African state, even with a legitimate invitation, because it is perhaps more sensitive to the immediate and volatile reactions of some neutralist leaders than it is to the long term interests of the African states and the larger interests of peace and stability in the world.

This is simply to say that there is no moral or political presumption in favor of United Nations action over bilateral action, or of alliance action over unilateral action. The political wisdom and moral justification of sound foreign policies are derived from the intention and consequences of the policies rather than from the channels through which they are expressed.

CHAPTER 10

THE NEW DIPLOMACY:
THE 1955 GENEVA SUMMIT MEETING

PAUL C. DAVIS

I. Introduction

It may seem puzzling to have selected a summit conference as a case for the examination of modern diplomacy. A summit conference is, after all, but one manifestation of diplomacy, and in the long sweep of history perhaps a unique one at that. For purposes of analysis, however, it is peculiarly opportune because a summit conference is a microcosm of the diplomacy, the foreign policies and the strategies of the major states, telescoped in time, focused in intensity, bringing the power and methods of each to bear upon common problems.

Nor are its processes so entirely distinct from normal diplomacy as the common criticisms of "summitry" would suggest. Issues, techniques, public and private representation, ceremonial actions, and the personal impact of leaders are manifestations which summit conferences share with foreign ministers' conferences, state visits, missions of special emissaries, and the day-by-day conduct of diplomacy by resident plenipotentiaries. If the summit conference is unique, its uniqueness lies in its apparent brevity [1] (with all that implies about accomplishment), the public expectations and attention it invites, and the aura of publicity in which it proceeds. Even in these respects it differs from most forms of diplomacy only in degree. Of these apparently unique features of the summit conference I shall have a good deal to say.

PAUL C. DAVIS is a senior staff member of the Institute of Naval Studies. He is a contributor to *United States Representation Abroad* (to be published in 1965 by the American Assembly).

[1] "Apparent" because as I develop in the concluding section of this paper, the actual conference is but one phase of a negotiative process.

It is not my purpose, then, to scrutinize the summit conference as a special phenomenon. I want rather to see what one particular summit conference can teach us of the general nature of modern diplomacy, in order to see how diplomacy can more effectively be used as one of the foreign policy instruments.

I say "modern diplomacy" for the significant reason that there is a widespread sentiment among those with experience in diplomacy—and they tend to be the only ones who write about its nature—that diplomacy has changed for the worse. Their criticism usually rests on three propositions. The first is that diplomacy properly has as its sole aim accommodation, or the reaching of agreement in accordance with mutual interests, and that an unhealthy tendency to conduct diplomacy for "victory," for prestige, or for other allegedly irrelevant purposes has become the norm. Thus Sir William Hayter (who, incidentally, participated in the summit conference of 1955) says: "The Russians always negotiate for victory. It never occurs to them that the proper object of negotiation is not to defeat your opposite number but to arrive at an agreement with him which will be mutually beneficial." [2]

The second proposition grows naturally out of the first: negotiations, to be successful, must be, as they once were, conducted quietly, "far from the madding crowd." Publicity tends to compel rigidity in negotiation, for a negotiator's departure from previously announced positions is popularly construed as appeasement. Today there is altogether too much publicity, they assert. Often they imply that we must somehow exorcise the modern press or that the diplomats could by sheer exercise of will induce silence. Some, recognizing that public silence is impossible, try to distinguish between "good" and "bad" publicity, between the airing of issues to educate the public or to learn its will, and publicity intended to create hostility or embarrass opposite numbers.

In the third place these critics bemoan the use of conferences "for propaganda." This they see as something different from and more insidious than the mere "vice of publicity." In their minds the cold war has brought with it a misconception that the function of conference diplomacy is to provide an occasion for fighting a war of words. It is not always clear whether the implication is that propaganda is conducted without purpose. At the least the proposition seems to suggest that diplomacy and propaganda, like oil and water, do not mix.

These are serious criticisms uttered by very responsible people. It is one of the purposes of this study to discover what light the 1955 Geneva

[2] Sir William Hayter, *The Diplomacy of the Great Powers* (New York, 1961), p. 28. Also Lester Pearson, *Diplomacy in the Nuclear Age* (Cambridge, Mass., 1959), p. 42.

Meeting of the Heads of Government [3] sheds on the validity of this indictment.

Beyond this, the Geneva Conference was quite generally thought to have had profound significance, yet involved no substantive agreement. The mystery of its pay-offs and its influence in the absence of agreement challenges our curiosity, and suggests that here if anywhere insights could be had about the nature of modern diplomacy. As we shall see, the anomaly of its impact is explainable in terms of a complex interplay of psychological and substantive factors which distinguish the new diplomacy from the old.

II. PREPARING THE CONFERENCE

The idea and the name for a "summit" conference were Churchill's. He first raised the idea in the British general elections of 1950. The time seemed to some more propitious when, as Prime Minister, he again proposed it, this time in the House of Commons in April, 1953, after the death of Stalin and before the impending Korean armistice. His idea seemed to conform to the old diplomacy: no fixed agenda, and ". . . conversations on the highest levels, even if informal and private. . . ." [4]

The Soviet government welcomed the idea. But it was thought unpropitious by Washington in the absence of encouraging Soviet actions; this was the period of "liberation" policy, and in any case Churchill's illness prevented the British from pressing the issue. Russia exploited the British-American difference in a steady flow of diplomatic correspondence over the next two years, and it is significant that when the 1955 conference was finally held the most active private Russian discussions were with Eden.

In 1954 Russia's general interest in a conference—to enhance Soviet prestige and decelerate Western unity measures—acquired a more specific rationale. Moscow now took the initiative in proposing a *formal* conference, apparently in order to forestall the rearming of Germany. Churchill, with U.S. sympathy, prolonged the preliminaries in order first to ensure the incorporation of Germany into NATO. France, under Mendès-France, settled reluctantly for the postponement, and under his successor Faure, France came to the conference apparently still

---

[3] Hereafter referred to for brevity as the Geneva Conference or simply the conference. The Geneva Meeting of Foreign Ministers, which grew out of it and took place the same year (Oct. 27–Nov. 16), is referred to hereafter as the Foreign Ministers' Conference.

[4] David J. Dallin, *Soviet Foreign Policy After Stalin* (New York, 1961), p. 128, quoting the *New York Times* of April 21, 1953.

hoping faintly for some Russian concession which would make the arming of West Germany unnecessary. If there was a legitimate element of hope for an accommodation between East and West, it must have lain in this common concern of France and the U.S.S.R.

American motives were mixed and obscure. Certainly there were strong Right-wing Republican pressures against any negotiation with the Russians. The evolution of Dulles' perspectives, always complex, we shall examine at a later point. It is fairly clear that he was at first opposed to a conference because he thought the Kremlin struggle for power was not yet over nor was their policy line established. Dulles is thought to have accepted the idea initially as a reward to France for the Paris Accords and as an aid to Eden in the British general elections. If Eden privately agreed to the latter, his memoirs gainsay it; indeed, he had it in his power to postpone the election and seriously considered, as an argument for doing so, the completion of the conference, which he was certain would take place.[5]

Underlying the general impetus toward a conference was the popular sentiment favoring a way out of the arms race which the Soviet development of the H-bomb had stimulated. Unstructured and difficult to assess as such sentiments always are, they were certainly in the minds of the Western leaders (and possibly the Soviets as well).

Being impelled toward a conference by a variety of pressures and having specific objectives for the conference are not the same thing. At the least we can say that the causes which gave rise to the idea of a conference were more general than the purposes developed as the conference approached. Perhaps only the United Kingdom had its negotiating objectives in mind all the while. But before discussing objectives it is worth reciting, very briefly, a series of attendant political events which bore upon these.

Most had to do with the Soviet Union, and of these a number prompted speculation as to whether the Soviet line was not changing and softening. In April the Bandoeng Conference took place. The U.S.S.R. was not represented but sent its blessings. On May 10, 1955, the Soviet delegation to the U.N. Disarmament Commission tabled the most radical change in the Soviet position since World War II, accepting so many of the Western points as to cause the U.S. to take a second look at its own position. On May 15 the Austrian State Treaty was signed, providing for Austrian neutrality and the withdrawal of Soviet and Western troops, which followed ten years of Soviet intransigence.[6] This had come

[5] Anthony Eden, *Full Circle* (Boston, Mass., 1960), pp. 298–99.
[6] On the background of this treaty see David Dallin, *Soviet Foreign Policy After Stalin,* chapter 3.

only two months after a public change in Soviet policy on Austria. The Treaty was followed shortly by an announced reduction of Soviet armed forces of about 600,000 related seemingly to abandonment of the line of communications to Austria. In May the U.S.S.R. surrendered its military rights in Port Arthur. The last week in May Khrushchev made his pilgrimage to Yugoslavia, foreshadowing a fundamental shift in Soviet-satellite relations. All these Soviet acts were subject to various interpretations; there followed, however, one month before the Geneva Conference, the Soviet diplomatic recognition of West Germany, the purpose of which in the light of the conference agenda was not at all obscure.

This, then, was the environment in which the four powers prepared to meet. What were the respective objectives of the powers as they prepared for the conference? The immediate aim of the U.S.S.R. is now so well documented in Soviet diplomatic correspondence and propaganda as to admit of no doubt. Initially it was to forestall the arming of West Germany, but before the conference began that was acknowledged a *fait accompli* and their object became the delay of German reunification.[7] Of more interest is the light recently shed on the relationship of the conference to Soviet global strategy revealed by David Dallin. Based in part on documents still secret,[8] Dallin's disclosures are however supported in part by the published testimony of Seweryn Bialer, a Polish defector. At a Plenum of the Central Committee which opened July 4 and closed six days before the Geneva Conference, the basic Soviet global strategy was revised. The Soviet Union would take the offensive in Asia to detach the underdeveloped countries from capitalism, sealing the fate of the West by the "capture" of India. Meanwhile the strategy of "defense in Europe" must be actively conducted, while avoiding conflict. Certainly any modification of the German problem other than stabilization of the status quo would not have fitted this strategy.

The British objectives were not at all based on a global strategy. As Sir William Hayter has pointed out, the British Foreign Office is chronically poor at this sort of planning.[9] Moreover, Eden shared what we have called the conventional diplomatist's view; he believed in making progress through specific but modest settlements out of which the confidence for broader settlements might grow. He considered German reuni-

[7] Bulganin announced the shift in July, 1955. (Dallin, *Soviet Foreign Policy After Stalin*, p. 279.) This objective was not thought an adamant one at the time by either Eden, Dulles, or Adenauer for reasons I develop later. See for example, Eden, *Full Circle*, pp. 323–26.

[8] The so-called "D Papers," which will be made public in 1976. See Dallin, *Soviet Foreign Policy After Stalin*, introduction.

[9] Sir William Hayter, *The Diplomacy of the Great Powers*, p. 46.

fication by far the salient question to be dealt with, but he had no confidence in the possibility of a short, direct route to unity at a single conference. He wanted rather to approach it through piecemeal disarmament measures. He favored a demilitarized strip at the Iron Curtain, some measures for control and inspection in the area, and, in one variation of his idea, a general European security pact. His experimental and pragmatic approach, designed to create confidence, is confirmed in his memoirs: "I wanted to try out such a system with the Russians taking part in it. . . . The Russians were suspicious of control. . . . When the great powers have accepted a system of international control in some sphere and begun to work it, we may emerge from the cold war." [10]

Eden seems to have had no thought that pressure, other than the pressure of reasonableness, ought or indeed could be put on the Russians. Indeed, quite unlike Dulles, he thought time to be on the Russian side.[11] His memoirs do not mention either propaganda or the European satellites as appropriate levers for extracting agreements at Geneva. Finally, Eden's interest focused on Europe. He did conduct private conversations with the Russians at Geneva about Formosa. But he avoided discussion of wider Asian problems. Like Dulles, he wanted the agenda limited to Europe in order to get substantive results, in his case on his arms control plan. It is clear from his memoirs that Eden was apprised rather late of the Russian moves in the Middle East, and felt no strong concern about Soviet Asian moves as late as 1956.

France, as we have noted, had seen value in a conference only as a hope against having to rearm Germany. Under Faure there appears, however, to have been full acceptance of a rearmed Western Germany. Nonetheless, France remained but mildly interested in reunification, and probably gave support at Geneva to the United States-inspired position on Germany and European security only out of the expectation that nothing would come of it. France played but a minor role at the conference, having gone to Geneva mainly to appease a very anxious public extremely fearful of a nuclear holocaust, fears typified in the hostile French reaction to Dulles' ebullient pre-conference tactics.[12]

[10] Eden, *Full Circle*, pp. 324–25. His emphasis on "making a practical start" toward German unity through arms control measures is also reflected in his opening statement at the conference. See Department of State, *The Geneva Conference of Heads of Government, July 18–23, 1955, International Organization and Conference Series*, I, 29, pp. 32–33 (hereafter cited as *International Organization and Conference Series*).

[11] See Eden, *Full Circle*, p. 320.

[12] Typical of French reaction was that reported by Gênet from Paris in the *New Yorker* for June 4, 1955: that Eisenhower's remark made in May, "There is no alternative to peace," was very well received, while Dulles' hard-boiled pre-conference television chat with the President was thought "dans un style bon

When we turn to United States objectives we enter the realm of modern diplomacy wholeheartedly, as evidenced in the differing perspectives and aims of President Eisenhower and Secretary Dulles, in the evolution of their aims, and in the roles they assigned to mass communications.

Both Eisenhower and Dulles began by doubting the value of the conference and both came to favor it, but for different reasons. Dulles' reasons were substantive, Eisenhower's psychological. Dulles began by thinking the Russian leaders too weak in personal power and too unyielding in foreign policy purpose to make negotiations at all profitable. An analysis of the bloc situation, however, brought Dulles to believe that the Russians might require a settlement because of their weakness. Eisenhower began by fearing the domestic reaction to hopes unrewardingly raised, but his optimism led him to see in Geneva play for his special talent at conciliation. Eventually, however, he came to believe that he might bring the Russians to trust in the possibility of settlements with the West. But his sense of mission in this aim obscured from him the fact that in working for a spirit of trust he would raise the very hopes at home he was at the same time trying to allay.[13] His pre-conference statements were, therefore, a long series of self-contradictions. On balance, the President's public statements, no doubt at Dulles' behest, were cautionary although his private hopes were high, while Dulles, privately wary of a spirit without substance, expressed publicly some optimism (with an occasional dash of caution), as befits a loyal cabinet member.[14] At times the cautionary statements of the two were evidently coordinated.

Eisenhower took the lead early in expressing the hope that a new start

---

enfant," intended "for the use of simple souls." In this connection the French (and the Italian) Left-wing and Communist press gave the coming conference a build-up as a Soviet initiative to end the cold war. If the Soviets led anyone to the conference as captive of a peace-making propaganda it was Faure, though such pressures had some bearing on the attitudes of all the Western leaders.

[13] These self-contradictions are in part attributable to his need to appease the Right wing of his party.

[14] See for example Dulles' May 17 radio-television report to the President, which reveals the cautionary approach, which Eisenhower promptly qualified in an interjection; and Dulles' May 24 press conference, where in reply to a question, he supported the President's aim: "What we need is a new impetus and a new spirit . . ." (Department of State Bulletin, Vol. 32, pp. 875, 915). While speaking the next day at West Point, Eisenhower warned against the danger of expecting a "miraculous cure" and of our need to keep our guard up. (Ibid., Vol. 35, p. 988.)

The President's mixture of public caution and private hopes is evident in his statements at the conference, which contained a large measure of the latter and a small dose of the former; it is confirmed by Donovan (Eisenhower: The Inside Story [New York, 1956], pp. 346–47); and it comes through even in his public statements before and after the conference.

might be made in negotiating differences, provided the air was cleared of tensions and hostility. It seems clear that Eisenhower, conscious of his forte for composing differences through his personal magnetism and aura of sincerity, hoped to establish himself as the great peacemaker, a nice counterpoint to his role as great warmaker. At the same time he understood the dangers of nuclear parity, and even more the popular worries about it. Essentially of a harmonizing nature, he did not, like Dulles, see nuclear power as a weapon of diplomacy, nor does he seem to have been so confident of Soviet military inferiority. Tending to reduce politics to problems of human personality, and not overly informed about Marxism, he was ready to accord universal human attributes, notably essential goodness, to his adversaries. About his own ethics he had that element of self-deception so common to idealists. Thus he wanted to approach the Russians with the objective of creating mutual confidence so that negotiations could be approached in a new atmosphere. This began to show in his early statements and appeared regularly until the conference.

The President's pre-conference optimism reached its apotheosis in his television address on the eve of his departure for Geneva. "Our many post-war conferences have been characterized too much by attention to details; by an effort apparently to work on specific problems rather than to establish the spirit and the attitude in which we shall approach them. Success, therefore, has been meager." [15] His attitude, of course, reflected a tendency to underrate substantive differences, as well as the danger of reaching misleading agreements couched in confusing generalities, which the conventional diplomatist so abhors.[16] In Eisenhower's case, however, this was compounded by an ambivalence and lack of clarity, which caused him to contradict his strategy of creating a new spirit. Thus at the conference he said in his opening statement, "The new approach . . . cannot be found merely by talking in terms of abstractions and generalities. It is necessary that we talk frankly about this concrete tension between us. . . ." [17]

There was the second ambivalence—that between the President's urgent desire to create a new spirit and his concern lest its failure injure domestic morale. The quest for a new spirit dominated, however, breaking through the membrane of caution in his public utterances, and

[15] "Radio-Television Address of July 15, 1955," *International Organization and Conference Series,* I, 29, p. 14.

[16] See Sir William Hayter, *The Diplomacy of the Great Powers,* on similar weaknesses in the diplomacy of Lloyd George, Woodrow Wilson, and Neville Chamberlain.

[17] Opening Statement, July 18, *International Organization and Conference Series,* I, 29–31, p. 19.

appearing in a form more exaggerated even than his private hopes, evidently because of his sense of the dramatic quality of his own destiny. All this is evident, for example, in one sentence from the television address previously referred to: "I say to you if we can change the spirit in which these conferences are conducted we will have taken the greatest step toward peace, toward future prosperity and tranquillity that has ever been taken in all the history of mankind." It was his sense of mission as peacemaker which led him also to exaggerate the dangers of war. Other Presidents had gone abroad in their war-conducting or war-settling capacities. "But now," he continued, "for the first time, a President goes to engage in a conference with heads of other governments in order to prevent war. . . ." In the light of such a statement it is interesting to recall that, though the ominous cloud of the H-bomb then floated over the world, there were at the time of Geneva no military crises such as had existed the year before or have dogged the world since the year after.

Dulles, as we have seen, gave reserved support to Eisenhower's optimism. But his sense of mission and optimism were rooted quite differently from Eisenhower's. He believed not at all in Soviet sincerity; his religion was no bland belief in people-to-people togetherness, but a stern distrust of the sinner, combined with the lawyer's zeal to outwit him and the determination of the *Realpolitiker* to overpower him. Dulles' pessimism turned to optimism not because he thought the character of Russian leaders had changed but because he sensed that their power had greatly deteriorated.

It seems clear that Dulles, who before the signing of the Austrian State Treaty and the Paris Accords was against the conference, began to favor it immediately after, and with each intervening month became more confident of results.[18] On May 18, two days after the Austrian Treaty was signed, and five days after the Tripartite Invitation to Russia, Dulles was mildly encouraging: ". . . it may possibly be the case that the Soviet Union, after this experience of trying to buck everything, may be feeling that it may be more convenient for them to conform to some of the rules of a civilized community." [19] Late in May, Dulles began to show marked optimism, and, according to Eden, he assured Adenauer at this time he was confident the talks would lead to the reunification of Germany.[20] From this time on, Dulles returned again and again, with

[18] There are, however, some who argue that Dulles never changed his view and went to the conference grudgingly. This is the thesis of Goold-Adams (*John Foster Dulles* [New York, 1962], chapter 11), but he does not document it. I know of no source that does document this view.

[19] *Department of State Bulletin*, Vol. 32, p. 876.

[20] Eden, *Full Circle*, p. 323.

guarded optimism, to the theme that the events of the spring (the Austrian Treaty, incorporation of the German Federal Republic into NATO, Khrushchev's pilgrimage to Yugoslavia, and Russian troop withdrawals) offered the West real opportunities to capitalize upon what seemed a radical Soviet policy shift. In this his focus was constantly upon the liberalization (though probably not liberation) of Czechoslovakia and Hungary.

The behavior of Dulles in preparing for the conference included a pattern of public cue-giving statements, which ought properly to be looked upon as negotiative propaganda, for they were effectively though not openly addressed to the Russian leaders with a particular negotiating purpose. These centered about two propositions: that the United States was negotiating from a position of strength and that the agenda ought to include not only German reunification but two items that would affect the very stability of the Soviet Bloc and system—the question of the independence of the European satellites and the question of the activities of international communism. A careful scrutiny of Dulles' statements and Soviet counterstatements concerning these questions demonstrates their negotiative character.

The "position of strength" concept and Dulles' interest in the "problem of the satellites" were probably first raised in his May 17 radio-television report to the President on his return from signing the Austrian State Treaty. Eisenhower, as an opening remark, reminded Dulles that they had agreed in 1953 not to meet the Russians in conference until the rearming of West Germany was assured; Dulles then spoke with circumspect interest of the possible consequences of the Austrian Treaty for the Eastern European nations. The following day Eisenhower at his weekly press conference indicated that he favored the two agenda items (the problem of the satellites and the international activities of communism), attributing their previous mention to Dulles.[21] On May 22 *Pravda* criticized Eisenhower and Dulles for raising the question of the satellites.

On May 24 Dulles issued his most definitive negotiative communication in a prepared statement at a press conference, the pertinent portion of which follows:

> It is not possible as yet to grasp the full significance of what is taking place. But it is clear that we are seeing the results of a policy of building unity and strength within the free world. It is that policy, the failure of the Soviet Union to disrupt it, and the

---

[21] *New York Times,* May 29, 1955, section 4, p. 1; and May 22, 1955, section 4, p. 3.

strains to which the Soviet Union has itself been subjected which undoubtedly require a radical change of tactics on the part of the Soviet Union, which is now particularly illustrated by new Soviet attitudes toward Austria and Yugoslavia. No doubt these new tactics will involve some risks to the free nations. Also they will surely bring vast new opportunities. The essential thing is that we should adhere to the principles which we now know produce good fruits.[22]

In reply to a reporter's question he then said that the question of the satellites certainly should be discussed, because subjugation of these nations was a genuine source of international tension.

The Soviet Union in its May 26 letter accepting the Tripartite Invitation to the Conference took exception to ". . . certain statements of leaders of the U.S.A. made after receipt by the Soviet Government of the aforementioned note . . . ," which, it said, asserted that the United States was acting from "a position of strength." It took exception also to statements to the effect that the United States had ". . . the necessity of interference in the internal affairs of other states . . . ," which the U.S.S.R. implied would foredoom the conference.[23] Its acceptance notes to the U.K. and France, otherwise identical to that sent the U.S., included an additional paragraph implying that it would not accept the satellites as an agenda question. Whether these powers interceded with the United States is not known, but certainly this was the Russian purpose. The complaints quite evidently referred to Dulles' May 24 statement.

On July 4 Khrushchev, at an American Embassy garden party, made a little speech to the American chargé J. W. Walmsley, saying that there were some in the West spreading rumors of Soviet weakness in agriculture and elsewhere, that there were many who think that if the U.S.S.R. makes a good decision ". . . there is something that forced it to make that decision and even that the Soviet Union fears some catastrophe if she does not." Khrushchev stated that Russia would not go to Geneva if the West were not serious, but clearly he meant only that he wanted all questions about Communist Eastern Europe excluded. His repeated denial of agricultural weakness, a kind of peroration after Walmsley's reassurance that no inference of weakness was intended by the United States, was a transparent evidence of insecurity.

At the President's next press conference on July 6 he denied he knew anyone who had said the Soviets were going to the conference in a

[22] Press release 288, May 24, 1955, *Department of State Bulletin*, Vol. 32, p. 914.
[23] *International Organization and Conference Series*, I, 29, p. 8.

position of weakness. On July 8 the press revealed that testimony Dulles had given in executive session June 10 before the House Appropriations Committee on the subject of Foreign Aid, but not released until July, had indeed made comparisons of the United States and the Soviet Union to show that Russia was wilting under the competition. The press gave the impression that it was in the context of economic competition alone that Dulles had made his comments, though the implication was clear that Dulles' testimony had been intentionally withheld for a month.[24] The White House promptly explained that the comparison was not directed to any immediate crisis. Given the delayed publication of the testimony and its apparent aim of supporting the foreign aid program, these press and governmental interpretations seemed persuasive.

The full testimony gives, however, quite a different picture. The delay in publication was at Dulles' request, simply to afford him the opportunity to review his transcript.[25] At Dulles' specification, the bulk of his testimony was "on the record," and it was these remarks, not any declassified remarks, which the press (and the Russians) picked up. Moreover, almost all Dulles' remarks about Russia and the European situation *were* directed to the immediate situation and went beyond anything needed merely to support the foreign aid program. He made three basic points: that recent Soviet actions showed they realized their old policies had failed; that the Austrian Treaty opened a "new frontier of freedom" to Czechoslovakia and Hungary; and that the Soviet "pilgrimage" to Yugoslavia would "have a very great repercussion upon the hold which the Soviet has upon the satellite countries in Europe." It appears then that Dulles was the conscious cue-giver. In any event Khrushchev responded in a way which seemed both to confirm Dulles' estimate of Soviet weakness and to be designed to defeat his purpose. The careful staging of Khrushchev's remarks and the fact that they were not published in the Russian press suggest this. Khrushchev now became cue-giver in his turn; his response served to exploit the difference in perspective between the President and Dulles and to impel the President toward a position independent of his Secretary, for the White House response validated Khrushchev's condition for the conference. Explicitly, this was to negotiate sincerely on a basis of equality (a condition which Eisenhower shared). But in reality it was to shift the propaganda power struggle from the sensitive subject of liberalization in Eastern

[24] *New York Times,* July 8, 1955, p. 3.
[25] U.S., Congress, Hearings before the Subcommittee of the Committee on Appropriations, *Mutual Security Appropriations for 1956,* 84th Cong., 1st Sess., p. 1.

Europe to the ambiguous subject of relaxation of tensions, which the Russians felt to be greatly to the advantage of their global strategy.

It is noteworthy that every position publicly put forward by the Russians before the conference was in fact maintained there. Perhaps the most interesting was the Soviet acceptance as *fait accompli* of the incorporation of West Germany into NATO, for on this their position was publicly reversed between April and June,[26] rather than at the conference. The United States similarly maintained the positions it had publicly advanced. It might seem therefore that the statements of position had no influence on the conference. But it is significant that those agenda items (two American, three Russian), aired publicly prior to the conference but which in fact had been, with one exception, in the category of propaganda not related to substantive issues, were thereby quickly eliminated. (The one exception, the Far East, may well have been raised by the Russians to insure its elimination; in any event they accepted its elimination readily.) Indeed, as we shall see, the only symbolic ideas of a non-negotiative character actually pushed at the conference came as a surprise and were not listed as agenda items.

It would appear then that pre-conference negotiative communications (those in which leaders were clearly speaking to each other) served to shape the course of the conference. Each party wanted the conference, to be sure, mainly for symbolic reasons, for each wanted its version of relaxed tensions. Indeed, the conference may be viewed as bargaining over the shape of reduced tension. Moreover, the desire of each for a conference caused each, in more or less degree, to respect the other's choices of subject areas designed to serve symbolic aims, but only so long as these seemed ambiguous or universal (e.g., development of contacts between East and West), and to respect each other's sensitivities about symbolic subjects that were not.

If we reflect upon the respective aims and methods of the protagonists we see that three approached the conference with psychological means or purposes in mind: Eisenhower sought a new spirit, hoping thus to dispel the fear of nuclear onslaught; Dulles, in the Foreign Ministers' Conference, used psychological pressures to bring about substantive changes in the power balance; the Russians sought a relaxation of tensions in the West. But all dressed them in substantive problems—the German problem, European security, or disarmament. Of these Germany received priority. The conferees were not sure whether Germany might or might not prove a pay-off, but they labored as though it might, since if the pay-off was to be substantive it could only be in this area.

---

[26] See Dallin, *Soviet Foreign Policy After Stalin*, p. 279.

Because of this mixture of purposes, the first conference itself took on a mixed style of negotiative and symbolic communications, and so too did the second.

III. CONDUCTING THE HEADS OF GOVERNMENT CONFERENCE

We do not dwell upon the substantive agenda items in spite of the fact that they were most seriously discussed. They were not, however, the things for which the conference will be remembered. As James Reston has said, the real lessons lay not in the substantive discussions but ". . . in the techniques of modern international diplomacy." [27] It was in part a conference of manners. This was evident from the start. All brought huge press delegations. Bulganin and Khrushchev for the first time rode in an open tonneau from which they greeted the crowds bareheaded and paused on the steps of the Palais de Justice to wave in "politician" style. Eisenhower, recovering early from the somber obscurity of his bullet-proof car, greeted the Russian leaders with something between a Mexican abrazo and a Russian bear-hug and took Zhukov to his bosom like a long-lost brother.

It must not be thought, for all the preparatory maneuvers, that the U.S. delegation came to Geneva with a full-blown theory of modern diplomacy ready to be put into practice. The delegation was composed of persons with different purposes and different styles for carrying them out, so that we see in their performance combinations of the old and the new. This is nowhere more evident than in the American handling of press relations. In this respect the size of the press delegation was misleading. Both Charles Bohlen and Lewellyn Thompson were at first considered for the role of press spokesmen; both declined on grounds that this was inconsistent with their role as diplomats. Here were the new and old concepts confronted practically. As a compromise, James Hagerty acted as spokesman, and for that purpose attended all sessions. This seems to have proved either inhibiting or overwhelming. Of all four government representatives, he proved the most close-mouthed. Here again, attendance of a spokesman at sessions was new, uncommunicativeness was old.[28]

Indeed, the spokesmen of all four powers were new to the job of interpreting diplomacy and foreign policy. Oddly enough, the French and British reportedly performed the best, even though their leaders held

---

[27] "Two Parleys in Geneva," *New York Times,* July 23, 1955, p. 4.
[28] See Michael Straight, *New Republic,* Aug. 8, 1955, pp. 11–13.

the conventional view that diplomacy should be quiet.[29] Perhaps this was because the Soviet and U.S. proposals dominated, and the British and French spokesmen were unencumbered with the duty to reinforce or to conceal the psychological motivations of the proposals.

The behavior of the Russian leaders was marked by a new set of manners, which Philip Mosely has pointed out was the only change in the normal Soviet diplomacy.[30] While Bulganin and Khrushchev were no match for Eisenhower's simple effusive sincerity, they did play down all occasions for possible friction and addressed themselves to touchy questions with temperate dignity rather than the usual Russian acerbity. Accordingly, Bulganin and Eisenhower were able to promptly eliminate five symbolic agenda items which they had evidently proposed only "for the record." [31]

Eisenhower relentlessly pursued his aim of convincing the Russians of his sincerity and thus creating a "new spirit." In his opening statement, after outlining the difficulties that lay before them, he called upon the participants to ". . . create a new spirit that will make possible future solutions of problems . . ." and ". . . try to take here and now at Geneva the first steps on a new road to a just and durable peace." He had some nasty things to say about international communism, but he said them in an un-nasty tone. He closed the first day, in his capacity as chairman, with an appeal for a continued spirit of friendship and sincerity as they got into the substantive questions.

At one point, Eisenhower, pledging his personal honesty as assurance the Russians could trustfully enter into agreements with the West, turned to Zhukov for confirmation that ". . . I have never uttered a single word that I did not believe to be the truth." [32] As Drew Middleton put it, day after day Ike was ". . . aggressively friendly and the Russians ruthlessly amiable." Michael Straight describes the closing scene: "Then, when the Conference ended, he went over once more to embrace and to reassure the Soviet leaders. The final impression that the Ameri-

[29] *New York Times,* July 21, 1955, p. 5; this view is generally substantiated by Richard Rovere, in a series of articles from Geneva which appeared in the *New Yorker.*

[30] Philip Mosely, *The Kremlin and World Politics* (New York, 1960), p. 434 and chapter 20.

[31] Eisenhower clearly did not share Dulles' conviction that "the problem of the satellites" or "the activities of international communism" should trouble the waters of the conference. The statement in which he abandoned them revealed that he had "seen his duty" because of a joint resolution of Congress. Dulles of course had favored these items not to appease Right-wing congressmen but because he had genuine hopes of thus hastening the liberalization of Eastern Europe.

[32] *International Organization and Conference Series,* I, 29, p. 46. Thus the Soviet cue of friendliness in the presence of Zhukov was returned verbally in the symbol of military frankness and incapacity at duplicity.

can experts brought away was of Bulganin, Khrushchev, and Zhukov, beaming and basking in the warmth of the President's personality." [33] Already on the opening day of the conference the East European press and radio were applauding the optimism and "spirit of conciliation." On July 24 *Pravda* stated that the Geneva Conference will go down in history because of its contribution to the strengthening of confidence between the U.S.S.R. and the Western powers. In the wake of Eisenhower's enthusiasm Eden echoed his hopes for peace and a new spirit, much as in 1918 the European leaders emulated Wilson's new diplomacy—though no doubt with *arrière-pensées*.

Unlike the negotiative communications, the Open Skies proposal came as a surprise, and achieved by the manner of its announcement an aura of apparent spontaneity. At the fifth plenary session, July 21, Eisenhower interrupted the reading of a memorandum to inject the following extempore statement:

> Gentlemen, since I have been working on this memorandum to present to this Conference, I have been searching my heart and mind for something that I could say here that could convince everyone of the great sincerity of the United States in approaching this problem of disarmament. . . . I propose, therefore, that we take a practical step, that we begin an arrangement, very quickly, as between ourselves immediately. These steps would include:
>
> To give each other a complete blueprint of our military establishments, from beginning to end, from one end of our countries to the other; lay out the establishments and provide the blueprints to each other.
>
> Next, to provide within our countries facilities for aerial photography to the other country—we to provide you the facilities within our country, ample facilities for aerial reconnaissance, where you can make all the pictures you choose and take them to your own country to study, you to provide exactly the same facilities for us and we to make these examinations, and by this step to convince the world that we are providing as between ourselves against the possibility of great surprise attack, thus lessening danger and relaxing tension.[34]

The influence of the Open Skies proposal upon the European press and public and upon American journalists was profound. They treated

---

[33] "How Ike Reached the Russians at Geneva," *New Republic*, Aug. 1, 1955, p. 7.

[34] *International Organization and Conference Series*, I, 29, p. 58.

this as an act of spontaneous sincerity, and journalists such as Richard Rovere and Max Ascoli took pains to reject allegations that this was propaganda.[35] The fact nonetheless is that it was propaganda. And this brings to our attention the presence at Geneva of persons representing a third American policy-orientation besides those of Eisenhower and Dulles, that of the psychological warriors.

The Open Skies proposal had been worked out at a conference at Quantico, Virginia, designed to contribute to a basic study on psychological strategy. The idea is generally credited to the President's cold war adviser, Nelson Rockefeller, but reportedly it was originated by his assistant, Colonel William R. Kintner. Rockefeller persuaded Admiral Radford, Chairman of the Joint Chiefs of Staff, and Secretary of Defense Anderson that it had merit. But Harold Stassen, heading the newly formed Disarmament Agency, was less enthusiastic, particularly because his staff was just being formed and had not had time to review its consistency with our wider disarmament proposals. Rockefeller pressed the President by cable to go ahead, and he and Stassen were forthwith ordered to Geneva two days before the idea was presented. That afternoon Eisenhower sounded out Eden, who concurred. At a full dress conference the next day (July 20) Eisenhower decided to use the idea, reserving the timing of his statement for his own judgment. The next day Eisenhower made his "spontaneous" proposal. The precaution had been taken to inform key congressmen such as Senator George, so that it received immediate public support from leaders in both parties. The inconsistency between the Open Skies proposal and Eisenhower's "spirit of Geneva" approach, accounted for by the influence of advisers with differing assumptions (Rockefeller and Dulles favoring pressure rather than accommodation through trust), seems not to have disturbed the President, if indeed he recognized it.

Interestingly, the responses of the Russian leaders and the public did not expose the inconsistency either. The Russians went along with the

---

[35] Thus Max Ascoli, taking exception to the quotation marks many put around the term *spirit of Geneva*, stated: "This last feature [aerial inspection] . . . has been called by many people, even in our own country, propaganda—a word that perhaps more than any other deserves to be sterilized by quotation marks" (*The Reporter*, Sept. 22, 1955, p. 13); see also Richard Rovere, "Letter from Geneva," *New Yorker*, Aug. 6, 1955, pp. 62–63; and *Christian Century*, Aug. 3, 1955, p. 883, where it similarly takes issue with the *Chicago Tribune*'s doubts about Ike's sincerity over Open Skies. Rovere reported at the time that even though spokesmen for the President insisted that the proposal had been carefully planned, ". . . most other observers here, and evidently most observers throughout the world, were backing the President's offer as a master stroke of diplomacy. Exactly what made it a master stroke is a question that the Americans . . . still find it difficult to answer to their own satisfaction. . . ."

myth of sincerity, apparently for two reasons: first, they wanted to salvage the "spirit" and second they were caught on the horns of a dilemma and knew it. To have openly rejected the proposal immediately would have been foolhardy, for the world's press took the proposal to heart; it was a great psychological coup. The Russian leaders of course were not taken in. Talking to Eden immediately afterward, they heaped scorn upon the proposal.[36] But they played it straight publicly. The Soviet press spokesman, Leonid F. Ilyichev, said that "the frank declarations" on disarmament around the table would have "a great significance for the examination of this point in the future," and Pierre Baraduc, the French spokesman, reported that Bulganin described Eisenhower's speech as a "sincere statement" that would have a "wide effect" and that it provided a "good augury" for the discussion of disarmament. However, Bulganin did not discuss it officially with the West until September 19.

Eisenhower and Dulles gave impetus to Open Skies upon their return from the conference. In his May 26 news conference, Dulles stated: "This is the most dramatic, and at the same time most serious and sober, peace proposal that history records." [37] And the President in his July 25 radio-television address, speaking of Open Skies, said, "The principal purpose, of course, is to convince everyone of Western sincerity in seeking peace," and at another point, "there is a realization that negotiations can be conducted without propaganda and threats and invective." [38]

As the conference drew to a close, the lines between the Western and Russian approach to German reunification and European security had been firmly drawn, but the differences were muted by manners and by avoidance of details. So the conference closed on a note of expectancy and hope.

The old and the new were mixed at the conference. For the Russians it was "old" to talk over the heads of diplomats to the people; what was new was how little they did this and how much their communication continued to be negotiative. Eden's diplomacy was "old" in that he quietly sought specific agreements over a narrow range and met frequently with the Russians in private discussion. Eisenhower's was "new" in that he sought through gesture and word to create a new spirit; the effort to convey sincerity was in the old tradition, but the effort to define it and catalogue it as an essence prerequisite to concrete talk was new.

---

[36] Eden, *Full Circle,* p. 337.
[37] *International Organization and Conference Series,* I, 29, p. 87.
[38] *Ibid.,* pp. 85, 86.

IV. POST-CONFERENCE EXPLOITATION: NEGOTIATIVE AND
NON-NEGOTIATIVE PROPAGANDA

In the West the "spirit of Geneva" had for a time a major influence
upon public opinion. The press of France and the United Kingdom, for
example, gave it much the same favorable treatment as the political
journalists in the United States. At the opening of the Foreign Ministers'
Conference in October, Foreign Minister Pinay could legitimately say,
"The Conference held in Geneva last July aroused tremendous hopes
throughout the world."

In the United States the "spirit" at first merged with hero worship of
Eisenhower. As Robert Donovan has said, "His performance . . . had
won universal acclaim. . . . Indisputably he was the leader of the free
world." [39] However, public opinion was skeptical for the greater period
of the interim between the Heads of Government and the Foreign Ministers' Conferences. Not only were Americans more used to living under
the cloud of the bomb than Europeans. Soviet efforts at penetrating the
Middle East quickly soured a public ever inclined to doubt the Russians'
honesty; and the administration conducted no systematic propaganda to
maintain the atmosphere of a new spirit.

Indeed cautionary advice was offered by both Eisenhower and Dulles,
just as before the conference. It readily became evident that the Eisenhower target had been the Soviet leaders and he felt he had completed
his task. It is nonetheless difficult to explain how Eisenhower came to
lose momentum in pushing an aim he could hardly have discarded so
quickly. The seeming duplicity of the Russian mission to Cairo would
appear insufficient cause to have abandoned his missionary purpose,
given the great fruits he hoped from it. It may simply be that as Eisenhower was not himself to participate in the second conference he lost
interest. The West did seek to revive the spirit, as we shall see, in the
earlier days of the Foreign Ministers' Conference; but preparation for
the second conference included no public drum-beating for a new spirit.
The last gasp by Western leaders in support of the "spirit" was probably
that uttered by Dulles on his return from the Foreign Ministers' Conference. Stating that neither the President nor he had ever thought it a
"magic elixir," he nonetheless claimed that the spirit still existed in the

[39] Robert S. Donovan, *Eisenhower: The Inside Story*, p. 352.

sense that both parties at the conference had refrained from threats and invective and that war had become less likely.[40]

Russia had larger purposes for the "spirit of Geneva" and kept it thriving much longer than did the West. Support for the new spirit began, as we have noted, while the conference was still meeting. In the last days of the conference the reports of Russian correspondents were as euphoric as those of Western correspondents. One of the underlying themes in Russian foreign audience periodicals was that the West had abandoned its "positions of strength" policy in favor of relaxing tensions in accordance with "the Geneva spirit." In a rare departure from normal practice the *New Times* complimented the Western leaders and press on their moderate tone.

Support for the Geneva spirit was carefully maintained by Bulganin afterward. His optimistic appraisal of the results was accompanied by continuation of the Geneva manners. This was particularly noticeable in his report on the results of the conference to the U.S.S.R. Supreme Soviet on August 4. He carefully avoided criticism or recriminations against the West, and in his concluding speech the following day gave credit to the Western leaders for their display of goodwill and sincerity.[41] At the Foreign Ministers' Conference, after the West had finally abandoned efforts at restraint,[42] Molotov still defended his positions in the name of the "spirit," concluding that "the 'Geneva spirit,' in reality, is appropriate because it leads to the strengthening of peace, to the reduction of international tension, and to the establishment of real security in Europe." [43]

After the Foreign Ministers' Conference there was a change in Soviet handling of the "spirit." Still supporting it themselves, the Russians now attributed failure of the second conference to Western abandonment of the spirit. Holding out some hope of a renewed spirit, *International Affairs* stated, "A frantic campaign is being conducted in the West to kill 'the Geneva spirit' and inflame the cold war. . . ." [44] Thus Russia began to claim the very pay-off that many Western analysts believe was a pay-off for the West: proof to the doubters that the adversary was to blame for international tension and cold war.

At the final session of the Supreme Soviet held at the end of 1955, Khrushchev asserted that Eisenhower had ". . . swept aside whatever remained of the Geneva spirit" by his proposal of Open Skies and his

[40] "Radio-Television Address of Nov. 18, 1955," *International Organization and Conference Series,* I, 30, pp. 6–7.
[41] *Current Digest of the Soviet Press,* VII, 29, pp. 13–20.
[42] See section V below.
[43] *International Organization and Conference Series,* I, 30, p. 168.
[44] "In the Service of Peace," *International Affairs,* Nov. 1955, pp. 11–13.

Christmas message to the people of Eastern Europe.[45] We can probably date the end of Soviet support of the "Geneva spirit" from this pronouncement. At the Twentieth Party Congress, convened the following February, it received no mention and America was once again declared communism's enemy number one.

The Open Skies proposal was for the Russians only a tactical problem, but inept handling might have impeded their exploitation of the "spirit." They continued for some time to handle the proposal gingerly. Even Communist press and radio commentary on Open Skies was sporadic and contradictory. For example, L'Humanité expressed "unreserved satisfaction" with the proposal in the same period in which the East Berlin radio stated that the President had presented it "with much rhetoric" but that "unfortunately he did not propose real disarmament and the banning of atomic and hydrogen weapons." The deliberateness and uncertainty with which the Russians handled the proposal is confirmed in their official correspondence.

Some order in the Soviet line began to emerge with Bulganin's report to the U.S.S.R. Supreme Soviet. Saying that Russia stood ready to consider seriously any proposals by other participants, he went on: ". . . President Eisenhower's proposal on organizing an exchange of military information between the Soviet Union and the United States and on carrying on aerial photography of each other's territories is just such a proposal." [46] The context in which he spoke suggests that the Soviet strategy was to incorporate Open Skies into the "spirit of Geneva," which in turn of course was to be a sub-strategy of "peaceful coexistence."

On September 19, after the West had had a new occasion to air Open Skies at the sub-committee meetings of the U.N. Disarmament Commission, Bulganin addressed a letter to President Eisenhower on the subject of disarmament, in which he proposed adding provisions for inspection teams at control points (from the Soviet May 10 disarmament proposal) to provisions for exchange of blueprints and for aerial photography, the sincerity of which he again specifically praised. President Eisenhower promptly agreed. Bulganin also asked for aerial photography of overseas bases, which the President found acceptable in principle after its application to the U.S. and the U.S.S.R. and subject to approval of the nations concerned.[47]

---

[45] Both were laid on as psychological operations. The Christmas message was part of an annual food offer to both East and West European countries, which, first carried out in 1953, invariably invoked refusals from the East European nations and acceptance in the West.

[46] Current Digest of the Soviet Press, VII, 29, p. 20.

[47] Department of State Bulletin, Vol. 33, pp. 643–47.

Again, during the Foreign Ministers' Conference, Molotov, expressing "not the slightest doubt" of the President's good intentions about aerial photography and exchange of blueprints, set about drawing the proposal carefully into the wider web of disarmament problems, and concluded that unfortunately it did not meet the aim of reducing armaments and the danger of atomic war. Alluding ever so subtly to the possible use of Open Skies to aid rather than deter attack, he did not reject it but relegated it to the last stage of disarmament.[48] Thereafter the Russians alternately attacked or resurrected Open Skies to fit their tactics of the moment. Meanwhile public enthusiasm over Open Skies subsided. Early in 1956 Khrushchev bluntly called it a Western espionage scheme. Yet in July, 1956, Bulganin informed President Eisenhower that the Soviet Union would accept aerial photography, though only in an area 500 miles each side of the Iron Curtain.[49] This and the later series of counterproposals for photographing limited areas of the two powers, while evidencing the psychological potency of the proposal, ultimately dissipated much of the initial embarrassment and loss of prestige which the U.S.S.R. had suffered.

V. The Foreign Ministers' Conference

On October 27 the Foreign Ministers' Conference began; it was to last nearly three weeks. The meeting divides into two phases. The first lasted from October 27 through November 4, when Molotov returned to Moscow presumably for new instructions. The second lasted from his return November 8 to November 16. The first was a period of quietly but unsuccessfully testing whether the Geneva spirit would survive. The second was one in which Molotov proved less willing, even than before his Moscow trip, to yield on any position, and one in which the West abandoned negotiation in favor of mass-consumption propaganda.

Pinay opened the conference with a dramatic appeal to carry out the quest for settlements in a "spirit of dialogue." So true was his statement to Eisenhower's approach, it seemed for a moment that the first conference had never adjourned. Molotov the same day praised the historic significance of the first conference. But immediately he set the tone of all his later remarks. He claimed for Russia certain unilateral deeds already taken in the "spirit," but made veiled assertions that others were seeking

---

[48] *International Organization and Conference Series,* I, 30, pp. 181–83.
[49] John W. Spanier and Joseph L. Nogee, *The Politics of Disarmament* (New York, 1962), pp. 99, 100. They incorrectly call this the first Soviet acceptance. Molotov's statement at the Foreign Ministers' Conference constituted formal acceptance, though just as unreal in practicality as the one they cite.

to obscure the success of the first conference and were failing to use unilateral "opportunities" as benevolent as those Russia had acted upon.[50]

The Western foreign ministers continued to avoid similar aspersions. Nonetheless, their temperate tone and their pains to expose carefully the reasoning behind their proposals as well as to analyze the Soviet proposals *in extenso* with an air of objectivity could not brook the fact that on all three agenda items (European Security and Germany, Disarmament, and Development of Contacts between East and West) there was no ground whatsoever on which East and West could agree. Still the West consistently retained in this phase a posture of restraint and hope, epitomized by Mr. Dulles' remark on the eve of Molotov's return to Moscow, "I find it hard to believe that this rigid and unresponsive position of the Soviet Union is final." [51]

It is clear that in this first phase communication was almost entirely negotiative, designed on the part of the West both in manner and substance to induce Molotov to modify his position, and in his case to withstand these efforts. This was conventional diplomacy.

When the conference reconvened on November 8, the French and British ministers, speaking first, pressed for the Soviet views but nonetheless continued to be temperate. Then Molotov spoke, rejecting the Western proposal for reunification *in toto* and declaring that elections in Germany were no longer possible. This last was the one change he made from the former Soviet position.

The next day Secretary MacMillan set an entirely new pattern of hard talk and frank criticism, clearly designed no longer to influence Mr. Molotov but to apprise the world that Russia had killed any chance for settlement. Using the refusal of elections as proof that Molotov was no longer sincerely carrying out the Directive,[52] he accused Russia of treating the German people as "pawns in this game to break up the defensive system of the West" and of seeking to Bolshevize all Germany through the use of puppets. From the irony of "this . . . is their contribution to the Geneva spirit," he turned finally to grave indictment: "I do earnestly beg the Soviet Government not to incur so grave a responsibility before history." [53]

[50] In this obscure statement may lie revealed one of the results Russia really entertained for the "spirit"—unilateral Western withdrawals analogous to Soviet abandonment of Porkkala Udd, knowing that no Western withdrawals could be *negotiated* without additional costs to Russia.

[51] *International Organization and Conference Series*, I, 30, p. 128.

[52] Bulganin and Khrushchev had approved "reunification of Germany by means of free elections" in the Heads of Government Directive to Foreign Ministers.

[53] *International Organization and Conference Series*, I, 30, p. 154.

Dulles, who followed, was no less severe. "My first observation is that the Soviet position if persisted in will perpetuate conditions which put in jeopardy the peace of Europe. My second observation is that it strikes a crippling blow at the possibility of developing relations of confidence with the Soviet Union." He stated that Molotov's position had done severe damage to the spirit of Geneva, which would "affect adversely the overall relations of the Soviet Union with other countries, including the United States." [54]

From then on the moves of both sides aimed no longer at negotiation, but at propaganda intended for use outside the conference room. For example, on November 10 Dulles made a strong defense of Open Skies. The next day, citing Molotov's statement that "no doubt President Eisenhower was guided by the best of intentions" but that his Open Skies proposal would in fact heighten tensions, Dulles went on:

> In essence the Soviet Union says that . . . he has bad judgment regarding these matters of war and peace. With this conclusion, we cannot agree, and we believe that most of the world will not agree. It is not easy to disparage the judgment of one who won world-wide renown as the military leader of the great coalition which won the victory in the west for freedom. When President Eisenhower made his proposal . . . it was greeted with a wave of acclaim throughout the whole world." [55]

Clearly meant to catch headlines, this was symbolic propaganda in the best cold war style.

Similarly on November 9 Molotov sought to pin the West to a meaningless nonaggression treaty, and on November 15 to a list of platitudes on which they had supposedly agreed, including continued negotiation. And on November 15, before the conference had ended, the Western powers released a "Tripartite Background Paper for the Press Containing Observations on the Proceedings of the Expert Committee on East-West Contacts," and another summarizing Soviet responses to the Western proposals on East-West contacts, both exposés of the intransigence of the Soviet position.[56] Finally, in his closing statement of the conference Dulles attributed Russian rejection of German elections to fear of instability and of the "peoples' choice" throughout the satellite area,

---

[54] *Ibid.*, pp. 155, 158. I have been unable to discover whether Dulles' abandonment at this time of his effort to reap the dividends of the "spirit" had the President's explicit approval. As the President returned from his illness in Colorado on Nov. 11, it is quite possible it did not.

[55] *Ibid.*, p. 201.

[56] U.S. Delegation Press Release No. 21, Nov. 15, 1955, in *Ibid.*, pp. 279–83.

and indicted the Soviet system for its inability to tolerate freedom of communication and freedom of thought.[57]

This non-negotiative personal communication of the Western leaders was "for the record." This does not mean, however, that Dulles (or the other Western leaders) had conscious plans for post-conference exploitation. The perspective of modern diplomacy has not yet gone this far. Rather they saw themselves as establishing for history the responsibility for failure. This is not a new technique. Insofar as it is not motivated by the diplomatists' pride (a conference which does not "settle" is a conference which fails), it is a diplomatic debating device to write a record which can be quoted at future meetings as part of the argumentation. Unlike the Russians, Western diplomats have as yet hardly learned to use this record to establish a propaganda campaign.

VI. CONCLUSIONS

At the outset we cited three propositions widely maintained by diplomats of experience as to the proper characteristics of diplomacy and the conditions which have recently degraded it.

The first was that diplomacy should properly limit itself to the quest for accommodation. Applying this proposition to summit meetings, Sir William Hayter has said: "The truth is that if there is a desire to settle, a Summit meeting is unnecessary, while it is useless if there is no such desire." [58] I have already described how much the objectives of the participants ranged beyond and how much they ran counter to a quest for accommodation. This point merits brief review in the context of a second question. Since the Geneva Conference did have wider purposes than accommodation, were the pay-offs of those purposes significant or was the conference, as Sir William Hayter would prognosticate, indeed useless? What did each participant want? What did he get?

President Eisenhower valued the first conference as the occasion to create conditions of mutual confidence as a prelude to accommodation in the second. He succeeded notably in achieving a new "spirit" at Geneva, but how much this influenced the Soviet leaders is problematical. If there were vacillations in the rigidity of Bulganin and Khrushchev under the magnetism of the President, these reaped no obvious fruits. All we can record with confidence is that the new spirit did not advance the substantive negotiations. It did not even stimulate the Russians to

[57] *Ibid.*, pp. 285–87.
[58] Sir William Hayter, *The Diplomacy of the Great Powers*, p. 67.

take a new initiative in their own interest at the Foreign Ministers' Conference; their defensive strategy precluded that. It may even have forced them to be more rigid at the conference than they had intended. The President viewed the "spirit" as an accommodative move, meant only to influence the Russian leaders. In this it proved nugatory, whereas its symbolic effects were great.

Secretary Dulles sought in vain through his negotiative propaganda not to reach accommodation, but rather to weaken the Soviet hold on the European satellites. He failed both because of Soviet negotiating tactics and because his objective conflicted with the President's. Geneva was a manifestation of the thaw in Eastern Europe, but the thaw owed far more to the Soviet decision to liberalize its controls than to the maneuvers of Dulles. His purpose was not accommodative. On the other hand his nonaccommodative aims proved unproductive.

French hopes of deferring German unity benefitted from Soviet rigidity on this issue. But neither the French aim nor its result can be characterized as accommodative. Accommodation assumes change. The French success lay in changing nothing. Indeed a far more significant pay-off in the eyes of the French was the relaxation of tensions. Not only were the French leaders more driven to the conference by their public than were other governments; the public response to the "spirit of Geneva" was probably greatest in France.

Eden's purpose was to gain a settlement of modest nature—limited demilitarization. He hoped from it both a substantive accommodation and a contribution to mutual confidence which might lead to further settlements. It was viewed in this light by all parties and was seriously negotiated. Eden's aim was, then, accommodative, and we have no reason to discredit it as a meaningful effort. It fits Sir William Hayter's prescription well. We must, however, recognize that the other participants did not place it high among the reasons for the conference.

The Russians went to Geneva to perform a blocking action in Europe and through diversion to gain time for their Asian offensive. In this they were mildly successful. They would have been more so had they conducted the second conference as adroitly as the first. Certainly they needed no conference in order to postpone German reunification: simple inertia could have accomplished that. But the relaxation of tensions in Europe was well worth the effort, and it is difficult to visualize another way which could have been as dramatic and as persuasive of their sincerity as the Geneva Conference.

The Russian leaders no doubt viewed the symbolic pay-offs of Geneva as closely related to their more concrete global strategy. For Western leaders many of the symbolic pay-offs were ancillary. This difference notwithstanding, the symbolic pay-offs are in many respects the most interesting for what they suggest as to the limits of *accommodation* as the prime occupation of diplomats.

Clearly, the almost total acceptance of the idea that there had been a tacit agreement against nuclear war, and its variant that the likelihood of war had receded, have had consequences for the post-1955 style of East-West negotiations which are incalculable. They reach beyond the modest aims of accommodation. Geneva marked the beginning of a flexibility in the strategy of both major powers, which has opened up great opportunities, great uncertainties, and great risks. It led to an alteration in strategies and negotiating styles. While this change has embraced elements that are accommodative, it has also included elements which are far more ambivalent and complex.

This ambivalence is exemplified in the contrast between the promise and the fate of the "spirit of Geneva." For the slogan, "spirit of Geneva," which was received at its inception so euphorically in so many places, afterward acquired an opprobrium probably in the main deserved. Over-dramatization, partly by the President but more particularly by journalists, gave rise to self-deception in the West. The "spirit" which President Eisenhower wanted only for the negotiations became in fact a public trauma. This could have had unpleasant consequences but the new mood proved insufficiently structured for that, and new events quickly brought a more sober view of the dimensions of the cold war Had the "spirit" been used after the Foreign Ministers' Conference to reinforce Dulles' aim of subverting the satellites, it might have had greater effect, though Hungary showed how little we could have capitalized upon it. In any event, the "spirit" was not immediately very productive, perhaps was even counter-productive, but revealed the possible dimensions of policy leverage which diplomatic conferences will afford once the planned use of such atmospheres becomes better understood.

The second ancillary pay-off—Open Skies—was an intended one. But it was a spill-over nonetheless, because it was not consistent with the President's object of creating a climate of confidence for further negotiation. Open Skies nonetheless illuminated the possibilities of symbolic negotiation. It revealed for just a moment the tremendous vulnerability of the Soviet Union to the well-conceived psychological operation: one which appeals superficially to dramatic and simple truth while it exposes beneath the surface basic flaws in Soviet society. Though the President gave Open Skies the appearance of an accommodative move, it was in fact an offensive cold war maneuver, and for a time it was a successful one.

In sum, to view the Geneva Conference as an effort at accommodation would be greatly to distort its character. Probably no one save Eden can be thought to have played the traditional diplomat in a quest for what can fairly be called accommodation. Both purposes and results ranged beyond the traditional pattern. Yet neither can be thought either irrelevant or insignificant. The Geneva Heads of Government Meeting was a significant milestone in post-war world politics, not only because the participants pursued an unprecedented variety of objectives, but also because the pay-offs, intended and accidental, successful or not, were strategically significant.

The symbolic pay-offs were among the most interesting. Perhaps no other event in the entire cold war so mesmerized the public, or so suddenly transformed expectations, popular and elite, about the possibilities of future policy. This, it might be alleged, is the very danger to which such conferences are subject. But that can only be judged by the ways leaders profit from this newly discovered capacity to restructure opinion. It reveals that leaders are not necessarily prisoners of an inflexible public opinion. There is an interplay that the conventional statesman has too often failed to exploit by giving the public appropriate opinion-molding cues. There are occasions, it seems, when leaders can escape the power-dissipating pressures of conflicting interest groups and acquire through dramatic symbolism the chance to act strategically and decisively in the name of a universal consensus—a consensus such as Rousseau once favored as the prime mover of states. The summit conference may occasionally serve this purpose, particularly when the issues are elemental and universal.

The second proposition held essential to conventional diplomacy was that diplomatic negotiation should be conducted quietly, to avoid rigidity. It is difficult to conceive how the first such meeting since Potsdam could possibly have been held in quiet. Not alone was it bound to excite public expectations. The impetus to bring the conferees together included and probably required the pressures of publicity and propaganda. When nations have endured a long period of hostility one cannot simply leap into amiable negotiations without overcoming the resistances posed by the suspicions of leaders, the opposition of political factions, or public distrust.

Extensive publicity during the negotiations might have been avoided. The leaders used the press positively if somewhat uncertainly, revealing most of the formal discussion daily. Did it prove inhibiting? The first conference, far from being forced into rigidity by its openness, was conducted in a friendly and flexible manner. Not only did this flexibility favorably influence the public, but public reactions (as in the case of Open Skies) compelled a flexibility of response on the part of some participants which they did not privately feel. The second conference was characterized by rigidity, but this arose from the private negotiating purposes of the participants, not from public pressures. Public acclaim for the "spirit of Geneva" was not transformed into pressures on the Western foreign ministers to yield; public opinion proved both unstructured and highly adaptive to the new pessimistic turn of events. It appears that whether rigidity is induced by public opinion depends on a variety of environmental factors, and often as much on leadership aims and estimates as on the excesses of public fervor.

The press, which was made privy to much of the negotiation, far from constituting a distractive element, reflected the views of the diplomats quite accurately (though admittedly with simpler optimism).

The third proposition of the conventional diplomat is that conferences are often mistakenly conducted "for propaganda," as a forum for the invective of the cold war. To deal with this charge effectively requires examination of larger aspects of the interplay of diplomacy and propaganda, which we discuss below. Suffice it to say at this point that both propaganda and diplomacy are usable for a number of purposes. Perhaps the diplomatist means really to question the wisdom of those purposes. Insofar as propaganda supports diplomacy, its range of purposes is as wide as those of the particular diplomacy it supports. And at Geneva these purposes were wider than those the conventional diplomat finds suitable.

The possible purposes of diplomacy go even beyond those embraced by the West in the Geneva Conferences. A conference may be used, for example, to seek to avert war (by clarification of intentions and capabilities or by ambiguous or frank preventive ultimata); to enhance prestige or diminish an opponent's; to illuminate public opinion or allay public fears; to assess the adversary's strategy or take the measure of his strength of will and mind; to achieve delay, diversion, subversion, or deception; to register or confirm an objective situation; or even to reach accommodation on substantive issues. There are as many symbolic as substantive purposes possible, and there is no a priori reason why one kind of purpose need be less useful than another.

The Western uses of diplomacy at Geneva were, then, many. But they did not have the strategic sweep of the Russian and their accomplishments suffered by the fact their objectives were evident to the Russians. Negotiative propaganda is *meant* to be evident, but the larger purposes to be served by the particular diplomacy need not be.

There will always be propaganda going on at the time of negotiations (and for that matter negotiations in one form or another go on continually too). Some of the propaganda will not be directly related to the negotiations. If it does violence to the negotiative aims this is quite likely an accidental spill-over, such as often develops between our various policies; otherwise the propaganda must be truly purposeless, which is an absurdity. There will also be propaganda directly related to the negotiative aims. If we are clear which diplomatic aims we have, the choice of an appropriate propaganda becomes a rational exercise in policy execution. Propaganda must serve to facilitate the object of the diplomacy. If we are seeking simply "to gain propaganda advantage," this is probably not a deficiency in the propaganda itself but in the precision of the diplomatic objective. Many diplomats probably entertain this vague notion of the functionlessness of propaganda, a notion which propaganda planners by their laxity all too frequently reinforce.

If diplomatists need not limit themselves to diplomacy conventionally defined, it is equally true that propaganda need not be conducted only by the "conventional" propagandists. This is one of the points which the Geneva Conference best illustrates. The American negotiative propaganda was not conducted by a propaganda agency. Indeed it could not have evoked the necessary responses if it had been. Top leaders are inevitably propagandists, and the Geneva case suggests that they are often consciously so. In this modern age of symbolic communication, in which most life is experienced vicariously, propaganda cannot be restricted to a narrow range of officially identified propaganda media. Nor if it could be, would it be effective in its purpose.

If we look at the Geneva Conference as a total process this supportive interplay of diplomacy and propaganda becomes evident. Neither conference was a discrete event in itself. It was a continuum [59] consisting of three phases: preparation, conduct, and exploitation. In all three phases both diplomacy and propaganda played a part. In the preparatory phase diplomatic correspondence and diplomatic conferences took place, including a preliminary meeting between East and West. But propaganda received priority. Propaganda was used first to make the conference possible, then to negotiate and delimit the agenda, and finally to establish and communicate the basic aspects of the respective agenda positions.

In the conduct phase, though conventional person-to-person diplomatic intercourse was the normal mode of communication, many of the pay-offs were sought through symbolic action. This is to say they were aimed at influencing leaders indirectly through public pressures, and not

---

[59] Actually part of the larger continuum of the policy process, evident in the difficulty I have had in finding a starting point, end, or geographic limits of the process. Nonetheless, it was relatively isolable as a unique aspect of the larger process.

solely concerning the agenda. In the exploitation phase, propaganda media were the main but not exclusive vehicles. In all three phases, real targets were mixed (sometimes mass, sometimes leadership), and the medium of communication used is not necessarily a clue to the target. It is an arbitrary convenience to think of public communication as propaganda, hence intended for the masses, and to think of personal communication as diplomacy, hence meant for the leadership. In reality, there was negotiative communication and non-negotiative communication, and both were communicated person-to-person as well as by the mass media.

At this point conclusions as to the precise nature of negotiative propaganda and its function are in order. Negotiative propaganda is designed to focus leaders' thoughts upon the scope of the agenda and the considerations affecting one's negotiating position, and to influence their perceptions and expectations concerning both so that one's diplomatic aim may be served.

Negotiative propaganda is conducted publicly when one (a) has an obligation or occasion to speak publicly for an ancillary purpose; (b) wants to commit oneself publicly as a bargaining device; (c) has an obligation or occasion to speak publicly for an ancillary purpose; or (d) when silence might be disadvantageously construed, typically when one is the cue receiver in a negotiative communication process.

In the present case, non-negotiative propaganda was of two kinds. First was the cumulative, non-strategic propaganda which the information agencies conducted normally, some of which no doubt had relevance to the conference though handled in accordance with the routine policy planning procedures. This we did not examine. Second was the single instance of the Open Skies proposal. Because of the attention-getting forum in which it was announced and the audience officially addressed, it was strategic in character. It could, however, be thought negotiative only had its primary intent been to influence the disarmament negotiations of the two conferences. The Russians pretended to treat it so and in fact we did as well. But its aim was actually to influence public attitudes about the nature of a closed society, and by reshaping popular images of the Soviet Union to gain a general initiative in the conduct of our global strategy. It was indeed inconsistent with the immediate American aim and cannot therefore properly be thought negotiative. For these reasons Open Skies should be classified as strategic non-negotiative propaganda.

The combination of audiences which the "modern diplomatists" addressed is instructive. Mr. Dulles often talked publicly for the ears of Khrushchev, and Khrushchev in turn replied publicly for the ears of

Eisenhower or Dullles. At the first conference, Eisenhower offered the "spirit" to his opposite number and Open Skies to the public. But the Russians and the press converted the "spirit" into symbolic propaganda, and indeed Eisenhower was unable to keep its negotiative separated from its symbolic consequences. All seemed at least partly conscious of these distinctions. No Western leader used negotiative communications so consciously as Dulles. But when he failed in his diplomatic aims (German reunification and weakening the Communist Bloc), he did not carry out fully his final shift to symbolic propaganda. For this the close support of the United States Information Agency would have been required, and it is unlikely that Dulles saw symbolic communication as other than a one-man task.

I have said earlier that at Geneva the old diplomacy mingled with the new. I do not suggest that the Geneva Conferences were in any sense a consciously rationalized model of modern diplomacy. At the same time, Soviet diplomacy is in this context not, as some have suggested, a gauche and amateur old diplomacy but a modern Marxist diplomacy. It has the limitations *and* the advantages of the Marxist perspective, of which the great advantages are clarity and unconventionality of objectives and the skill to conceal the objectives. Western diplomacy is at a transitional stage. American diplomacy has abandoned the old but not yet perfected the new. It supports a new range of purposes. It does not yet derive these purposes from a broad strategy, for that strategic perspective does not yet exist. Nor has it yet fully elaborated the role of propaganda in modern diplomacy. Our leaders are experimenting with the interplay of propaganda and diplomacy as the modern American statesman becomes his own natural propagandist.

This interplay, so evident in the international conference, is naturally less evident in day-to-day personal diplomacy, but hardly ever absent. The international conference, however, enjoys advantages over representative diplomacy akin to those enjoyed by the television political debate over whistle-stop speeches. The widened range of negotiative purposes that we have enumerated can find their full play best when public attention is focused as only a foreign minister's or summit conference permits. There will no doubt always be scope for quiet negotiation, notably when the prospects of accommodation are evident. But for the wider range of diplomatic aims, especially (but not exclusively) when they deal with adversary states, the international conference is probably here to stay and governments will probably continue the process of rationalizing this kind of modern diplomacy as a communicative process.

CHAPTER 11

ORCHESTRATING THE INSTRUMENTALITIES: THE CASE OF SOUTHEAST ASIA

ROGER HILSMAN

For more than a decade—ever since the French defeat at Dienbienphu in 1954—the United States has had the major responsibility for the frustrating complexity that is Southeast Asia.[1] Here all the problems that face us in the various underdeveloped regions of the world are combined—teeming population, illiteracy, endemic disease, undeveloped resources, the bitterness of a colonial experience, "bloody-shirt" nationalism in an extreme form, and over all the steady probing of Communist aggression, both politically and through guerrilla terrorism. Understanding the peculiar, interacting problems of Southeast Asia is a baffling effort; meeting them requires a confusing array of the different instrumentalities of foreign policy which must be orchestrated with exquisite precision. Yet there is perhaps no more urgent order of business on the American foreign policy agenda.

Partly this urgency comes from the importance of the area itself. Here, in the great arc of Asia from Japan and Korea in the north to India and Pakistan in the South, live half the world's people and, once developed, some of the richest of the world's nations. Partly the urgency comes from the fact that the Communists, and especially the Chinese Communists, feel that they have discovered a new and potent tactic in "internal war" through guerrillas and organized terrorism. But partly it comes from the fact that Southeast Asia has become a test case of the

---

ROGER HILSMAN is professor of government at Columbia University. He is the author of *Strategic Intelligence and National Decisions* and a contributor to *Alliance Policy and the Cold War*.

[1] An earlier version of this chapter appeared in the *New York Times Magazine*, Aug. 23, 1964, under the title, "Plea for 'Realism' in Southeast Asia," and is reprinted here by permission.

United States' ability to learn how to mesh the different instrumentalities of foreign policy so they all further the same political goal. For whether or not we are successful in devising effective ways of meeting the challenge depends not on any single instrumentality of foreign policy—aid, or military power, or psychological warfare, or diplomacy—but on our ability to blend them all.

I

If the United States is to arrive at an effective policy in Southeast Asia, the first step is to be clear in our thinking about our political objectives. We must be certain that what we are trying to achieve in Southeast Asia is realistic.

It would be dangerously unrealistic, for example, to attempt to make Southeast Asia a base for American power and a bastion of anti-communism. Certainly it is by now clear that the power of the United States to dictate the course of history in Asia is limited. Southeast Asia is far from the sources of American power and close to the sources of Chinese Communist power, and the effort required to make Southeast Asia an anti-Communist bastion in the teeth of Chinese Communist resistence would far exceed the possible gain.

But it would be equally unrealistic and dangerous to withdraw from Southeast Asia, as Senator Wayne Morse has advocated. Under present circumstances, withdrawal would in effect turn the area over to the Communists, which we cannot afford. Politically, economically, strategically, and psychologically, the United States' stake in Asia is high, and Southeast Asia is a strategic salient into the arc of Asia that we cannot allow the Communists to control.

It is sometimes argued that Peking will inevitably dominate Southeast Asia and that it would never agree to anything less than total domination. But there is a difference between what Peking would like to have in Southeast Asia if the costs were not excessive and what it could be brought to accept, just as there is a difference between what Peking could be brought to accept and what it would not tolerate no matter what the cost. The United States does not have to resign itself to Southeast Asia's becoming a satellite of Communist China—and clearly it should not.

Thus the United States' political objective in Southeast Asia should be something between the two extremes of attempting to make the area an American base or letting it become a Communist satellite. The ideal objective is easily stated—independent countries free to develop in their own ways. In practice, however, we must recognize that this would mean a wide variety of political shadings among the individual countries, some of which would cause the United States difficulties, and an over-all situation that both we and Communist China would find distasteful but still less dangerous and exacting than the alternatives.

In one sense this goal is no different from the goal President de Gaulle envisions for Southeast Asia when he talks of neutralization. But the practical differences are significant. French motions imply an international conference followed by the withdrawal of outside powers under the supervision of international inspectors. A conference may well be desirable at some stage, and international inspection might be useful, but certainly neither would be the end of the matter—the United States would have to continue to be very active if any agreement that might come out of such a conference is to work.

Although the Geneva agreements on Laos were far from perfect, they did maintain relative peace in Laos; they did permit the neutralist government to gain in strength and influence; and most importantly they did keep the Mekong lowlands out of Communist hands, thus providing some insulation for both Thailand and South Vietnam. But even this limited success was possible only so long as the United States was active and involved, making it clear that this country stood fully and honestly behind the Geneva Accords as an acceptable middle course for both the Communists and the free world, while at the same time making it equally clear that the United States would do whatever was necessary to prevent the Communists from taking over the country if they abandoned that acceptable middle course. Even the essentially modest goal of an independent Southeast Asia may require some difficult decisions on the part of the United States and a determination to fight if fighting is required.

II

If setting realistic goals is the first step in arriving at an effective policy in Southeast Asia, the second is cutting through to the real nature of the problems we face there. We call what has been going on in South Vietnam a war, for example, but is it really? We have thought of Laos, Cambodia, and each of the other countries of Southeast Asia as separate problems, but isn't there also a problem of our attitude toward the region as a whole?

Any analysis of the nature of the problem we face in South Vietnam should probably start with the proposition that what we are dealing with is not a war—at least in the sense that the problem is more political than military, more concerned with acts of terrorism than battles. Out of a population of 14,000,000 in South Vietnam, the Communist Vietcong number only an estimated 28,000 to 34,000 regular guerrilla troops plus 60,000 to 80,000 part time auxiliaries. In a very real sense the F.B.I. has had more relevant experience in dealing with this kind of problem than the armed services.

The fact that the fighting in South Vietnam up to now has been organized terrorism rather than orthodox warfare does not, of course, relieve North Vietnam of the guilt of committing aggression. Hanoi trained the officers and noncommissioned officers that form the cadre of the Vietcong; Hanoi directs their activities; and Hanoi has supplied them with at least some arms and equipment. But the vast bulk of the Vietcong are recruited in the South; their food and clothing are procured in the South; and they collect "taxes" in the South to import other supplies through Cambodia. They have operated more as small bands of guerrillas than as armies. For even when the Vietcong guerrillas have operated in groups as large as battalions, they have not attempted to take and hold territory in the manner of regular armies; instead they strike and disappear.

The basic reason the Vietcong can get supplies and recruits in South Vietnam is not that the villagers are against the government or for the Communists, but because the villagers are vulnerable. The villagers are turned inward on themselves and have little sense of identification with either the national government or Communist ideology. They are isolated in every way, physically, politically, and psychologically. In such circumstances, certainly, it is not at all difficult to develop a guerrilla force. In Burma during World War II, for example, about 150 Americans created a guerrilla force of well over 25,000 and did it with white faces. It is hardly surprising that the Vietcong could do as well or better.

The villagers of Asia are not seeking a revolution. What they want is their old way of life with the cruelties removed. In Vietnam the villagers desperately want security, and their loyalty will go to the side that fills this need—providing also that security is followed with some simple progress toward a better life and, most importantly, action to convince the villagers the government cares about them and their future.

A recent survey of one of the worst provinces in the delta of South Vietnam illustrates the point. In very insecure villages, subject to frequent visits from the Vietcong, 75 per cent of the people resented both the government and the Vietcong, while 25 per cent were silent. In relatively well protected villages—those which could be penetrated by large Vietcong groups but not by small patrols—50 per cent of the people took a view that was essentially "a plague on both their houses," while 50 per cent were mildly pro-government. But in very secure villages—which had also received some benefits, such as a school or a well—the people were almost 100 per cent pro-government, and they openly expressed their opposition to the Vietcong.

III

The need for multiple policy responses and a variety of instrumentalities in such circumstances is obvious. The first principle of an effective strategic concept would call for giving the villagers physical security— coupled with a civic action program of wells, schools, and simple medical help to demonstrate what is for Asia the truly revolutionary idea that governments exist for the benefit of their people. The tactics are the so-called oil-blot approach—starting with a secure area and extending it slowly outward, making sure no Vietcong pockets are left behind, and using police to winkle out the Communist agents in each particular village. The role of the police, which has been much neglected in Vietnam, is vital, for the movement of both people and things must be absolutely controlled through police techniques, identity cards, road checks, and curfews.

The second basic principle is that to fight the guerrilla one must adopt the tactics of the guerrilla—the night ambushes, small patrols, and constant movement emphasized by the United States Special Forces trained at Fort Bragg, who have had some role in South Vietnam but not the major responsibility.

A strategic concept keyed to the peculiar nature of the problem in Vietnam, in sum, calls for careful coordination of military operations, police efforts, and rural development—all directed toward the primary objective of giving the villagers security and winning their support. And it calls for using military forces in a different way from that of orthodox, conventional war. The air bombardments and artillery barrages of conventional war hurt the innocent and recruit more Vietcong than they kill, while large scale, set piece operations using battalion-sized or larger units telegraph their moves to the enemy. Guerrilla warfare calls for small patrols blanketing the back roads and trails the guerrilla regards as his own and for the clear-and-hold operations and rapid reinforcement of villages under attack that give the peasant physical security. "Over-militarizing" what is essentially a political struggle by relying too heavily on bombers, artillery, and large-scale conventional operations is dangerous. Purely military measures by themselves can only postpone a Communist takeover in a place like Vietnam and then only for as long as the South Vietnamese and we are both willing to pay the price. Even the very best of generals and the most modern of military equipment will not bring about a satisfactory conclusion to the fighting. For that, the major means must be political.

It is, of course, understandable why advice from the United States has not always been as much to the point as it could have been. The major responsibility of the Pentagon is to prepare for large-scale war, whether nuclear or conventional. Guerrilla warfare is rightly far from the center of their major concerns, and the Special Forces, which is the organization charged with both guerrilla and counterguerrilla operations, is something of an orphan. Similarly, in the economic aid agency, the major concern is with economic development, with industrial plants and highways and agriculture, and the Public Safety Division, which is responsible for whatever training the aid agency can offer in police work, is also something of an orphan. Yet the central problem in Vietnam is precisely the area with which these two orphans are concerned—the area where guerrilla tactics and police work intersect.

We must also understand that tempting though it is for Americans to take charge completely in the name of speed and efficiency, the slower, more indirect way is in this case the surer. Beginning in 1962, there has been a tendency to "over-Americanize" the fighting in Vietnam by too many high level visits, by talking about "the only war we've got," and by Americans coming closer and closer to taking actual command. But the political nature of the struggle in a place like Vietnam means that if Americans play too big a role the peasants will begin to believe Communist propaganda about U.S. "neo-colonialism."

IV

In Southeast Asia as a whole, the problem also constitutes a mixture of elements, demanding a subtle orchestration of political, economic, and military instrumentalities. In Laos, for example, the Communists pursued a two-track policy. With one hand, they scratched away at the neutralist and conservative positions, pausing on each occasion to assess the United States reaction. With the other hand, they kept up the negotiations to implement the Geneva Accords. In general, the Communists were careful to keep both lines open—ready to go ahead with the Geneva Accords if they had to and ready to nibble away entirely the neutralist and conservative positions if the United States would permit it. If the United States reaction to a probe was prompt and strong, the

Communists stopped or drew back. If the United States hesitated, the Communists were encouraged to take another bite. In February of 1964, for example, the Communist Pathet Lao began again to nibble, coming to within fifteen miles of the Mekong River and the vital north-south road. There they paused for several weeks, but seeing no reaction from the United States they were then encouraged to go ahead and destroy the neutralist position in the Plain of Jars. Thus they kept their intentions ambiguous, avoiding an open, clear-cut challenge so they could either continue to nibble or return to the Geneva Accords if and when they finally became convinced that the United States would permit them no acceptable alternative.

The Communists are clearly not stronger than the free world. But they are closer to the scene of struggle in Southeast Asia, and the forces they have at hand are more suitable to the problem than most of the forces we have so far committed. The peoples of Southeast Asia, of course, are on no side but their own—which is why the outcome will ultimately turn on political factors and why "winning" will never be in terms of black or white for either the Communists or the free world.

Politically, the problem for the United States is one of maintaining flexibility and developing support for what is admittedly a subtle and sophisticated policy message—that our ambitions in Southeast Asia are limited and contain no threat to others, that we are willing to negotiate a middle way, but that we are determined to prevent Southeast Asia from becoming a Communist satellite.

Militarily, the problem is one of developing military means that are appropriate to the political goals we seek and that support those goals. Asian Communists will move cautiously in the face of the kind of verbal threats they heard from Washington in the spring of 1964 and such implied threats as that contained in the appointment of a famous and highranking general, Maxwell D. Taylor, as Ambassador to South Vietnam. But given the facts of life in a nuclear world, Asians in general are not impressed with the totality of American power. For even though they know the world-wide strategic balance tips heavily in our favor, they cannot see how nuclear power is applicable to jungle and guerrilla warfare. What does impress Asians and what both free and Communist Asians are looking for as they scrutinize our words and actions are signs of United States determination to use the kind of power that is appropriate to the threat—and in Southeast Asia this means ground forces. When the United States, for example, introduced ground forces into Thailand in 1962, following the fall of Nam Tha, the Communists stopped their nibbling attacks in Laos and went ahead promptly with the Geneva Accords.

V

Appealing though they are, the simpler, more direct means of dealing with the Communist threat in Southeast Asia are both ineffective and so blunt as to be self-defeating. The trouble is, of course, that Asians are well aware of interservice rivalries in the Pentagon, of the disputes in Washington revolving around the question of air power versus ground power in Asia, and of both the public and the supposedly top secret debates about bombing North Vietnam. Nothing has gone unnoticed— from the debate in the Eisenhower administration preceding the fall of Dienbienphu in 1954 and the reluctance expressed at that time to fight anything but "immaculate" wars using only air power, right through to the 1961 pressure on President Kennedy to ignore his strong words about Laos and Southeast Asia in the television press conference shortly following his inauguration. Whether or not it is true, many Asians have understandably come to believe in the existence of what Joseph Kraft, writing in *Harper's* and Hanson Baldwin in the *New York Times,* called the "Never Again" club, a group of Army and Air Force generals who are supposed to hold that never again should American ground troops be committed to large scale fighting in Asia. It is for this reason that displays of American air power in Asia—by reconnaissance flights over Laos or even bombing attacks such as those on the North Vietnamese P.T. boat bases in the summer of 1964—are sometimes interpreted as a sign of weakness, as an unwillingness to commit ground forces.

Paradoxically, it is also ground forces that better communicate the political part of the message we must convey to the Communists. A display of air power over Laos and North Vietnam, for example, violates the Geneva Accords and puts the United States in the same bad political light as the Communists. It is not effective in stopping infiltrators on the ground, and it implies an offensive threat and ambitions against the Communist homelands. The introduction of ground forces into Thailand, on the other hand, would not only be interpreted as a much stronger move, more indicative of determination and more effective against infiltrators, but it would also be interpreted as defensive, signaling restraint and respect for the Geneva Accords as an acceptable middle way for all concerned.

As to striking at the North, it seems clear that the United States has little to gain and much to lose by "escalating" the fighting in a situation such as that presented by Vietnam, as for example by bombing North Vietnam. My own view is that at a certain stage, after noticeable progress is made in winning the peasants and the only prop remaining for the Communist terrorists is support from the North, it might be useful to hit certain selected installations whose sole function is to support the fighting in the South. But if anything more extensive were attempted— such as bombing Hanoi itself or taking out the twenty-five to thirty power plants, factories, and so on the North Vietnamese have sacrificed to build—the result would probably be to take the restraints off the North Vietnamese army entirely.

It would be well for the advocates of bombing and other "easy" solutions to such problems to remember that Hanoi's policy was not to infiltrate *North* Vietnamese into South Vietnam—the infiltrators have almost all been southerners sympathetic to communism who went North in 1954. Hanoi has kept to this self-imposed limitation partly to maintain the fiction that the origins of the fighting in South Vietnam were internal, but partly to minimize the risk of retaliation against their precious factories. Once the factories are gone, so is the deterrent.

Our retaliation against the P.T. boat bases in response to the attack on an American destroyer in international waters in the summer of 1964 was, of course, different from attacking North Vietnamese factories and power plants as a means to force the end of the guerrilla terrorism. It could be argued that our own loose talk about escalating the fighting and attacking the North alarmed the Communists and made them feel they had to take action to deter us, but once the attack took place the United States had no honorable choice but to respond. An increase in our naval forces in the Tonkin Gulf and a forceful exercise of our right to be there was certainly a minimum response.

Whether the further step of bombing the P.T. boat bases was necessary is more open to question. On the one hand, the bombing was itself measured and restrained, limited as it was to the source of the attack on American forces. It punished an aggression; it showed American determination; and it demonstrated that the Communists could not assume that their territory was immune to retaliation. On the other hand, there is clearly a political liability in appearing to be no different from the Communists in their disregard of the Geneva Accords and an undoubted risk in an action that tends to remove the tacit limitations on the fighting in Southeast Asia. The only judgment that can be passed on such a move as the bombing of the P.T. boat bases is that the immediate consequences seem in this case to have been beneficial, while the long term consequences do not lend themselves to calculation.

VI

The foregoing only emphasizes the importance of creating in Southeast Asia as a whole an atmosphere of confidence about United States intentions and about our willingness and ability to follow policies and use instrumentalities that are appropriate to the problems. The most effective way to do this would be to strengthen our over-all military posture in Southeast Asia in ways which would make it clear that we are single-mindedly improving our capability to take whatever military steps may be necessary to halt Communist aggression in the area, but which at the same time would demonstrate our limited objectives, our respect for the Geneva Accords, and our willingness to negotiate.

Thailand is a loyal friend and ally and the keystone of our position in Southeast Asia. Introducing substantial ground and air forces into Thailand would (1) signal clearly to the Communists that we are prepared to go on into Laos if necessary, and (2) guarantee that, whatever else happened, Thailand itself would not be left to the mercy of Communist aggression.

Although there is periodically discussion in Thailand about returning to their past policies of balancing off the rivalries of the Great Powers, most Thais are prepared to stick with the free world. But they will also be stubborn, matching vigor with vigor and American indecisiveness with Thai policies that are more and more independent. In an emergency, they will not beg for U.S. troops in Thailand, for example, nor will they accept them unless the United States makes it clear the move is not just a bluff and the troops will actually be used in Laos if it becomes necessary to deny the Communists the north-south road and the Mekong lowlands. But in the latter circumstances, the Thai would welcome such a move and cooperate with it.

I scarcely need add that these forces could not accomplish their political purpose if they were put into Thailand and then quickly taken out again. A temporary troop movement sufficed in 1962, but today a more permanent arrangement will be necessary. Our problems in Southeast Asia are not going to vanish overnight no matter what we do, and we must recognize that any acceptable political accommodation, whether it is arrived at tacitly or by negotiation, will still require the United States to be prepared to maintain a strong military posture in the area quite indefinitely.

Ground forces in Thailand, coupled with a policy of scrupulous support for the Geneva Accords, would go far toward stabilizing the situation in Southeast Asia as a whole and toward deterring open and direct Communist aggression. But the decisions are not ours alone to make, and if the Communists choose to enlarge the war, what kind of war should we fight? Such a vast subject, of course, calls for thorough study and debate, and reasonable men may hold very different views. Recognizing this limitation, my own view is that we should fight, but also that the basic political factors in Southeast Asia would still operate and that we should therefore fight a limited war tailored to the same realistic political objectives discussed above. Even so, the Communists—and others—should realize that once this Pandora's box is opened, it may not be possible to keep the fighting limited.

If the over-all situation could be stabilized by such means as troops in Thailand, we could then concentrate in South Vietnam on the kind of politically oriented program to deal with the Communist guerrillas envisaged in the strategic concept outlined above. The ideas in this strategic concept are not new. They were developed, in fact, in Malaya and the Philippines, and successfully applied against Communist terrorism in both places. But they have never been fully and vigorously applied in South Vietnam. Partly this has been the fault of the Vietnamese. Under the influence of President Ngo Dinh Diem's brother Nhu, whose purposes were mainly ideological, the Vietnamese government adopted the name of the program but ignored its basic principles. The army relied on conventional tactics, large units, bombing, and heavy fire power rather than the small group tactics of the guerrilla. And rather than the oil-blot approach, Nhu sought to blanket the whole country with so-called strategic hamlets which in many cases were nothing more than wire enclosed villages doused with political propaganda. The result was a country of little Dienbienphu's—indefensible, inadequately armed hamlets far from any reinforcement. In effect, they were storage warehouses of American arms that the Vietcong could seize whenever they willed.

But the United States must also accept some of the blame for the failure to apply the basic strategic concept of counterinsurgency fully and vigorously in South Vietnam. From 1954 to 1961, we ignored the possibility of guerrilla warfare and trained and equipped a Vietnamese army suitable only for conventional, Korea-type wars. And even since 1961, we have probably been slower to understand the exigencies of guerrilla warfare than we should have been, too willing to rely on conventional forces, bombers, and artillery, and certainly too prone to proceed in all directions at once, with each service and department going its own way with little over-all direction.

A politically oriented counterinsurgency program, as described above, calls for giving the villagers security through clear-and-hold operations gradually spreading outward, for guerrilla tactics to fight the guerrillas, and for police techniques to control the movement of goods and people. For its part in implementing a program of this kind, the United States needs to give the Special Forces a much larger role in the delta of Vietnam as well as the mountain regions, and perhaps over-all command of the United States advisory effort. We also need more emphasis in our training and advisory functions on police work and police techniques. And most important of all, we need to ensure that all American personnel from all departments and agencies understand the political objectives of our presence in South Vietnam and are effectively subordinated to political direction.

Stationing United States ground forces in Thailand will dispel doubts in the minds of both free and Communist Asians about our ability to understand the nature of the problem in Southeast Asia and our willingness to do what is necessary to keep it out of Communist hands. Although it may be too late in South Vietnam to win the population—the failure to give the villagers protection and enlist their support and the emphasis on an essentially military approach to the problem of guerrilla warfare may have gone on too long—yet a politically oriented counterinsurgency program will for the first time begin to strike at the roots of the problem. To these two actions must be added a third, a political and diplomatic offensive. Such an offensive is needed, first, to explain and gain support for the admittedly subtle political objectives we seek and the admittedly onerous measures that are required to achieve those objectives. Its second purpose is to bring the Communists to realize the wisdom of the middle way—that we will not accept defeat, but that neither will we insist on total victory.

We have not yet lost the struggle for Southeast Asia, and we do not need to lose it. But we need a more realistic assessment of what it is we seek—of our political objective—than we have made as a nation in the past, and a more sophisticated orchestration of military power, economic resources, and diplomatic skills in the pursuit of that political objective. For we can be sure that if we do not meet the politically skillful but highly ambiguous challenge the Communists are presenting us in Southeast Asia we will soon meet the same tactics somewhere else in the world.

But the need for a better blending of our different efforts in foreign affairs would continue even without the Communist challenge. Human misery and human ambition would exist even if the Communists did not, and so long as they do the challenges will continue to be complicated mixtures of many factors, requiring equally complex responses. We have yet to learn, as a government and as a people, to mesh fully the many different instrumentalities of foreign policy and to obtain the full benefit from mutually reinforcing actions—which is the essence of the policy craft.

PART III

Statecraft and Moral Theory:
The Perennial Issues

CHAPTER 12

BALANCE OF POWER AS A PERENNIAL FACTOR: FRENCH MOTIVES IN THE FRANCO-SOVIET PACT

WILLIAM E. SCOTT

The balance of power has been a recurrent factor in international relations, but it would be hard to prove it by reference to the interwar years. As a concept it became very unfashionable in the United States, in England, and in socialist circles on the continent. Woodrow Wilson was only the most famous of many who regarded it as an evil thing, one of the very roots of war. Statesmen, if they practiced it, would not admit it; they spoke instead of "collective security" and "regional agreements." The League of Nations had rendered the balance obsolete.

Practice seemed to follow theory. On the level of the great powers, the balance of power often did not function at all in the years 1919–39. Despite her defeat and the losses imposed by the Versailles Treaty, Germany emerged as potentially the strongest power in Europe. Yet from 1924 to 1933, the United States, England, and Russia gave Germany financial, economic, military, and diplomatic assistance. The feeble and erratic performance of Hitler's enemies in the late thirties dominate our impressions of that decade. Chamberlain sincerely thought that peace would be served by aiding Hitler to recover Germany's "natural" hegemony in Central Europe. We are still astounded to read how the French threatened the Czechs that if the Czechs did *not* surrender the Sudetenland to Hitler, the Franco-Czech alliance would not be honored. Stalin could point to Munich as justification for his own connivance with aggression, but nonetheless the Nazi-Soviet Pact

---

WILLIAM E. SCOTT is associate professor of history at Duke University. He is the author of *Alliance against Hitler: The Origins of the Franco-Soviet Pact*.

amounted to giving Hitler easy conquests of Poland, Holland, Belgium, and France. All these things have led to the feeling that the balance of power did not operate until Hitler literally forced it into operation by attacking a great many countries.

Such a view ignores the first three years after Hitler's accession to power. From 1933 to 1935 the balance of power did function. Russia and Italy were alienated by Hitler's ambitions, and France grasped at both opportunities for alliance; the Russians began to revive their Slavic ties. Out of these realignments came the Rome Accords of January 7, 1935, the Franco-Soviet Pact of Mutual Assistance, May 2, 1935, and the Czech-Soviet Pact of Mutual Assistance, May 16, 1935. The balance of power was operating according to tradition. A group of states previously at odds with each other had dropped their own quarrels and were forming a coalition against the potential aggressor.

The Franco-Soviet Pact was the most important link in this chain. Did the men in Paris who made it reason consciously in terms of the balance of power? If not, what were their calculations? Let us look briefly at the conditions of European diplomacy which faced them and then at the personal motives of the principal French architects of the Pact: Herriot, Paul-Boncour, Barthou, Flandin, and Laval.

I

Painful memories held back the Franco-Soviet rapprochement: Brest-Litovsk, Soviet repudiation of the French debts, French intervention in the civil war. The subversive activities of the French Communist party were daily provocations. Had the two countries been strong, there would have been no alliance. But they were weak: economically, militarily, and diplomatically weak.

In Moscow, Stalin faced staggering problems, accentuated by a serious famine. The grim winter of 1932–33 was the low point of his regime and to survive he needed peace. His nightmare was a two-front war, for the Far East was already aflame.

It is the vulnerability of Russia which explains the sharp reaction to Hitler. The Soviet leaders knew that Germany could not strike immediately, but they could not stand the uncertainty. They waited two, three, four months, watching the destruction of the powerful German Communist party, listening to Hitler's exalted pledges that Germany had a mission to save Europe from Bolshevism. Then came worse: Hitler started to court the friendship of Poland, and one of his Ministers, Hugenberg, publicly proposed that Germany be allowed to colonize

Russia. The Soviet press began to snarl, Litvinov bitterly chided the German Ambassador, and the secret collaboration between the Reichswehr and the Red army was cut off. For some seven years, German officers and technicians had used training stations in Russia for airplanes, tanks, and poison gas. Both armies had profited from testing of prototypes and training with arms forbidden to Germany by the Versailles Treaty. Early in June, 1933, the Soviet government demanded that the training stations be terminated. Berlin acceded, the Reichswehr regretting the breach, Hitler welcoming it, and in September the Germans took their leave.

Soviet foreign policy in the interwar period seems to have followed an unwritten law: Russia must have one friend among the European great powers. Lenin had put it in Marxist terms but the meaning was the same. "We must know how to exploit the contradictions and antagonisms among the imperialists. . . . We, as communists, must use one country against the other." [1] In 1933, there were four great powers in Western Europe. England was indifferent; Italy was not strong enough. That left France and Germany. No sooner had the split with Germany become serious than the Russians turned to France. In September, 1933, they pressed the French for a secret military alliance—each country to support the other wherever attacked. They also made suggestions that the French army fill in for the departed Reichswehr.

Where did France stand in 1933? Spared at the beginning, she was now pinned fast by the grip of the world economic depression. The prestige of the French army was still high, but the price of its victory in the world war was coming due. In 1935, the annual class of conscripts would drop from around 230,000 to 118,000. The gap would open for five years, the "hollow years," the result of five years of heavy casualties.

Hardly anyone but the diplomats knew how weak was the French alliance system. Seldom has a coalition been so unmercifully riddled by the evidence. There has been a natural tendency to remember its fate in terms of a collapse against overwhelming odds. The historian will have to write that as a coalition, as a system, there was nothing to overwhelm. As allies against Hitler, Belgium, Poland, Rumania, and Yugoslavia did France more harm than good; for Czechoslovakia, unfortunately, the reverse is true.

Since 1931, the Belgian government had been trying quietly to slip

---

[1] Speech by Lenin to a meeting of Moscow Communist Party Secretaries, Nov. 27, 1920, in *Soviet Documents on Foreign Policy*, Vol. I, 1917–24, ed. Jane Degras (London, 1951), pp. 221–22. At that time, Lenin was arguing for an alignment with Germany.

out of the bonds of the Franco-Belgian Military Convention. The public knew little of this and the luminous figure of King Albert still symbolized the wartime comradeship. But the relaxation had gone so far that in the judgment of a French general staff officer, "the French must not count on immediate intervention on the part of Belgium in case of German attack." [2]

Poland was supposed to be the sturdiest French sentinel in the east; the reality was not merely disappointing, it was almost incredible. The Quai d'Orsay was weary of the Poles' pretentions, annoyed by their arrogance, and disturbed by their feud with the Czechs. Marshal Joseph Pilsudski, in turn, flaunted his contempt of democracy and correctly sensed the weakness beneath the French desire for security. All that was needed was the appointment of Colonel Joseph Beck as Foreign Minister. Beck's ambition and ill-concealed grudge against France, combined with Pilsudski's suspicions, were fair game for Hitler's most brilliant maneuver—his startling offer to Poland that the two countries should pledge to renounce force. The Polish-German rapprochement, which began in May, 1933, was regarded in Paris as an insult and in Moscow as proof of Hitler's hostility.

The ill will and distrust with which the Polish and Czech governments regarded each other made French coordination of their eastern allies impossible. Even the threat of Hitler could not bring Warsaw and Prague together; after a momentary détente in March, 1933, they drifted further apart. At best, the French system was an army with two headquarters, one in Warsaw and one in Prague. The Little Entente itself was an entente only against Hungary. Each of the three suffered from a nightmare of a different color. For Rumania it was Red Russians, for Yugoslavia Mussolini's black shirts; only for Czechoslovakia was brown-shirted Nazi Germany the main enemy. Rumania and Yugoslavia were highly vulnerable to German trade pressure; indeed, the latter looked upon the Germans as friends whose support was vitally necessary to ward off Mussolini's support of Croatian separatism.

France had no alliance system in 1933. She had allies, friends, clients (two of them scarcely on speaking terms). After World War I the French had taken Poland, Czechoslovakia, Rumania, and Yugoslavia and rolled them all up to make an *alliance de revers*. Some diplomats and soldiers in Paris had never believed that this group of "succession" states constituted a new balance of power against Germany. When

---

[2] Colonel de Lattre de Tassigny (aide to General Weygand) to the British Military Attaché, Colonel Heywood, Nov. 10, 1933, in *Documents on British Foreign Policy, 1919–1939*, Second Series, Vol. VI (London, 1957), p. 50 (hereafter cited as *B.F.P.*).

Hitler came to power, its fragility became obvious. It was not surprising that Frenchmen began to think more fondly of the old pattern, the Russian alliance.[3]

Were there no other feasible allies against Hitler? Was it necessary to take the risk of embracing a power that controlled a subversive party in France? By 1933, the French were resigned to the different conceptions of security and the sharply divergent policies toward Germany that plagued their relations with the British. Arnold Wolfers, whose analysis of Anglo-French disunity has been impressively confirmed by the evidence disclosed since 1945, makes Germany the central point. "The basic issue underlying the controversy between Britain and France was not a matter of general attitudes, but the concrete political problem of Germany's power and position." [4]

Adolf Hitler posed the concrete problem of German power in his first year as Chancellor. He pulled Germany out of the World Disarmament Conference and the League of Nations, serving notice that he would not wait to be given "equality of rights" in arms. Equality of rights had only one real meaning—the right to compete. Competition in rearmament between France and Germany, when the latter had a twenty-five million lead in population and a five-million-ton superiority in annual steel production, was a dire prospect. Meanwhile, he launched an all-out campaign to take over Austria by internal revolution. What were the British reactions to these moves? Sir John Simon washed his hands of the common disarmament program which had provoked Hitler's reaction and began to put pressure on France to concede limited German rearmament. He would agree only to a guarded reference to support of Austrian independence. The British attitude toward Nazi Germany remained until 1939 (with brief periods of hesitation) basically the same as their attitude toward Weimar Germany. Germany had been unjustly treated at Versailles; justice and her vital role in the European economy counseled the appeasement of her grievances. With such an attitude there was no sense hoping that the British would join the ring against Hitler. Once in a while, the French did ask and they were told with unvarying courtesy that no British cabinet could give France a further pledge of security beyond that contained in the Locarno Accords.

The French did not hope for more than diplomatic support from the United States, but even there they were disappointed. Hitler's rise coin-

[3] The evidence for this and subsequent interpretations of French foreign policy will be found in my book, *Alliance against Hitler: The Origins of the Franco-Soviet Pact* (Durham, N.C., 1962).

[4] Arnold Wolfers, *Britain and France between Two Wars: Conflicting Strategies of Peace since Versailles* (New York, 1940), p. 381.

cided with the deepest isolation in the interwar period, 1933–37.
Two days after the German withdrawal from Geneva, Mr. Norman
Davis, chief of the United States delegation, read a statement which had
been sent to him by President Roosevelt and Secretary Hull. "We are
not . . . interested in the political element or any purely European
aspect of the picture. We again make it clear that we are in no way
politically aligned with any European Powers. Such unity of purpose as
has existed has been entirely on world disarmament matters." [5] It is
hard to know whether that official declaration of policy was more noteworthy for its naive distinction between disarmament and politics or for
the comfort it gave Hitler. From October, 1933, to October, 1937, there
was no reason to consider the United States as any more of a factor in
European diplomacy than Japan. From the great crises of those years—
the assassination of Dollfuss, the reintroduction of conscription in Germany, the Italo-Ethiopian war, the remilitarization of the Rhineland, the
Spanish Civil War—the United States stood aloof.

Incidentally, from a strictly military point of view, the question of
British and American aid against Hitler was academic. Both countries
had reduced their armies to such a ridiculously low level—around
150,000 men—that they could not possibly have sent any expeditionary
forces to France for years. The same was the case with their air forces.
In effect, the two powers could only offer their navies.

There was one other state with enough power to help in restraining
Hitler; that was Mussolini's Italy, whose air force was currently the
most modern in Europe. When Hitler came to power it was assumed
that Mussolini would be his partner, and this Hitler sincerely desired.
However, his coveting of Austria crossed the Duce's desire for an active
role in controlling the Danube valley. The French widened the gap by an
assiduous courtship of Mussolini. Mussolini threw his weight behind the
Austrian Chancellor, Dollfuss, and when Austrian Nazis assassinated
Dollfuss during their vain effort to seize power in Vienna on July 25,
1934, Mussolini swung hard over to the French camp. The realignment
was promoted when Mussolini decided to invade Ethiopia, an adventure
for which French benevolence was essential. The French rapproche-
ments with Italy and Russia were pursued simultaneously, and they were
a perfect combination for French public opinion.

Against Hitler, then, the French could not rely on their original "alliance system"—Belgium, Poland, and the Little Entente—nor could they
hope for any solid support from England and the United States. On
calculation of the fundamental elements of power—demographic, in-

    [5] Declaration by Mr. Norman Davis in Geneva, Oct. 16, 1933, *Foreign Rela-
tions of the United States,* Vol. I, 1933 (Washington, D.C., 1950), p. 277.

dustrial, and military—Russia and Italy were the only two states which could effectively aid France in forging a new balance of power against Hitler.

II

Such were the principal factors of the European state system at the time Hitler came to power. They were the daily stuff of the diplomats and soldiers. To what extent did the French politicians calculate in terms of power? How sophisticated were their analyses, how much a product of tradition? How did their politics affect their calculations?

The first French politician of stature to promote the Franco-Soviet rapprochement was M. Édouard Herriot, leader of the moderate Left wing party, the Radical-Socialists. Herriot had been one of the first French visitors to Moscow, and, as Premier in 1924, he had pushed through French recognition of the Soviet Union. These actions had sprung from a sentimental comparison of the French and Russian revolutions. Herriot, however, had become disenchanted owing to the intransigent attacks of the French Communists on his own party. When he returned to power as Premier and Foreign Minister in June, 1932, he did not show any enthusiasm for the negotiations for a Franco-Soviet nonaggression pact. Suddenly, in September, 1932, he became urgently interested in the negotiations and pressed them to conclusion of the pact on November 29, 1932. Herriot had been antagonized by the driving demands of the Papen-Schleicher government for German rearmament; his revival of the Russian talks came directly after the German demand for samples of "defensive" weapons and, following its refusal, the first German withdrawal from the disarmament conference. The democratic Germany in which he had put his faith was collapsing, militarists were in power, the Nazis were not far behind, and Herriot felt that his fingers had been burned. He was a classic case of an idealistic conciliator whose disillusion turned him back to *Realpolitik*.

Although his cabinet fell in December, 1932, Herriot retrieved a direct influence on foreign policy by election as president of the Foreign Affairs Commission of the Chamber of Deputies in February, 1933. He organized a full scale debate on the Non-Aggression Pact and he launched a campaign to educate public opinion by lectures, political speeches, articles in the press, and a book. The climax of Herriot's campaign was a trip to Russia in August and September, 1933, organized as virtually a triumphal progression in honor of his pro-Russian reputation. He had talks with Molotov and Litvinov, the latter entrusting him with a message urging a closer entente. Herriot returned to spread his now ardent conviction that Russian manpower and industry must be secured on the French side. Hitler had turned his suspicions into a profound, almost clairvoyant fear of Germany. He became obsessed with the weakness of France and her inability to stand up to Germany alone. Already in March, 1933, the British Ambassador in Paris, Lord Tyrrell, noted that the new situation in Germany had "turned Herriot into an impassioned advocate of a Franco-Soviet alliance." [6]

After the riots of February 6, 1934, Herriot joined the "National Union" cabinet formed by Gaston Doumergue. He and André Tardieu were paired off as symbols of Left and Right. As the most prominent leader of the Radical-Socialist party, 160 strong in the Chamber, his position in the cabinet was extremely strong, as it was in the subsequent Flandin and Laval cabinets. All three governments, which ruled France from February, 1934, to January, 1936, were heavily oriented to the Right, coalitions of two-thirds conservatives and one-third moderate Radical-Socialists. Yet they were dependent for existence upon approval by the Chamber of Deputies which had a Left wing majority. They were tolerated because of the need for order after the riots and because of the general prejudice in favor of their deflationary financial policy. Herriot's presence was regarded by the Left as a guarantee that these cabinets would not tamper with the Republic and as a brake on their anti-Leftist policies. As long as Herriot gave his certificate of good conduct, the cabinet survived. When he resigned, as in November, 1934, and January, 1936, the Doumergue and Laval cabinets immediately fell.

For two critical years, Édouard Herriot was the most powerful politician in France. He never relaxed his pressure for a Franco-Soviet pact. He vigorously supported the pro-Russian policies of Louis Barthou, Foreign Minister until October, 1934, and he watched with vigilance the pro-German policies of Barthou's successor, Pierre Laval. When Hitler announced German rearmament in March, 1935, he joined with the Premier, Pierre-Étienne Flandin, in imposing upon Laval the decision to conclude the Franco-Soviet Pact. He also played a major role in two defense decisions: the termination of disarmament negotiations with Germany, expressed in the April 17, 1934, note, and the increase of service in the French Army from one to two years, March 15, 1935.

Édouard Herriot justified his Russian policy in the traditional terms of the balance of power: population, geography, troops, and matériel. He was forever quoting statistics from Soviet officials, Tukachevsky for example, to show the growth of the Red army and its experimentation with new weapons. He returned again and again to the theme of

[6] Dispatch of March 20, 1933, *B.F.P.*, Vol. IV, pp. 462–66.

France's low and static population and her less industrialized economy vis-à-vis Germany. He was accustomed to studying the map of Europe and he frequently emphasized the impact of geography upon military strategy. As a former professor, who was well versed in European history, Herriot invoked precedents as far back as the sixteenth century for the French concept of an *alliance de revers*. Two entries in his memoirs show his attitude in April, 1934, and April, 1935, and illustrate his mode of thought.

> I have reflected on this as best I could. Hitler has taken his stand; he is already in full execution of his program and his maneuvers are only feints and lies. It is on the side of Russia that England and France must seek their security and that of the small states of Europe. The map talks; that is sufficient.[7]
>
> Alone, France, with her 40 million inhabitants, cannot resist a nation of 60 million inhabitants. An agricultural country, she cannot arm as rapidly and as powerfully as a country with a great industrial concentration. . . .
>
> I consult the map. I see only one country which can bring us the necessary counterweight and create a second front in case of war. That is the Soviet Union. I have been saying it and writing it since 1922. People call me a communist or an imbecile. In the old days, the Tsar, despot that he was, agreed to ally with a Republic.[8]

Herriot considered the alternatives. Although he valued the friendship of the United States and England, he believed that the British navy was all that France could count on and that was not enough to constitute a second front. Out of the original French alliance system, he rated only Czechoslovakia and Yugoslavia as reliable and he feared that the assassination of King Alexander in Marseilles would snap the loyalty of Yugoslavia to France. Poland he wrote off completely as an ally, even as a friend; he went so far as to suspect her of collusion with Germany.

Strangely, Herriot, who was willing to trust Stalin, would not trust Mussolini. He merely accepted the Rome Accords and probably would not have made them had he been Foreign Minister. He liked to repeat the formula: "From Italy we have everything to fear and nothing to hope for." [9] His distrust of an alliance with Fascist Italy flatly contradicted his willingness to subordinate ideology for the sake of alliance with Communist Russia.

What about the French Communists? Herriot once had been alienated

---

[7] *Jadis*, Vol. II, *D'Une Guerre à l'Autre, 1914–1936* (Paris, 1952), p. 411.
[8] *Ibid.*, pp. 522–23.
[9] *Ibid.*, p. 523.

by their intransigence and their obedience to Moscow. How did he reconcile alliance with their master, Stalin? He was influenced by the fact that in 1933 the French Communist party was small and its morale poor. Like others who made the pact, Herriot was a parliamentary politician and his view of the Communists was shaped by their insignificance in the Chamber of Deputies, 10 out of 600, no competition for 160 Radical-Socialists and 130 Socialists. Herriot's conclusion was to ignore the Communist danger; he did not try to embrace it. As the leader of the moderate wing of the Radical-Socialists, he leaned toward cooperation with the Center parties. The February 6th riots set in motion a powerful rally of the Left, which produced the *Front Populaire* coalition of Communists, Socialists, and Radical-Socialists. The driving force was the Communist party, suddenly instructed by Stalin to switch from intransigence to brotherly love. Herriot distrusted and resisted the drive for this coalition. It was Herriot's bitter rival, M. Édouard Daladier, who pushed the Radical-Socialists into the *Front Populaire*. Daladier, as befits the paradox, was willing to cooperate with the French Communists, but not with their master, Stalin. He distrusted the traditional balance of power, and never showed any enthusiasm for the Franco-Soviet Pact.

The man who took the critical step of opening formal, secret alliance negotiations with Russia was M. Joseph Paul-Boncour. An independent Socialist who had resigned from the party because of its refusal to support defense budgets, he was deeply patriotic. Paul-Boncour was one of the few advocates of collective security who acknowledged the decisive role of power. He yielded to no one in his devotion to the League of Nations, yet he well knew that it would be emasculated unless it had force behind its decisions.

Paul-Boncour was Foreign Minister from December, 1932, to January, 1934. Immediately, he set out to improve relations with Italy, to end the sour, often venomous quarrel which had opposed Rome and Paris since 1919. Accepting the Four-Power Pact to indulge Mussolini's vanity, he utilized the improved atmosphere to initiate negotiations for a comprehensive Franco-Italian settlement.

Simultaneously, Paul-Boncour speeded up the tempo of the Franco-Soviet rapprochement. However, he was reserved in his reception of the sudden Russian overtures for an alliance made in September, 1933. What erased that reserve was the German withdrawal from the disarmament conference and the League of Nations on October 14, 1933. This coup confirmed his suspicions of Hitler and revealed the flabby nature of the Anglo-French-Italian-American disarmament bloc. "It was a clear signal that Hitler would not be slow to begin the series of achievements which he had announced in *Mein Kampf,* that astonishing book where he had warned his victims more openly than any other statesman had ever done." No one in London or Washington seemed to draw this conclusion, and although Mussolini did he also tried to preserve his position as mediator. Hitler's defiance showed Paul-Boncour that the common western front, which he had painfully constructed, was a mirage.

> The duty was no less clear: to fortify our alliances and to search out new ones. . . . It was once again that *"alliance de revers,"* a constant of French policy through the centuries, at first vis-à-vis Austria then vis-à-vis Germany, which France had sought successively in Turkey, Sweden, and Tsarist Russia. The Treaty of Versailles and subsequent accords had found that alliance to some extent in Poland and the Little Entente. But Russian power, which French diplomats and travellers in Russia . . . assured me had revived, represented a formidable handicap for Poland and Roumania, if Russia were not on the same side as they or at least were not benevolently neutral.[10]

After conferring with his two top aides, M. Alexis Léger and M. Paul Bargeton, Paul-Boncour decided to shoot for a mutual assistance pact with Russia. Litvinov was enthusiastic, Stalin gave his approval, and secret Franco-Soviet negotiations began early in December, 1933. They made rapid progress before Paul-Boncour had to leave office at the end of January, 1934. Moscow requested absolute secrecy, to which Paul-Boncour willingly acceded. He did not inform the British nor any of the French allies; he did not even inform his own cabinet, only the Premier, M. Camille Chautemps, who approved.

Paul-Boncour shared Herriot's affection for the English and Americans; he also shared the feeling that it was impossible to count on them for immediate armed support against Hitler. Herriot had given up on the original French alliance system. M. Paul-Boncour had not, and that colored his view of the Russian alliance. He attached three conditions to his offer: no obligations concerning the Far East; Soviet entry into the League of Nations; and, if possible, coordination with the Franco-Polish and Franco-Rumanian alliances. The Soviets made no trouble about the Far East, though they wanted French help against Japan; they also declared their willingness to enter the long despised League of Nations. But they fought hard to avoid any commitments to Poland and Rumania.

[10] *Entre Deux Guerres,* Vol. II, *Les lendemains de la victoire, 1919–1934* (Paris, 1945), pp. 361–62.

M. Paul-Boncour's insistence on leading the Russians gently to Geneva was more than the recruiting instinct of a devotee of the League. League participation was necessary to avoid injury to the Locarno Accords. If Russia joined the League, Poland and Rumania might be more amenable to military cooperation with her. Paul-Boncour faced squarely the deep Polish and Rumanian distrust of Russia; he recognized their real fear. "To make mutual assistance agreements with Russia . . . was to accept the probability that, in case of German aggression, Russian troops would fight along side of them [Poland and Rumania] and pass through their territories." Paul-Boncour, nevertheless, believed that the problem could be solved and he set out to construct an Eastern Locarno, in which a Franco-Soviet pact would be complemented by Polish and Rumanian accords with Russia, and Czechoslovakia would play a part.

> Above all, this plan was in our own interest; without it, we would have given more than we received. For Poland and Roumania it was already a considerable advantage to have the assurance that Russia would be an ally of France in case of war with Germany. But, for France, what good was Russian power if it had to remain behind its own frontiers, separated from Germany by Poland and Roumania? [11]

After he left office, his conception of an Eastern Locarno was formally proposed and failed; his successors went ahead and signed the Franco-Soviet Pact. Paul-Boncour thought they had not tried hard enough to bring in Poland and he hinted that he might not have signed the Franco-Soviet Pact. However, when it came up for ratification in 1936, he piloted it through the Senate. His justification was as follows:

> One thing is missing, and that is not the fault of France nor of Russia. This treaty is not the sort of treaty we desired, a regional treaty of mutual assistance concerning all of eastern Europe. You know that the signature of this regional pact . . . was offered to Germany and Poland. It was not our fault that these nations and all the other neighbors of Russia and countries of eastern Europe did not join the treaty. [12]

Germany and Poland had refused; therefore they should not complain about the result, a Franco-Soviet axis.

Paul-Boncour's handling of the balance of power was more realistic than Herriot's in one sense. Although a Socialist with a long record of

---

[11] *Ibid.*, p. 373.
[12] *Journal Officiel*, Sénat, *Débats Parlementaires*, March 12, 1936, p. 264.

opposition to fascism—he had called Mussolini a "Caesar de Carnéval" —he dropped ideological considerations and sought the Italian alliance as tenaciously as the Russian. He invoked geography and historical precedent as naturally as did Herriot. In another sense, he was less realistic. He was so devoted to the League of Nations that he was determined to place Franco-Soviet mutual assistance inside and dependent upon the League machinery. Russia had to become a member of the League; that in itself would not mean much more than conformity. But Paul-Boncour apparently conceived of the two allies going to the League, consulting carefully with England, Belgium, Poland, and Rumania, and not launching their forces until the League had approved or had shown its complete inability to agree. By that time, the war might be over.

More than any other French architect of the Pact, Paul-Boncour was preoccupied by the problem of coordinating the old and the new. He refused to slide over the uncomfortable fact that Germany and Russia did not have a common frontier, that to attack Germany, Soviet troops had to cross Polish soil. Yet his insistence on the need for a Russo-Polish accord was academic. No power on earth, let alone M. Paul-Boncour, could have persuaded the Poles to permit Russian troops to enter their country. (The course of the Anglo-French-Soviet negotiations in August, 1939, is proof of that.) For Paul-Boncour to insist upon protecting the old alliance was to risk losing the new. In that sense, and in his devotion to the League, Paul-Boncour was less realistic, less brutal, in his use of the balance of power than Herriot.

Louis Barthou, who was Foreign Minister in the Doumergue cabinet, was the oldest of the principal architects of the Franco-Soviet Pact and he conceived of the balance of power in the most old-fashioned terms. At 72, his political career seemed finished, distinguished by seventeen cabinets and forty-five years in Parliament. Yet his "inspired direction and blunt speech" made his nine-month reign at the Quai d'Orsay so exciting that it is remembered as a golden interlude in the decline of French power.[13]

A conservative senator, Barthou was fearless; he cared not at all about political popularity. Subtle and clever to the point of deception, he misled friends as well as enemies. His motives were seldom admitted and the historian often must fall back on deduction. Barthou's whole career had been dominated by patriotism and the struggle with Germany. He grew up in the fervent nationalism of the *revanche* movement. In 1913, as Premier, he pushed through the three years military service

---

[13] The words quoted are those of Anthony Eden, *Facing the Dictators* (Cambridge, Mass., 1962), p. 120.

law. In the early months of the war, his only son, Max, had been killed. After the war, Barthou returned to prominence in the cabinet of his close friend, Raymond Poincaré, for whom he often served as trouble-shooter. He fully approved, and carried out with what seemed to many a spirit of revenge, Poincaré's tough German policy which led to the occupation of the Ruhr. He was one of the few Frenchmen who had read *Mein Kampf*. Hitler to him was simply a new manifestation of the dire threat which the Germany of Bismarck and William II had posed to out-numbered, out-produced France. Everything that happened in Germany in the spring and summer of 1934—rearmament, the Blood Purge, the assassination of Dollfuss, Hindenburg's death and Hitler's succession to his posts—confirmed his suspicions and fears.

Barthou's first step was to investigate the condition of the existing French alliances. Trips to Brussels, Warsaw, Prague, Bucharest, and Belgrade revealed their fragility and disunity. In Warsaw, Barthou, as befitted one of the signatories of the Franco-Polish alliance, tried hard to revive the old spirit. He found that Pilsudski and Beck were determined to stick to their "independent" attitudes and were proud of their recent No-Force Declaration with Hitler. Only Czechoslovakia seemed to be a solid ally against Germany. Barthou never said so publicly, but it is clear that he came to the conclusion that Belgium, Poland, and the Little Entente were likely to be liabilities rather than assets against Hitler.

Louis Barthou did not even consider the United States as a possible ally. He ruled out the possibility that England would be an effective ally against Hitler in the near future. Herriot and Paul-Boncour had done the same; where Barthou differed was that he did not share their regret and reluctance. Barthou never let himself be put on the defensive in arguing with the British; if they wanted to indulge their guilt complex about Versailles, if they wanted to test their theory that Hitler could be appeased by concessions, that was their affair but he could not be expected to applaud, let alone to follow. His blunt criticism of British policy recalled the old duels of Poincaré with Lloyd George and Curzon; indeed, that was where he had learned it.

Barthou's friend Poincaré had tried to pursue a tough policy against Germany unilaterally. It had worked momentarily but had ended in exhausting France. Instructed by that example and alarmed by the February 6th riots in Paris, Barthou realized that France badly needed help if she were to stand against Hitler. He resolved to secure powerful allies and he decided that the only candidates were Russia and Italy.

Barthou revived the negotiations by meeting with Maxim Litvinov in Geneva in May–June, 1934. Together, they devised a scheme of mutual assistance pacts known as Eastern Locarno. This step coincided with the funeral session of the World Disarmament Conference. Barthou threw into the teeth of the British his insistence that security take precedence over disarmament. He flaunted his dislike of Sir John Simon—"mon cher collègue et presque ami"—and flayed British tenderness toward Germany in the most sarcastic speech the conference had ever heard. In contrast, he applauded M. Litvinov's obstinant promotion of security. "M. Litvinov was not a man who tried to please everybody. . . . He was a man who accepted realities." [14] The first public demonstration that France and Russia were thinking of an alliance was given a sharp anti-British twist. In that sense, it had a striking resemblance to the origins of the Franco-Russian Entente of 1891, in whose conception hostility to England had been very prominent.

Eastern Locarno was the most unlikely piece of pactomania of the interwar years; it was a tactical move and neither Barthou nor Litvinov took it seriously. Russia, Germany, Poland, Czechoslovakia, Lithuania, Latvia, Estonia, and Finland were to sign an Eastern Pact of Mutual Assistance. France and Russia would sign a separate treaty of mutual assistance, a sort of "guarantee" of the Eastern Pact. It will be seen that when Paul-Boncour had insisted on adding Poland, Litvinov had replied by loading on the Baltic states. Louis Barthou took this treaty with him on a fence-mending visit to London in July, 1934, and made an eloquent defense of his Russian policy.

> Did His Majesty's Government think it good to try to turn Russia, with a population of 160 millions, towards peace? . . . There was a danger that Russia might go to the other side of the barricade, as before the Hitler revolution. A disappointed Russia might go over to Germany. . . .
>
> If the French Government did not succeed in this matter, either owing to a German or Polish refusal, and then the proposed arrangements did not mature, the problem of security would remain open as between Russia and France. The French Cabinet had not yet deliberated on what would happen in those circumstances. But long ago Republican France had signed a treaty with Tsarist Russia, though the two regimes had been very different. Geography, however, commanded history, and there had been a Franco-Russian alliance.
>
> Would the France of today also be obliged to ally herself with Soviet Russia, who would abstain from propaganda in her terri-

[14] Speech of May 30, 1934, League of Nations, *Conference for the Reduction and Limitation of Armaments, Minutes of the General Commission,* Vol. III, pp. 665–70.

tory? It was possible, that if the Eastern Locarno failed, the dangers of the European situation would oblige France to do so.[15]

Barthou assured his hosts that the French government did not wish to offend by their Russian policy, but they could not be choosey; "they must take guarantees of peace where they could find them."

Barthou knew perfectly well that Eastern Locarno had little chance and his language strongly implies that he had made up his mind to go ahead alone with Russia. In fact, Finland turned down Eastern Locarno before it could be offered to her, Germany and Poland pretended to study it and then rejected it in September, the Baltic states wobbled into an embarrassed acceptance, and only Czechoslovakia showed any enthusiasm. This did not disappoint Barthou except to open his eyes to the extent of Polish alienation from France. Some time in the summer of 1934, Barthou made a verbal promise to Litvinov that if Eastern Locarno failed, France would be willing to join Russia in a bilateral mutual assistance pact.

Louis Barthou took great interest in Austria's resistance to Hitler's pressure and he demonstrated this concern by an interview with Dollfuss in Vienna on his trip to Bucharest. He was thus all the more shocked when, on July 25, 1934, the Austrian Nazis tried to stage a *coup d'état* in Vienna, shot Dollfuss, refused to let in a doctor or a priest, and watched him bleed to death. Barthou took the Dollfuss assassination and the Blood Purge as proof that Hitler's eulogy of ruthlessness in *Mein Kampf* was a key to his action. His interview with a Swiss journalist, Wilhelm Herzog, while on vacation in August, opens another window into his thoughts. Characteristically, what loosened Barthou's tongue was the mention of an English pacifist society which tried to stop war by "brochures and conferences."

> Against a power which wants war, which glorifies war, one cannot fight with fine resolutions in favor of the idea of right. The right is nothing without power. And the League of Nations has no power, at least not today. . . . We have had enough of speeches and conferences. Europe's security, not that of France alone, is more seriously in danger than ever. . . . It seems to me that there is no other solution than that all the peoples who hate war and want to prevent it should unite to work against the chaos which threatens to devour us all.[16]

[15] Minutes of the Anglo-French talks, London, July 9, 1934, *B.F.P.*, Vol. VI, p. 806.
[16] Wilhelm Herzhog, *Barthou* (Zürich, 1938), pp. 93–94.

How could a Frenchman read *Mein Kampf,* as he had done, without being terrified into action? "A document of hatred against France, against 'negroid' France, that he wants to annihilate. Does he not threaten to isolate us, the hereditary enemy, by means of a German-English-Italian alliance, so that he can strike us down with all the more safety?"

Utterly convinced of the mortal danger facing his country, Barthou threw himself into the work of constructing a new balance of power. With skill and driving insistence, he managed the complex negotiations for Russia's entry into the League. On September 18, 1934, after considerable resistance, in which two French allies, Belgium and Poland, participated, the Soviet Union became a member of the League of Nations. The essential condition for a Franco-Soviet alliance had been fulfilled.

The assassination of Dollfuss gave Barthou an opening which he did not neglect. It infuriated Mussolini, who had been subsidizing Dollfuss and thought he had Hitler's promise not to make a move in Austria without consultation. Barthou had not taken easily to Mussolini's diplomacy, but now the Franco-Italian rapprochement revived and, at Geneva, he and Baron Aloisi, Mussolini's *chef de cabinet,* collaborated on Soviet entry into the League and on the Austrian question. So well did this affair mature that Barthou promised the Italians that he would visit Rome in November. Before that, he needed to placate an old ally. That concern led him to his death, for he had scarcely welcomed King Alexander of Yugoslavia in Marseilles, on October 9, 1934, when they were both assassinated.

No one can tell what Louis Barthou planned to do, but it is almost certain that he intended to secure the Russian alliance as fast as possible, regardless of the cost. If the French Communists worried him he did not show it. A conservative in politics, he had quite a reputation as an anti-Communist. He did not change his opinions; he simply subordinated them. For him, the solution was that traditional formula: the primacy of foreign policy. For Professor J.-B. Duroselle, this was Barthou's distinction in a decade of doctrinaires. "Barthou, a committed and active anti-Communist, judged the Soviet Union in terms of power and had only profound mistrust for her regime." He arrived at his Russian policy "by pure realism, by a sort of implacable lucidity which derived from his character." [17]

Pierre Laval succeeded Louis Barthou; although he signed the Franco-Soviet Pact we do not need to examine his motives. The explanation of

[17] J.-B. Duroselle, "Louis Barthou et le rapprochement franco-soviétique en 1934," *Cahiers du Monde Russe et Soviétique* (Paris), III, No. 4 (Oct.–Dec., 1962), pp. 530–31.

that paradox is that Laval did not want the pact and did his best to stall it, until the cabinet ordered him to conclude the negotiations.

Pierre Laval began his career as a poor Socialist lawyer. Though now a rich man and a conservative senator, he retained some aspects of his Socialist formation, including a revulsion against war and suspicion of traditional balance of power diplomacy. He did not take it for granted that France and Germany were natural enemies. Reconciliation was the only way to avoid another war, which France could not survive, and it was also good business. Laval saw himself as successor to the great Aristide Briand, who had oriented French policy away from Poincaré's sterile intransigence into the conciliatory era of Locarno. The advent of Hitler did not cause Laval to change his mind; it simply made him more cautious.

Holding these beliefs, Laval naturally opposed the Franco-Soviet alliance. When the cabinet authorized the Eastern Locarno negotiations, on June 5, 1934, he had been the only Minister to offer vigorous resistance. "Laval declared himself categorically in favor of an accord with Germany and hostile to a rapprochement with Russia, which would bring us the International and the red flag." [18] Laval could not repudiate the Franco-Soviet negotiations. What he could do was to stall for time and simultaneously try to improve relations with Germany. The Saar plebiscite proved to be a convenient issue and Laval arranged a friendly settlement with the Germans. He moved closer to the British, who were delighted with the contrast between him and Barthou. Litvinov was furious and threatened that Russia might break off the negotiations, but that did not bother Laval.

In order to succeed in his effort to subtly transform French policy, Laval needed quiet in Germany. Hitler obliged until the Saar territory was safely back under the full legal sovereignty of the Reich. Then he set off an explosion. On March 10, 1935, he had Goering reveal the constitution of the Luftwaffe. On March 16th, Hitler announced the reestablishment of conscription and the constitution of a German army of thirty-six divisions. The reaction of French public opinion to this flagrant violation of the Versailles Treaty was very sharp and the cabinet decided on action. Herriot, who had been growing increasingly suspicious of Laval's aims, concerted with the new Premier, M. Pierre-Étienne Flandin. Their determination to force an anti-German policy on Laval was stimulated by resentment of the soft reaction in London; the British refused to make a strong common protest with the French

---

[18] Herriot's notes of the Cabinet meeting, *Jadis,* Vol. II, p. 437. Laval had been Premier at the time that the Franco-Soviet rapprochement began, spring, 1931. However, then the rapprochement had been limited to negotiations for a commercial accord and for a nonaggression pact.

and Italians and blandly insisted on maintaining the plans for Sir John Simon's visit to Hitler. Flandin, Herriot, and the nationalist leader, M. Louis Marin, swayed the cabinet against Laval's suggestion of a moderate protest. The cabinet imposed two vital decisions: a request for a special session of the League of Nations Council and the visit of Pierre Laval to Moscow, which was tantamount to the decision to sign a Franco-Soviet Pact.

Laval was above all a politician, and he turned necessity into a virtue. He was angling to become Premier, which he had been with much success in 1931. Laval knew that he, like Doumergue and Flandin, could not win the Chamber's approval without the cooperation of Herriot and his faction of moderate Radical-Socialists. In a sense, Laval signed the Franco-Soviet Pact in order to become Premier.

After difficult last minute negotiations, the Franco-Soviet Pact of Mutual Assistance was signed in Paris on May 2, 1935. Laval made an official visit to Moscow two weeks later, thus becoming the first Foreign Minister of a Western power to visit the Soviet Union. His talks with Stalin were cordial and successful; he persuaded the Russian dictator to declare publicly that he, Stalin, "expressed complete understanding and approval of the national defence policy pursued by France." [19] This was an unprecedented public order to the French Communists to stop their sabotage of the French army and their bitter opposition to the recently passed two-years military service law. As Laval journeyed back to Paris, the Czech-Soviet Pact of Mutual Assistance was signed in Prague on May 16, 1935. The Flandin cabinet fell on May 31, 1935, and on June 7, Pierre Laval became Prime Minister and Foreign Minister. Herriot, as Minister of State, and six other moderate Radicals were in the cabinet.

Laval's resistance to the Franco-Soviet Pact did not end at this point. He stalled on the ratification process, so that the pact was not ratified until March, 1936. Although he had promised Stalin that he would propose to the cabinet staff conversations between the Red army and the French army, which Stalin had said were necessary to give the pact its teeth, Laval did not do so and gave instructions to his War Minister to evade politely Russian requests for military cooperation. Laval's ban on a military convention was not only a product of his general attitude on foreign policy; it also reflected his fear of communism. Laval was still mayor of the Paris working class suburb of Aubervilliers, where he had to fight the Communists constantly. He was sure that a military alliance with Russia would boost Communist prestige and give them many openings for infiltration, particularly in the army. Feeling as strongly as he

[19] Communiqué of May 15, 1935, in *Soviet Documents on Foreign Policy*, Vol. III, pp. 131–32.

did, Laval should have refused to sign the pact, resigned, and led a campaign against it. That was too direct; his were tactics devious enough to be a match for the wily Stalin, with one exception—Stalin could not fall from power.

Pierre Laval did not hesitate about Russia out of respect for the original allies of France. He was quite willing to sacrifice Poland and Czechoslovakia—but to Germany, not Russia. He agreed with Herriot, Paul-Boncour, and Barthou in writing off the United States. Although he drew closer to British policy, it was not done out of any desire for a closer union with England but purely as a tactical device. He hoped to avoid war with Germany, and, therefore, he did not need further British commitments to French security. Locarno—a guarantee against German aggression in the West—suited Laval perfectly. He did not really care what Germany did in the East.

Pierre Laval did not entirely waive the balance of power. He restricted his use of it to the region of Western Europe. He secured a virtual alliance with Italy in the Rome Accords which he signed with Mussolini on January 7, 1935. In return for "a free hand" in Ethiopia for Italy, Laval secured promises of Franco-Italian consultation on the Austrian question and on German rearmament. When Hitler announced German rearmament, the French and Italians delivered strong protests to Hitler and finally persuaded the British to join them in a conference at Stresa to discuss the German violation. There Flandin and Laval agreed with Mussolini to put teeth into their protests. In June, secret army and air agreements were signed coordinating Franco-Italian operations in case Hitler should invade Austria. Laval hoped to induce in Hitler a reasonable frame of mind for negotiations by displaying the existence of the Franco-Italian-English coalition, the "Stresa Front." His aim was to "channel" Germany into a general settlement with the three Western powers. If successful, this alignment would have resembled the Four Power Pact of 1933 and the Munich constellation of 1938. But, if the effort failed, then the unwritten alliance with Italy would be a solid addition to French security. Laval, then, wished to construct what Arnold Wolfers has called an "isolated balance of power." [20] Laval's policy formed an interesting contrast to that of Herriot; Laval rejected Stalin but sought Mussolini's hand, whereas Herriot suspected Mussolini and trusted Stalin. Put them in the same cabinet and you have the Rome Accords and the Franco-Soviet Pact.

The Premier of France at the time of the conclusion of the Franco-Soviet Pact was M. Pierre-Étienne Flandin. Leader of a Center party, *L'Alliance Democratique,* Flandin was moderate in his convictions and flexible in his methods.

[20] Wolfers, *Britain and France between Two Wars,* p. 308.

M. Flandin has claimed that he regarded himself as the heir of Barthou. This claim is borne out by his actions, with the qualification that Flandin did not share Barthou's implacable hostility to Germany; he retained some hope of turning Hitler toward an eventual negotiation. Flandin's basic resemblance to Barthou was their catholic use of the balance of power; they wanted both the Russian and Italian alliances.

How did Flandin conceive of the Russian venture? He was impressed by three aspects of the Soviet Union: the industrialization pursued under the Five Year Plan, the reorganization and modernization of the Russian army and air force (he had been an aviator in World War I), and Stalin's realism. Regarding the Rapallo collaboration as a menace to France, Flandin was naturally tempted by the opening presented to France when Germany and Russia broke their ties.

As the German menace grew, French statesmen, those who remained imbued with the theory of the European balance of power, its value tested by history and enhanced by the failure of the Covenant as an effective guarantee of the peace, were the first to turn to Russia as the necessary counterweight to the ambitions and schemes of pan-Germanism.[21]

Flandin's doubts came on the interaction of foreign and domestic policy. He resented the subversive activities of the French Communists and feared the probable extension of their influence owing to diplomatic collaboration with their master. Like Barthou, he simply subordinated those fears to the primacy of foreign policy.

Flandin had a conception of the role which Russia might play which approached that of M. Paul-Boncour. He, too, was preoccupied by the relation of the old to the new. Although irritated with the Poles and skeptical of the Little Entente, he did not want to write them off. If they were afraid of Russia they could not give effective resistance to Hitler. The Franco-Soviet Pact thus might serve as "a guarantee of Russian non-intervention against the neighbors of Germany." This conception suggested a limited role for Russia, something akin to the arsenal and backstop. "We never wanted to give Russia a guiding hand in our destinies. We never wanted to bring the Russian Army into the center of Europe."[22]

III

Such were the motives of the principal French authors of the Franco-Soviet Pact. Let us ignore M. Pierre Laval, who, left to himself, never

[21] Pierre-Étienne Flandin, *Politique Française 1919–1940* (Paris, 1947), pp. 169–70.
[22] Interview with M. Flandin, in Paris, Dec. 8, 1950.

would have signed the pact. All the others, Paul-Boncour, Herriot, Barthou, and Flandin, consciously thought in terms of the balance of power. There were differences in their approaches: Louis Barthou was cynical and aggressive, Joseph Paul-Boncour scrupulously tried to fit Russia into the pattern of existing French obligations, Herriot rejected Mussolini, the others sought Italy as well as Russia.

There was also a difference in the intensity, the audacity of their realism. That difference concerned the relation of policy and force. Alliance with Soviet Russia was so risky that it made sense only if the highest stake—the independence of France—was in question. Nazi Germany posed a direct threat to French independence. In that case, Russian military power was essential and there was no sense worrying about "bringing the Red army into the center of Europe." As long as the United States and England had no ground forces to send to Europe, only a Franco-Russian military alliance could stop Hitler. Professor J.-B. Duroselle has insisted rightly that "military collaboration . . . was the key to effective mutual assistance" between France and Russia. Paul-Boncour and Flandin hedged on this agonizing issue. Only Barthou and Herriot accepted the full implications of their diplomacy.

> There is no doubt that Barthou wished to go all the way and that he would have led that collaboration to take a precise form, without doubt that of a military convention. . . . The death of Barthou was likewise the death of a true alliance policy, which, perhaps, would have permitted both countries to avoid many disappointments.[23]

But the similarities in the thought of Paul-Boncour, Herriot, Barthou, and Flandin were more significant than their differences. All four men were sensitive to the fundamental factors of geography, demography, industrial, and military power. They subordinated domestic politics to foreign policy. They were steeped in the tradition of the *alliance de revers* and they often cited the historical precedents, even comparing Stalin to Suleiman the Magnificent. They wrote off the United States as an alternative ally, they had no hope of immediate British support, they knew that Poland and the Little Entente were not strong enough to contain Hitler. Their analyses were not highly sophisticated, but they were practicing politicians who had little time for research and intense calculation. In a decade when there was so much wishful thinking about international relations, these four French politicians were thoroughly grounded in the traditional elements of the balance of power.

[23] Duroselle, "Louis Barthou et le rapprochement franco-soviétique en 1934," p. 536.

CHAPTER 13

THE ROLE OF POLITICAL STYLE:
A STUDY OF DEAN ACHESON

DAVID S. McLELLAN

If we are to judge a Secretary of State in the performance of the responsibilities of the office it is first essential to stipulate the criteria by which we propose to do so.[1] There have been many biographies of diplomats and Secretaries of State but few if any have attempted a systematic assessment of the individual's performance in the light of the scope and functions of the office. Furthermore while most such biographies probe into the actor's childhood, education, and career-line experience, very rarely do they undertake a systematic examination of the actor's mode of leadership, decision-making, and configuration of policy in the light of such biographical factors. And yet foreknowledge of an actor's personality in its public dimension ought to help illuminate the character of his leadership and decisions.

What then are some of the elements by which we may examine and distinguish Dean Acheson's performance from that of other Secretaries of State? Here we are on thin ice, indeed.

According to Alexander de Conde the principal functions of the American Secretary of State are two in number. First, it is his responsibility to seek the attainment of ends generally understood under the rubric of the national interest. Secondly, in the process of defining and maintaining the national interest, the Secretary of State must act within the limitations of a definite number of roles—as chief adviser to the President, as the advocate of the President's policies before the Congress and before other executive officers, as administrator of the Department

---

DAVID S. McLELLAN is associate professor of political science at the University of California at Riverside. He is the co-author of *Theory and Practice of International Relations*.

[1] I am indebted to Deane E. Neubauer for intellectual assistance and to Bette Forest for her aid in editing the manuscript.

of State, and as the figure principally responsible for the conduct of United States relations with foreign countries.

The choices that a statesman makes from among the alternative modes of political behavior and perspective available to him will determine how he defines the national interest, mobilizes support, and fulfills the functions of the office. For example the manner in which a Secretary of State views the office and the function of government will generally exercise a subtle influence upon his performance. Similarly a statesman's concept of leadership accounts for much. He may either act upon the principle that a statesman's task is to provide leadership based upon understanding the requirements of correct and effective action, or he may assume that the statesman's function is to reflect the views of his constituents.

The character of a statesman's performance will also be shaped by the manner in which he reacts to problems. A Secretary of State may either respond by attempting to maintain the status quo by the application of legalistic formulae, as James Byrnes attempted to do in dealing with the Soviets, or his performance may be characterized by a willingness to innovate when faced by new and challenging problems. This in turn will depend to a great degree upon his confidence in organized social intelligence to produce answers and to resolve or control problems. Finally, the Secretary of State's performance will depend upon the degree to which his assumptions about international politics correspond to reality. A statesman who deduces the national interest and the line of policy from a priori principles will differ fundamentally from one who eschews abstract principle in favor of a pragmatic approach. Neither view is capable of full implementation because the moralist is, by necessity, bound to bump up against conflicting principles and the pragmatist operates with some sense of an ultimate goal which implies moral purpose; nevertheless each perspective colors and may fundamentally alter the conduct of foreign relations.

In summary the statesman's attitude toward the sphere of politics and toward government, his conception of leadership, his capacity for innovation, his confidence in organized social intelligence, and his view of international politics are the elements which energize a statesman's performance and determine his definition of the national interest. They also help the Secretary of State define the role of the office and inform the choices he makes in mobilizing support and choosing among alternative policies. To govern is to choose and each Secretary of State's performance is characteristically a configuration of the way in which his perspectives and attitudes about government, leadership, innovation, reason, and the nature of world politics contribute to his choices from among alternative modes. The manner of performance that a statesman assumes and which imparts a distinctiveness to his handling of the office I shall call "style."

Since the standards and modes of performance that a leader relies upon in public office are generally those which he has acquired as he moves out of his family circle into the wider arena to build the reputation which has made him eligible for high public office, the statesman's social class, education, and career-line experience hold important clues to his later performance. Let us now examine Acheson's performance in the light of the choices that his personality characteristically led him to make from among the alternative modes of political behavior and leadership.

I. GOVERNMENT

There are few extant expressions of Acheson's conception of government, but one in particular fits in with what we know of his career. In a letter discussing why young men might be encouraged to choose a career in government service, Acheson wrote, "A career in public service is rewarding because there is no better or fuller life for a man of spirit. The old Greek conception of happiness is relevant here: 'The exercise of vital powers along lines of excellence, in a life affording them scope.' " [2] Far from regarding government as a rather second rate career Acheson seems to have had a higher regard for it than for his lucrative career as a corporation lawyer. Acheson took to Groton a lively social conscience inherited from his father, the Episcopal Bishop of Connecticut. His youthful admiration for "Teddy" Roosevelt and Woodrow Wilson opened his eyes to government as a career worthy of a young gentleman's ambitions. Somewhere in those early years he appears to have established the relationship between individual excellence, which he had always sought, and active participation in political life. This is to be seen in his persistent willingness to serve in government posts despite the frustrations and hazards which such service involved, especially during the 1930's and 1940's. Even when he was forced to resign as Under Secretary of Treasury in 1934 as the result of a clash with Roosevelt over monetary policy (FDR's decision to drop the gold standard), Acheson did not let the incident destroy his respect for government. Unlike Raymond Moley, Lewis Douglas, Walter Lippmann, and others who broke with FDR in the early years of the New Deal, Acheson continued

[2] Paul Nitze, "The Role of the Learned Man in Government," *Review of Politics,* Vol. 20, p. 282.

to view the creative role of government as essential to the well-being of society.

Out of Acheson's difficulties with Roosevelt in 1934 came his extremely close relationship with Truman. Subsequent to his resignation as Under Secretary of Treasury Acheson regretted very deeply his behavior in the gold episode.

> I wasn't particularly well satisfied with my performance in it. It wasn't that what I had done was wrong . . . [but] I did not have enough consideration for the problems of the President. . . . Whether I was all right or not it warned me that there are terrible problems that an assistant to the President can get into by allowing things to get to the point where trouble occurs, and that therefore one ought to be very alert and watchful to consider his position and interests twice as much as one's own.[3]

As a result of this chastising experience Acheson approached the Truman relationship with a keen sense of the President's problems and the delicacy of his prestige. "My troubles with F.D.R. had a very deep and very lasting effect on my judgment in many things." [4] Among other things Acheson's respect for the presidency led him to discourage James Forrestal from surreptitiously establishing a role for the cabinet outside the purview of the President.

Acheson speaks now with considerable regret of the years from 1934 to 1940 when he was obliged to stand on the sidelines while others played the great game of politics. He eagerly returned to government in 1941 when Roosevelt appointed him Assistant Secretary of State for Economic Affairs. It is characteristic of Acheson's zealous regard for governmental service that during the war years he labored unflaggingly in a post far removed from the center of high diplomacy then being conducted from the White House. Instead of drama, his post called for unremitting efforts to maintain America's wartime economic operations amidst a miasma of conflicting authority and red tape. Acheson only began to emerge into the public limelight in connection with the Bretton Woods Agreements which he helped to shape and negotiate.

If one were to try to account for Acheson's high regard for government, his legal career in Washington would need to be given considerable weight. If Acheson's respect for government was not already in bloom by the time he arrived in Washington to become Justice Brandeis'

[3] Princeton Seminar: transcript of a seminar held at Princeton University, 1953–54, with Mr. Dean Acheson participating.
[4] *Ibid.*

law clerk (1919–21), it undoubtedly blossomed under the influence of that champion of the public interest against the claims of unconfined and irresponsible economic power. One finds in Acheson's writings—as in Brandeis'—the view that government is an indispensable agent for helping men maintain an open society in which all may participate in defining the ends for which society exists. In fact Acheson goes a step further than Brandeis. Recognizing the complexity of modern society Acheson accepts the possibility that government must actively intervene to provide men with the knowledge of the means to attain social ends which are unattainable by private means. This must be done in such a way as to avoid giving government unrestrained and arbitrary power so that it, in turn, becomes a menace to the ends which it exists to serve. It is precisely the challenge of coping with these questions that seems to have motivated Acheson's enduring interest in government.

Oliver Wendell Holmes was another influence on Acheson during the twenties, and no one familiar with Acheson's mind and writings can doubt the influence of that worldly skeptic. But unlike Holmes, Acheson refused to withdraw to the Olympian heights of the bench. When Roosevelt told Acheson he was sending his name up to the Senate for appointment to the Washington Circuit Court of Appeals, Acheson was indignant. "Would you like to be a judge?" he queried Roosevelt. Whatever FDR answered, Acheson retorted, "Well neither would I," and with that made clear his commitment to the life of political action.[5]

Acheson's fierce pride in government and respect for its intrinsic worth and distinction is nowhere better revealed than in a speech attacking Wendell Willkie's quest for the Presidency in 1940. To Willkie's claim that the war required a production engineer in the White House, Acheson replied: "Government is not a branch of manufacturing. The leadership of a people is not learned by designing an assembly line. Churchill has never produced anything, if by 'anything' Mr. Willkie means electric current or business deals. . . . We are not voting for a production manager, we are voting for a President." [6] Acheson expressed the view more than once during the pre-Pearl Harbor years that the disaster which overtook the West could have been averted had the democratic governments really been leading instead of following public opinion.

Acheson then possesses a lofty notion of government. To demonstrate how that influence was a significant factor in Acheson's style, we must provide evidence of the policy consequences of his view of government.

[5] Personal interview, Sept. 8, 1959.
[6] Speech in support of re-election of President Roosevelt, Radio Station WBAL, Baltimore, Md., Nov. 1, 1940.

It is generally accepted that the years from 1946 to 1952 witnessed a revolution in American foreign policy. Less than ten years after a probable majority of Americans could still support the isolationist side in the debate over events leading up to World War II, the United States was the center of history's most far-reaching set of alliances. Almost overnight it had become the leader of the non-Communist world, which it endeavored to support by costly policies of economic and military assistance. It is doubtful if such a transformation could have been carried out had there not been leaders such as Acheson whose profound regard for government enabled them to use its capacity for ordering and stabilizing international politics.

Many of Acheson's "difficulties" with Congress also derived from his lofty conception of government. Acheson is convinced that the Congress is neither organized nor inspired to participate in the making of foreign policy as a fully responsible partner. Acheson sensed all too keenly that its collective and individual attitudes, conditioned as they were by the defense of local and parochial interests or by an anti-governmental philosophy, were out of phase with requirements for the sane and sensible conduct of foreign affairs. Furthermore, the power of Congress is farmed out to a score of congressional committees. Acheson quickly perceived that because of the excessive dependence in Congress upon committees, the Secretary of State need only concentrate upon a few key members of a few key committees to secure enactment of foreign policy. Contemptuous of the parochialism and petty politicking of its rank and file and knowing that he could secure passage of what he wanted by even a hostile Congress, Acheson took little care to hide his sentiments behind the mask of artifice and false good fellowship.

In this regard Acheson was extremely sensitive to the efforts of some congressmen to reduce the issues of international relations to the personal and parochial. During the hearings on the Bretton Woods Agreements when he was confronted by a series of utterances deprecating the honesty and good faith of the other signatories, Acheson burst out: "Who are we to sit around and suspect the motives of countries with whom we agree we must cooperate." [7] Whenever senators queried him about what America's allies were contributing toward mutual security, Acheson always reminded them that relations among sovereign states and allies could not be carried on in a bargain basement spirit, that governments conducted their policies with something in mind other than getting a return on their money. He goaded congressmen, not always successfully it must be added, to raise their sights to the level of state-

[7] U.S., Congress, House, Committee on Banking and Currency, *Bretton Woods Agreement Act,* 79th Cong., 1st Sess., p. 63.

craft. He lacked the indispensable political gift for believing that every argument has an equally legitimate intellectual background.[8]

This did not endear him to men whose political behavior was conditioned by the defense of local and parochial interests or by an anti-governmental philosophy. Senator Taft and his cohorts were irritated by the singular vehemence with which Acheson dismissed their argument that the main line of American security lay with a balanced budget. Since any efforts to explain the political and strategic "facts of life" to them always met with incredulity and doctrinaire resistance, he finally gave up even the pretense of trying to discuss the issues rationally. These men preferred to deal with a man like Louis Johnson who was willing to cut the military budget if he thought it would advance his presidential aspirations. Although Acheson was hardly a New Deal "braintruster" (his confirmation as Under Secretary of Treasury had been opposed because of his alleged connections with reactionary Wall Street interests), his zealous regard for the integrity of government policy made him the symbol of excessive governmental authority or, in the words of one conservative senator, "the very heart of the octopus itself." [9]

Similarly members of the Fourth Estate (especially the columnists) were offended by Acheson's refusal to let them plunder the State Department at will for news stories. As Reston put it, Mr. Acheson had "an exceedingly high conception of the office of Secretary of State," [10] meaning that he wasn't willing to take Reston into his confidence.

Again, Acheson's refusal to hand up sacrificial victims to the House Un-American Activities Committee reflected a regard for the integrity of government service not always shared even by his illustrious successor. All in all Acheson's conception of government and his style of conduct resembled too much Plato's "selfless instrument" to please this array of powerful interests.

Acheson's conception of government led him to value the advice of the expert over that of the legislator. It seems clear that Mr. Acheson's determination to be guided by the expertise and intelligence available to him in the Department of State created the impression, according to Senator Knowland, of a "Poppa knows best" attitude that many senators resented. In his determination to conduct foreign policy according to the highest canons of excellence, Mr. Acheson ignored Woodrow Wilson's prophetic words that the man of excellence can succeed in

[8] Personal interview with Lord Franks, Worcester College, Oxford, Eng., June 27, 1964.

[9] James Rosenau, *The Senate and Dean Acheson: A Case Study in Legislative Attitudes* (Ph.D. thesis, Princeton University, May, 1957).

[10] Personal interview, June 16, 1960.

politics only if he possesses the power of persuasion. "Men are not led," declared Wilson, "by being told what they don't know. Persuasion is a force, but not information; and persuasion is accomplished by creeping into the confidence of those you would lead." [11] Obviously Dean Acheson was not interested in creeping into anyone's confidence. He chose to command by the force of his logic. In other times and perhaps with a different President, Acheson might have been able to succeed in his relations with the Senate. Truman's failure, however, to fully perform the presidential function of mobilizing public support behind his administration's foreign policy left Acheson terribly exposed in his relations with the Congress. What surprises us is that in the face of a hostile Congress Acheson accomplished as much as he did.

Acheson's sensitivity to the importance and distinctiveness of government found its most successful outlet in international affairs. It is reflected most characteristically in his belief that international relations is a sphere of human intercourse in which only governments can come to any stable, lasting argreements. Acheson always supported the United Nations as an institution, but he never felt that it embodied those attributes of sovereignty and power which alone afford the basis for any real agreement in international politics. In accordance with the same principle he never allowed such notions as the conscience of mankind or the pressure for an ideological crusade to blind him to the reality that governments were, after all, still the final and effective expression of their people's consciences and interests and that until something occurred to alter that relationship the United States had better rely upon governments rather than abstract principles for the adjustment of its interests. Where he departed from this principle as, for example, in his refusal to recognize the Chinese People's Republic, it was no doubt reluctantly and under the extreme political pressure of the times.

While his energies were constantly directed toward encouraging Europeans as well as Americans to transcend the limitations of parochial nationalism, he recognized that the only stable basis for such advances lay in the hard currency of governmental agreements. The skill with which Acheson wove the lines of diplomacy into an effective system of Western security is accounted for by his sensitivity to the realities upon which government and international politics are based. As we shall see at a later point, Acheson's superb understanding of the creative potentialities of government contributed immensely to the confident and authoritative style with which he inspired other statesmen and secured their cooperation in delicate and trying diplomatic ventures.

[11] Woodrow Wilson, *Leaders of Men,* edited with an introduction and notes by T. H. Vail Motter (Princeton, N.J., 1959), p. 39.

.II. LEADERSHIP

Every leader operates according to some principle of leadership. In evaluating situations, making policy choices, and in carrying them out, each leader consciously or unconsciously expresses a characteristic mode of leadership. He may believe that his best prospects for success are to be found in keeping his policies in harmony with the prevailing desires of his constituents; or he may feel more at ease when he is molding public opinion to accept policies based upon knowledge and intelligence; or he may assume that there is no problem connected with leadership, that the "office" itself provides the necessary support for whatever needs to be accomplished.

A life dedicated to the pursuit of excellence and to respect for intellect and reason as crucial to the affairs of men engendered in Acheson a conception of leadership strikingly adapted to deal with problems of foreign policy, but peculiarly at odds with American political institutions and mores. We can most readily grasp Acheson's conception of leadership if we recall Plato's classic model of political leadership. In a discussion marked by a bitterness of tone rarely found elsewhere in the dialogues, Plato demands of Callicles if the ruler is merely to reflect the views of his constituents and practice such arts as will enable him to persuade them of the wisdom of whatever legislation or action best serves his own ends; or whether it is not the function of the ruler to cultivate the pursuit of knowledge and to act solely with regard to the requirements of correct and just action. "Does it seem to you," Plato has Socrates ask of Callicles,

> that orators always speak with an eye on what is best and aim at this: that their fellow citizens may receive the maximum improvement through their words? Or do they, like poets, strive to gratify their fellows, and in seeking their own private interests, do they neglect the common good, dealing with public assemblies as though the constituents were children, trying only to gratify them, and caring not at all whether this procedure makes them better or makes them worse.

Acheson shared Plato's belief that it is the task of the statesman to discover the best possible policy and not merely to carry out the mandate of the people. Unlike Plato, however, he did not shrink from competition in the political arena to establish and maintain the loftier view. Time and again in his pre-1949 utterances Acheson revealed a marked contempt and aversion for the principle that leadership involves representing the lowest common denominator of constituency desires. In an address given at Yale University, November 28, 1939, Acheson decried the American lack of will to resist the totalitarian powers (including Russia): "We should stop analyzing ourselves—stop Gallup polling ourselves—and start analyzing the needs of our situation and the potentialities of our power." [12] In the spring of 1946 he deplored the tendency of Americans to ascertain their convictions by "this mass temperature taking [polling]" and expressed the conviction that only leadership possessed of will and courage could meet the crisis that Americans faced in international affairs.[13]

About this same time Acheson gave a startling demonstration of what he meant. General MacArthur made an unauthorized statement to the effect that the occupation of Japan could be greatly curtailed in view of the docility with which the Japanese were accepting their defeat. The circumstances at the time were such that every congressman was under pressure to bring the boys home. MacArthur's statement had the effect of contributing to this pressure and thereby undermining the policy of the government in a very delicate and crucial area. The Pentagon prudently avoided rebuking MacArthur publicly and even President Truman was cautious in his public criticism of the hero. By contrast, Under Secretary of State Dean Acheson blasted the impropriety of MacArthur's statement. When Senator Wherry endeavored to make Acheson retract his criticism of MacArthur, Acheson curtly rebuffed him. Wherry never forgot nor forgave Acheson's forthright rejection of his defense of MacArthur.

It is not surprising, therefore, that once he had become Secretary of State Acheson acted upon the assumption that the guideline to foreign policy is not public opinion, or even congressional opinion, but the relatively objective knowledge of the expert and that his task was to make that knowledge the basis of action. At best, this is a difficult principle to uphold under the conditions of American society. It was rendered even more difficult because Acheson was not equipped, either by temperament or by conviction, to employ the techniques of public relations which had served FDR so successfully. His first few press conferences were brilliant affairs, but Acheson soon lost his zest for a function in which he sensed an inherent conflict between maintaining the integrity of political action and the type of information which the press wanted. In a revealing interview with James Reston on his last day in

---

[12] "An American Attitude Toward Foreign Affairs," speech to Annual Dinner of Davenport College, Yale University, Nov. 28, 1939.

[13] "Random Harvest," speech to Associated Harvard Clubs, Boston, Mass., 1946.

office Acheson explained why he and Reston had not enjoyed better working relations. Reston expressed the conviction that had Acheson been more willing to confide in the press some of the rip tides of adverse publicity which had swirled around him could have been avoided and a greater effectiveness of communications achieved. Secretary Acheson explained that "what Reston suggested would have been impossible since there was a basic conflict of purpose between the two." "A Secretary of State," Acheson said, "has to germinate new policies and to nurse them along until they have reached the stage of development where they can withstand the battering assault of the political arena. The reporter's primary purpose, on the other hand, is to get news for his paper, no matter what the effect on policy." [14]

So great was Acheson's contempt for pandering to public opinion that it pained him to have to seem to justify policy to the public. Here is a strikingly characteristic expression of this attitude:

> The United States, in my judgment, acts in regard to a foreign nation strictly in regard to American interests or those wider interests which affect American interests. And if it is to American interests or those wider interests which affect it, to do one thing in one country and another thing in another then that is the consistency upon which I propose to advise the President, and I am not in the slightest bit worried because somebody can say: "Well you said so and so about Greece, why isn't this true about China?" I will be patient, and I will try to explain why Greece is not China, but my heart will not be in that battle.[15]

Attitudes such as these cut Acheson off from many of the channels that are normally open to the decision maker in the process of eliciting support for his policies.

Acheson's relations with Congress present us with much the same dilemma. Did Acheson fail to permit the Senate to participate effectively in the policy process, or were the attacks upon him inspired solely by partisanship and personal malice? Findings by James Rosenau on the basis of a content analysis of everything said about Acheson on the floor of the Senate during his four years in office point to the latter as the cardinal explanation. Rosenau found that of some 121 senators who occupied office between 1949 and 1953 only 21 were actively hostile to Acheson, and of these only 13 were indiscriminating in their hostility. These 13 mounted a campaign against Mr. Acheson based upon alleged

[14] Douglas Cater, *The Fourth Branch of Government* (Boston, Mass., 1959), p. 20.

[15] Quoted in Norman Graebner, "Dean G. Acheson," in *An Uncertain Tradition*, ed. Norman Graebner (New York, 1961), p. 281.

communism and treachery which under the circumstances of the time other senators were either unable or unwilling, out of fear, to refute. Rosenau concludes that their image of Acheson was so irrational and distorted (and one might add vicious) "that it is apparent that he could have engaged in no actions which would have met with their approval." [16]

Confronted by such people, Acheson was probably wise in acting upon the premise that only leadership of the strongest intellectual and moral force could succeed. He perceived all too clearly that if the loyalty of our allies, the professional development of the foreign service, and rationality in our international behavior were to be protected, foreign policy must not be allowed to become a hostage to pathological or partisan elements in Congress. Therefore, rather than curry favor with such elements or allow them to prolong America's fitful slumber in an isolationist torpor, Acheson gambled on the premise that leadership based upon knowledge and skill would be its own best advocate and our only long-run salvation in the cold war.

When we examine the success of Acheson's style of leadership in specific policy arenas we discover a more mixed situation. The remarkable consensus upon which the administration's European policies (Marshall Plan, NATO) rested enabled Acheson to conduct policy based upon the logic and expertise of the State Department and its sister services. Thus troops to Europe and the principle of German rearmament easily met the challenge of the "Great Debate" and were quickly accepted as an established part of our foreign policy.

The same was not true of Far Eastern policy and here we may discover the Achilles' heel of Acheson's style of leadership. Many administration critics asserted, but few offered any proof, that prior to the fall of Nationalist China the administration's policy was not accepted by the Republican Party in Congress. Senator Vandenberg admitted privately and publicly that Republicans were consulted about China policy continuously over the post-war period and that, while they did not participate as directly in China policy as in the formulation of European policy, they never came up with any better alternative to that pursued by the administration. Where the State Department let itself in for more trouble than necessary was in not sufficiently committing the Congress to a policy position *after* the fall of Chiang Kai-shek. It was not enough for Acheson to announce that the department was in search of a policy, and until it found one it could only wait until the dust settled.

In a democracy this puts the cart before the horse. Under the circum-

[16] Rosenau, *The Senate and Dean Acheson,* p. 343.

stances what was needed above all was public confidence that the State Department knew what it was doing, and the only way to achieve that was by associating with it the appropriate committees of the Senate in the search for a new terrain from which to view the monumental events occurring in Asia. Acheson's principle of leadership seems to have inhibited him from doing this. Instead he had the department publish the China *White Paper* and a conference of China experts was held in the autumn of 1949. But neither of these actions produced beneficent results where they were most needed. It was not Acheson's style to let the Senate mess around with policy until the departmental experts had arrived at a clear decision. Unfortunately, since it was likely to be some time before the dust settled enough to get a clear decision, it would have been the better part of wisdom for Acheson to have sought to minimize the mistrust and suspicion of the department in connection with the fall of China. And this depended upon securing senatorial endorsement while public opinion was still open minded on the subject.

A similar ingenuousness characterizes Acheson's explanation for not urging the President to secure congressional sanction for the decision to go into Korea.

The question of congressional consultation was raised by Senator Kenneth Wherry (R-Neb.) at a Blair House meeting on June 30. Senator Alexander Smith (R-N.J.) asked Acheson informally whether it would not be a good idea to have a resolution in Congress approving the dispatch of United States ground forces to the Pusan bridgehead. It was the subject of full-scale discussion at a meeting of the President and his staff with Senate Majority Leader Scott Lucas (D-Ill.) on July 3. In each instance Acheson rejected so advising the President because by-and-large Congress acquiesced in the President's action and Acheson felt that it would be dangerous to gild a lily—"if you start gilding it, you may get into some trouble." This is how Acheson explains a decision frought with terrible consequences. Among the senators who spoke in support of the President's constitutional authority to commit ground forces to Korea was Senator William F. Knowland (R-Calif.): "I believe that he has been authorized to do it under the terms of our obligations to the United Nations Charter . . . [and] under his constitutional power as Commander-in-Chief . . ." When disaster overtook the expedition Knowland referred to the Blair House meetings as those which "led this country into war, but without a declaration of the Congress of the United States." [17]

What is the lesson to be drawn from the bitter fruit of these two

[17] Hearings, *Military Situation in the Far East*, p. 765.

policies? In his study, *A Citizen Looks at Congress,* Acheson views the administration's conflict with its congressional foes as nothing but partisan "power striking against power," which the people could understand as the efforts of the Executive to maintain the integrity of policy against the irrational forces gathered in Congress.[18] If Acheson understood that by the end of 1949 public confidence in the State Department's Far Eastern policies had been shattered, he failed to appreciate that the most urgent need was not a better or wiser policy but rather to restore public confidence in the department's activities. This was helped by appointing Dean Rusk Assistant Secretary of State for the Far East, but an even larger public effort at restoring confidence and consensus was needed, and until it succeeded rationality and knowledge would be at a discount in effectively determining policy. American foreign policy is often akin to a ship on a storm-tossed sea. No amount of competence on the part of the navigator can hope to avail against the natural forces of tempest raging in the public mind. Acheson may have failed to adequately appreciate that in a democracy like the American, public opinion is more than an obstacle, it is a natural force; and it is no shame for the statesman to reckon with it accordingly.

III. INTELLECT AND INNOVATION [19]

Logically, the impulse and capacity to innovate on the part of a decision maker derives from his belief that the existing situation is not being satisfactorily met, and from his willingness to do something about it. This in turn presupposes that the decision maker has certain standards of knowledge by which he judges the adequacy or inadequacy with which the situation is being met. It also asumes that he is willing to act because he believes that by acting he can improve his control over the situation. It stands to reason, therefore, that a decision maker who views the importance of his relationship to the decision-making process self-consciously, who possesses a well-developed sense of the standards and criteria for judging whether a situation is satisfactory or not, and whose social philosophy supports him in the belief that by acting he can im-

---

[18] Dean Acheson, *A Citizen Looks at Congress* (New York, 1956).

[19] Gordon A. Craig has testified to the importance of innovative capacity in an essay on Otto Von Bismarck. According to Bismarck's associates, Craig writes, he had "the quality that Thucydides admired in Themistocles: the ability, by some hidden force of mind or character, to fasten immediately, after short deliberation, upon what was needed in a given situation." Gordon A. Craig, *From Bismarck to Adenauer: Aspects of German Statecraft* (Baltimore, Md., 1958), pp. 14–15.

prove the situation, will be more likely to accept the value of innovation than a decision maker who lacks such qualities. Dean Acheson's capacity for innovation rested upon such qualities.

In Dean Acheson's life there is a long history of identification with that social philosophy which expresses the belief that by the steady application of intelligence and self-discipline man has a fighting chance to avoid the worst disasters of an unpredictable future. This is the same philosophy that nurtured Holmes, Brandeis, and FDR. A liberal, Acheson is neither wedded to an egotistic psychology, nor beguiled by a formal individualism into denying that man's problems are social or collective in nature, and that government affords an engine whereby man's intellect can be pitted against those collective problems. Like Brandeis, Holmes, and FDR, Acheson developed a deep aversion to all attempts to shackle human behavior with immutable laws, ". . . whether they are the laws expounded in the *Social Statics* of Herbert Spencer or those in *Das Kapital* of Karl Marx." [20] Dean Acheson was one of the very few men who broke with FDR in the early years of the New Deal who could look back twenty years later and declare that the New Deal "not only produced economic but spiritual results of great importance. The people were no longer called upon to bear their fate with courageous resignation and to learn the lessons which it taught. They had a leader who told them that by their own organized effort they could end their miseries and they had a government which could lead the way and mobilize the means." [21]

Acheson's confidence in man's capacity to manage his social existence is all the more striking because he does not believe in the innate reasonableness and perfectibility of man. He is too close to the Old Testament and too much of a New England skeptic to believe in notions about man's goodness and rationality. Speaking in 1946 of the problems that the world faced, Acheson remarked that "they come pretty directly from the medium with which one works, the human animal himself." [22] Acheson stresses the importance of will and self-discipline if men are to overcome their difficulties. Intelligence alone is neither sufficient nor easily come by. Whatever threads of wisdom man achieves must be spun from his "own innards." "Most of us," he continues, "can only splice those odd fragments of conclusion which this unaccustomed effort produces." [23] Nor does Acheson believe that man can exorcise the Old

[20] Dean Acheson, *A Democrat Looks at His Party* (New York, 1955).
[21] *Ibid.*
[22] "Random Harvest."
[23] *Ibid.*

Adam by recourse to agents outside himself. Moral salvation is a matter of the individual soul, not of society.

Acheson's view of the human prospect is redeemed by his knowledge that the problems men face in their social life are not all the direct consequence of man's fall from grace; they are problems created by the working or non-working of human intelligence and as such they are susceptible to human control. The implications of this outlook for Acheson's conduct of foreign policy were immense. It meant that he understood that the evil of power in international relations was rooted not so much in the sinfulness of man but in the context, the constellations, the situation, in which even good men are forced to act selfishly or immorally. In the conduct of foreign policy Acheson was *not* wedded to the so-called laws of power politics and man's *animus dominandi,* but acted in the knowledge that it was within his power to modify and influence the configuration of events. The chief thing that Acheson shares in common with Machiavelli is the belief that "a certain region of historical event which contemporaries were content to accept as the province of chance, could be brought under human control by systematic and self-conscious statesmanship." [24]

Long before the atomic bomb had rendered nugatory the easy assumption that civilization could survive the blind play of man-made forces, Acheson expressed the growing sense of man's need for a way out of his blind bondage to so-called natural laws. In a speech at the Annual Dinner of Davenport College, Yale University, November 28, 1939, Acheson called upon his listeners to recognize that the old European order was passing and that there was a need for vigorous reconstruction "from which we cannot stand aloof if we are alive to our interest." He rejected the idea of armed isolation as the solution, on the grounds that without Europe the democratic values of the United States would die. He argued that for the future America should devise a realistic policy consisting of a therapeutic and a prophylactic side. Among other remedies Acheson proposed that darkening winter evening in 1939 was one that came to life a decade later—that America join with other financially strong nations in making capital available to economically needy areas of the world. "Man," he concluded, "is an ingenious creature once he possesses understanding and the will."

Understanding and will sum up the ingredients essential to innovate action but they do not give adequate weight to the temper of mind and intellectual power necessary to overcome popular apathy and the force of events. In order to act in drastically new ways the decision maker must be supported by a powerful sense of the mutability of history and

[24] Herbert Butterfield, *The Statecraft of Machiavelli* (London, 1955), p. 18.

by a most profound personal self-confidence. Finally to be effective the decision maker's predisposition to act must also be accompanied by a knowledge of how to act. The one without the other is useless. We can best explore the significance of the innovative temper of mind if we compare Acheson's crucial role in the development of the Truman Doctrine and the Marshall Plan with the policy alternatives and criticisms of opponents such as Henry Wallace and Senator Robert Taft.

It is hard to imagine now just how new and radical these policies appeared at their conception and just how persuasive were many of the criticisms directed against them. Taft assumed that there was nothing the United States could or should do to preserve the European balance of power. His position was essentially the product of a static conception of the environment. It was also a recipe for disaster because it held that there were uncontrollable forces afoot in the world which rendered all human action unfeasible except the final desperate resort to war. The Wallace alternative was equally rigid and equally dangerous. It demanded that leadership put faith in pure, untarnished principle. It rested upon the assumption that only steadfast adherence to faith in the Soviet Union and to acts of generosity and trust unsullied by policy considerations could serve to avert a catastrophic breakdown of Soviet-American relations. Wallace made no allowance for the possibility that if his approach failed the resulting disillusionment might pitch Americans in the direction of a military showdown with the Soviet Union. Wallace assumed that the relationship between the Soviet Union and the U.S. was so fragile that the least deviation would have catastrophic consequences. Wallace, like Taft, ignored the possibility that resistance to Soviet expansionism need not result in a "hot" war.

To Acheson post-war Europe was a potential vacuum. Should its economic and political structure collapse, it would suddenly become a raging vortex into which both the United States and the Soviet Union would be sucked. While Europe survived, the deadliness of the Taft and Wallace positions were obscured, but once it fell into anarchy or under Soviet domination it would be too late. The trick was to re-establish Europe as a community capable of controlling its own destiny and by so doing reduce the Soviet threat to what Acheson likes to call "manageable proportions."

Acheson's superb confidence that the United States could by the application of collective social intelligence steady the tottering European edifice explains the decisive style with which he was able to act. Drawing upon the intellectual resources of the State Department, Acheson produced the Truman Doctrine in less than a month. The Truman Doctrine, contrary to the criticism made at the time, was molded almost entirely by a sensitive intellectual probing for that policy which would supply the "missing component." It is also characteristic of Acheson's innovative style that in the midst of preparing the Truman Doctrine for presentation to the Congress, he assigned the State–Army–Navy Coordinating Committee the task of preparing the studies which eventually led to the Marshall Plan. It was also Acheson who encouraged the Planning Staff to proceed with the formulation of the Marshall Plan in anticipation of its eventual necessity.

Only a mind accustomed to believing that by one's own action one can help to create alternatives as well as define the framework within which man operates, could have envisaged the potential for change present in the European situation. No one of the policies adopted under Acheson's guidance was an end in itself, any more than FDR viewed the New Deal as an end in itself. Each was part of an effort to restore the European community by contributing to the European's sense of security and self-confidence and to his belief that Europe still had a substance worth preserving. Beyond that, Acheson, like Roosevelt, recognized that even the quest for community is not a static end in itself so much as a means for enabling men to control the potentially disruptive influences in their lives. Just as Roosevelt viewed the New Deal as a means of bringing the American economy into an equilibrium that was manageable, so Acheson conceived of the Marshall Plan, NATO, and Point IV as means for making the international equilibrium manageable. By restoring the European and world communities, the sphere for the play of uncontrolled forces would be that much reduced and man would be enabled to struggle against his fate in a real match, not a mismatch. It is doubtful if innovation on the scale and style attained by post-war American foreign policy would have been forthcoming without such a profound belief in the mutability of history and in man's ability to influence his destiny by acting upon it rather than passively accepting it. His social philosophy predisposed Acheson to see in a desperate situation the potential for change which in turn encouraged and supported him in his determination to act.

Acheson likes to quote Dwight Morrow's words that "there are two classes of people: Those who talked about things, and those who did things. Competition in the second group was not keen." This statement epitomizes Acheson's pride in knowing how to get things done, in being able to take hold of a problem situation and mold it to his will. In this regard it is illuminating to compare Acheson's and Kennan's approach to the Marshall Plan. Joseph Whelan, a biographer of Kennan, has written:

In many respects the nature and purposes of the Marshall Plan seemed to fit perfectly into Kennan's general conception of the proper way in which to meet the Soviet challenge . . . the "containment" involved was subtle and indirect. It posed no overt threat to Soviet Russia. To this humanitarian appeal to reason and thoroughly "liberal," "positive" approach to the great problems of European recovery George Kennan had no objections. It, apparently, epitomized the kind of "mystical" containment-by-internal-virtue that he had in mind.[25]

Acheson's contribution to the Marshall Plan lay in his capacity to recognize in the European crisis a political problem susceptible of solution in relatively concrete economic terms. Acheson's readiness to act, to undertake a new departure, was supported by a sense of precisely what could be done to remedy the European economic crisis. Once he knew that the United States could reasonably supply the "missing component" that would make Europe a secure and viable entity, he experienced no hesitation in putting his plans into action.

Acheson invariably began policy-making with a searching appraisal of what was existentially desirable and what was humanly possible. He recognized that no policy is a universal solution or cure-all; no policy devised by men, no matter how morally satisfying, could hope to resolve the cold war overnight. Since the power that policy can call upon is always limited, Acheson's mind was on how to maximize its efficiency. The art of devising such policy lay in mastering a knowledge of all the elements present and potential in a situation and determining what new increment, if added, would make a difference. The trick was to produce a policy which by its form and substance would transform a hopeless situation into a viable one. Policy for Acheson began with knowledge of the problem, not with some a priori moral abstraction to which policy had to conform.

There is further testimony to and evidence of the powerful role of social intelligence in guiding and supporting Acheson's innovative and decision-making style. As Under Secretary and as Secretary, Acheson made the fullest use of the resources available to him in the State Department. It takes nothing away from General Marshall to recognize that it was Acheson who provided the inspiration for the brilliant staff work upon which the Truman Doctrine and the Marshall Plan ultimately rested. Marshall could and did weigh the alternatives but he was skepti-

[25] Joseph G. Whelan, "George Kennan and His Influence on American Foreign Policy," *The Virginia Quarterly Review*, Spring, 1959, p. 206.

cal, if not unappreciative, of the value of extended intellectual palaver. "Most discussions were largely 'hot air' anyway, he thought, and no way for a Secretary to spend his time." [26] Acheson, by contrast, valued those sessions in which he met with the working staffs to explore the problems, to bring his logic to bear, and to infuse the thinking of the participants with purpose and direction. "Meeting with members of his own staff," Joseph Jones writes,

> Acheson never stated an opinion or conclusion until everyone present had an opportunity to give his own ideas about the subject and suggest a remedy. By questions he stimulated others to talk, while he listened and took occasional notes. When every aspect of the matter had been carefully and fully understood, he would summarize what he had heard, point out conflicts in points of view, attempt to reconcile them, introduce facts and reasoning that might not have appeared and finally suggest a solution. It was as though he were aware that this logic and facility for expression might, if brought into play too early, intimidate full expression.[27]

No individual would have taken the staff work as seriously as Acheson did nor have exercised such care in bringing it to bear upon the formulation of policy had he not possessed a conscious respect for the value of collective organized intelligence.

Acheson has summed up the ingredients of sound policy-making in the following terms: ". . . information, carefully prepared; then a discussion of its meaning, conducted with spirit, criticism, and relevance; and an indication of the course of action. . . . To the staff this practice is a constant demonstration both that their contribution is important and that it is fairly heard and considered." [28]

Acheson built his relationship with Truman upon the same intellectual foundation. Far from deprecating Truman's intellectual abilities, Acheson insisted that the President know as fully as time and circumstances permitted what the problems were and what alternatives existed. While such an approach required that the President do an enormous amount of homework, it was precisely the relationship that Truman wished to achieve. As the result of the complete intellectual and policy rapport that Acheson established with Truman, it was possible for the President to step into the foreign policy picture without the least awkwardness or straining for contrived effects. At the same time Acheson

[26] Joseph Jones, *The Fifteen Weeks* (New York, 1955), p. 111.
[27] *Ibid.*, p. 101.
[28] Dean Acheson, as quoted in the *New York Times,* Oct. 11, 1959.

enjoyed great freedom of action because he knew that he had the President's confidence and support. Such a relationship favored the realization of policies based upon inquiry and the most complete intellectual understanding.

Acheson's domination of the late years of the Truman administration is not unrelated to the advantage that the use of collective intelligence gave him in proposing new policies or influencing events crowding in on the administration. The National Security Council recommendation to increase the military budget ceiling from $15 billion to somewhere between $18 and $20 billion (N.S.C. 68), was essentially an outcome of Acheson staffwork designed to enable the United States to cope with the deepening cold war crisis and the loss of our atomic monopoly. Whatever the fate of N.S.C.68 would have been, the Korean aggression clearly demonstrated its urgency.

It was also the essential logic of Acheson's staffwork that determined the sequence of Blair House decisions that put the United States at war with North Korea. On Saturday night, acting on the advice of his own counselors, Acheson took the initiative in presenting the President with a plan for handling the Korean situation within the framework of the United Nations. Acting on the request of the President, Acheson, on Sunday evening, laid before the conference a set of additional recommendations for our representative in the Security Council. Twenty-four hours later on his own initiative, he presented the Blair House conference with proposals for American military intervention.[29]

By the same token, major responsibility falls to Acheson for the decision or lack of decision that permitted MacArthur to take his ill-fated plunge across the 38th parallel. This is true on two counts, the political and the military. Politically, Acheson failed to adequately assess the likely Chinese reaction to MacArthur's advance to the Yalu. Militarily, there was no one except Acheson in the government, and least of all in the military, with enough determination to pass judgment on the military logic of what MacArthur was doing. We all know that MacArthur disregarded or interpreted orders to suit his own purposes. What is frightening is that for a variety of reasons no one in the Pentagon, least of all General Marshall, felt that he could interfere with the right of the local commander to exercise his discretion, even if it meant enlarging the war. Having let MacArthur slip the leash, Acheson, the only strong figure besides the President who might have put MacArthur back on the leash, felt constrained not to do so for fear of being charged with interference in military affairs. This "hands off" posture stood

[29] Glenn D. Paige, *The Korean Decision* [June 24–30, 1950] (unpublished manuscript, Northwestern University, 1959).

Acheson in good stead in refuting the charges—made against him in the course of the MacArthur hearings—that he had influenced military judgment against MacArthur's strategy. But it is frightening to know that civilian control of the government was at the mercy of such a rigid demarcation of functions as to inhibit the Pentagon from interfering with a local commander and the Secretary of State from making decisive use of his judgment.

No one knows how close to demoralization the Truman administration came in that disastrous winter of 1950–51. In Washington the Republicans were plotting to destroy Acheson, if not to impeach the President. The American people were demoralized and incensed by the failure of their government to act decisively in the face of provocation. At the United Nations the State Department knew that it had to sweat out a series of agonizing resolutions designed to mollify Communist China, before our allies, exhausted by appeasement, would return to the fold. Only by going through this nerve-racking process could the United States hope to regain the diplomatic initiative and leadership. Meanwhile in bloody Korea, MacArthur was clamoring for another Dunkirk, while 8,000 miles away the Pentagon struggled to regroup his shattered armies in a desperate holding action. The imperturbable style with which Acheson kept a steady flow of decisions and policies going out to all fronts is eloquent testimony not only of his nerves but also of his belief in the ultimate triumph of human will and collective human effort.

In short, the imprint of the Acheson style is on most of the foreign policy achievements and failures of the Truman administration, and these are substantially a reflection of the intellectual power that Acheson generated during his years as Secretary of State. This intellectual power derived in turn from Acheson's pragmatic commitment to the liberal principle that problems exist to be solved and that man can better his condition substantially if not infinitely by the application of intelligence to his affairs.

IV. STYLE OF INTERNATIONAL RELATIONS

Acheson was the architect of most of the policies which still constitute the main elements in the struggle against the Soviet Union. Ineluctably many of his policies contributed to the deepening of the cold war. Yet few of them created the uneasiness among thoughtful people that those of his successor did—policies such as "massive retaliation" and "brinkmanship."

I believe that this quality of reasonableness and sanity is attributable to the conscious and unconscious restraint with which Acheson handled power. In part his handling of power was tempered by a tremendous respect for the contingencies and inscrutability of foreign affairs.

What is occurring in that vast external realm is so complex, so complicated, and so voluminous that [the statesman] cannot fully comprehend it; nor until much time has elapsed grasp its full significance. This is not wholly, or even principally, because of man-made impediments to knowledge—iron curtains, censorship, and the like—but because of the obscurity and complexity of the molecular changes which combine to bring about the growth or decay of power, will, and purpose in foreign lands.[30]

Secondly, Acheson's style of handling power was tempered by a confidence born of humility and an awareness of the human capacity for error and for personal opportunism in evading the responsibility for one's acts.

"International politics," writes one scholar, "offers opportunities and temptations for immoral action on a vast and destructive scale which tend to present themselves in the guise of necessity of State." [31] Acheson expressed it with simpler elegance: "We are a moral people, but like others fall from grace and too often take an immodest view of our capacity to act morally."

How are we to assess the quality of moral responsibility which expressed itself in Acheson's style of international dealings? There are a number of points at which Acheson has gone on record with explicit or implicit denials of the tenets or canons of *Realpolitik*. To the pessimistic and amoral notion that in serving politics one is inevitably wedded to "the ethics of doing evil," Acheson opposes the assertion that the political process affords scope for human excellence and courage. To the claim that "the very act of acting destroys our moral integrity," [32] Acheson opposes the Holmesian dictum that "man is born a predestined idealist, for he is born to act. To act is to affirm the worth of an end and to persist in affirming the worth of an end is to make an ideal." [33] I

[30] Dean Acheson, "The President and the Secretary of State," in *The Secretary of State,* ed. Don K. Price, © 1960 by the American Assembly. Prentice-Hall, Inc., publisher, p. 35.

[31] *The Anglo-American Tradition in Foreign Affairs,* ed. Arnold Wolfers and Laurence Martin (New Haven, Conn., 1956).

[32] Hans J. Morgenthau, *In Defense of the National Interest* (New York, 1952).

[33] Oliver Wendell Holmes as quoted in Dean Acheson, "Morality, Moralism, and Diplomacy," *The Yale Review,* XLVII (1958), 492.

believe that Acheson's faith in the efficacy of human will and reason to overcome threatening situations sets him apart from the "realist" for whom power exercises a fatal attraction toward resignation, expedience, irresponsibility, and the glorification of amorality and war.

It is illuminating in this regard to examine Acheson's attitude toward the Soviet Union and the cold war. A great many of his difficulties could have been solved had he acquiesced in the popular clamor for a moral crusade against the Soviet Union. There were any number of occasions on which Acheson could have quietly let the tiller of responsibility slip from his hands and in the wake of an upsurge of xenophobia emerged as a national hero. This Acheson steadfastly refused to do. "I hear almost every day someone say that the real aim of the United States is to stop the spread of communism. Nothing seems to put the cart more completely before the horse than that. The thing to oppose is Russian imperialism," of which communism is but "the most subtle instrument . . . the spearhead." By refusing to place the Soviet-American conflict on an ideological footing, Acheson denied Americans that release from moral restraint for which so many yearned in the late forties and fifties.

I think it is safe to say that Acheson's greatest safeguard against irresponsibility in the conduct of foreign policy lay in his willingness to act upon the assumption that nothing was ever hopeless and that by planning and making sacrifices the worst possible alternatives or contingencies could be avoided. "We live in dangerous times," he remarked not long before assuming the office of Secretary of State in January, 1949, "because of the decisions of another power which are beyond the control of any or all of us. There is no formula which will exorcise these dangers. The decisions which create them will be affected by the facts which we are helping, and successfully helping, to forge from the unfolding future." [34]

Upon assuming office in 1949 Acheson had occasion to make some profoundly serious decisions affecting the whole future of our lives for many years to come. The establishment of the North Atlantic Treaty Organization involved the decision, in Acheson's mind at least, to push ahead with the restoration of Europe, including West Germany, without treating Soviet offers of negotiation with any great seriousness.

When Acheson went to the Paris Foreign Ministers' Conference following the lifting of the Berlin blockade, for the first time an American diplomat had no intention of playing the Soviet game of seeking compromise for the sake of compromise. For the first time, refusal to accept Soviet domination of Eastern Europe was an explicit tenet of American diplomacy. In a sense Acheson was saying: "Not even a united Germany

[34] Dean Acheson, address to Michigan State Bar Association, 1948.

is an end in itself—our basic policy and aim is to push freedom as far east as possible." [35]

No one will deny that there is a disturbing note of aggressiveness in that attitude; but the policy to which it gave rise—situations of strength —aimed at changing the Kremlin's outlook, not at physical roll-back and liberation. Acheson always recognized that any relaxation of the Soviet grip on Eastern Europe could only be brought about by modifying the expectations of the Soviet leaders.

We get a clearer view of Acheson's responsible temper in connection with the Korean War, although here Acheson cannot be fully absolved from the dreadful negligence which led to MacArthur's crossing of the 38th parallel. Amidst the disarray and panic which attended our defeat in Korea, Acheson stood out as a bulwark of sanity if not serenity. There was plenty of clamor for repeating the horror of Hiroshima and Nagasaki in the winter of 1951, but this time the world would not have forgiven us had Acheson or Truman acquiesced in such a course. Something of the restraint with which Acheson viewed the Korean operation even before it degenerated into MacArthur's *Gotterdammerung* is to be gleaned from a memorandum Acheson sent Philip Jessup concerning President Truman's speech to be given at San Francisco following his Wake Island Conference with the victorious MacArthur. In his memo criticizing a draft of the speech, Acheson ordered deleted all reference to Korean events as a victory.

> . . . the whole idea of victory should be taken out. We should not be talking about victory. This is out of keeping in the U.N. There are no victors or vanquished in this kind of situation, only an adjudication. The only victor is peace. . . . To talk in terms of victory makes this too much of a U.S.–U.S.S.R. conflict. This part of the speech should be done with great restraint, should be sober, somber, with a sense of responsibility.[36]

Acheson also objected to the speech's "hammering away at the theme of communist imperialism in this way. Not only stale and uninteresting but dangerous in the present situation." [37]

In assaying the sources of Acheson's style of handling these matters, a large place must be given to the temper of mind induced by the law. Take for example the following three passages of which the first two are from Holmes, the third from Acheson: "When I emphasize the difference between law and *morals* I do so with reference to a single end, that

[35] Princeton Seminar.
[36] Memo: Schulman to Jessup in the files of Charles Murphy, Truman Library, Independence, Mo.
[37] *Ibid.*

of understanding and learning the law. . . . It is for that I ask you for the moment to imagine yourself indifferent to other and greater things." Holmes continues:

> For my own part, I often doubt whether it would not be a gain if every word of moral significance could be banished from the law altogether, and other words adopted which should convey legal ideas uncolored by anything outside the law . . . by ridding ourselves of an unnecessary confusion we should gain very much in the clearness of our thought.[38]

Now listen to Acheson saying the same thing. In discussing questions of foreign policy, "I would not, for the most part, use the language of moral discourse or invoke moral authority," but would "state principles in terms of their purpose and effect without characterizing them as moral or immoral . . . not because moral principles can, or should be, excluded from the relations of states to one another. . . . It is rather because to characterize conduct between nations as moral or immoral will involve us in confusions of vocabulary and of thought, with which, despite their importance, we need not struggle. . . ."[39]

From his position on the bench Holmes could work out the logic of this cosmic skepticism to its utmost limits, upholding legislation which he personally considered foolish or in error. "We need," he declared, "to transcend our own convictions," to permit much that "we hold dear to be done away with short of revolution by the orderly change of law."[40]

It was far harder for Acheson, caught in the maelstrom of political events, to adhere to such a philosophy. Yet Holmes provided the lodestar by which Acheson navigated. "To those," Acheson writes, "who have any appreciation of the perils which surround us, of the lightning speed with which relative (indeed absolute) positions can change, of the effect which popular attitudes, so easily and often unworthily stimulated can have in forcing governments to foolish action or restraining them from wise action, a moralistic approach to foreign relations and by this I mean one which attempts to apply the maxims or ideology of moral teaching seems ill-adapted to the complexity of the task."[41] What approach then is adapted to the task? The method of the common law by which principle evolves out of the adjustment of conflicting claims in particular cases, a method by which the lines of principle are etched out a bit at a time by the process of inclusion and exclusion. It combines a

[38] Oliver Wendell Holmes, Jr., "The Path of the Law," quoted from *The Mind and Faith of Justice Holmes,* ed. Max Lerner (New York, 1964), pp. 78–79.

[39] Acheson, "Morality, Moralism, and Diplomacy," p. 481.

[40] Holmes, Jr., "The Path of the Law."

[41] Acheson, "Morality, Moralism, and Diplomacy," p. 485.

deep skepticism of the wisdom of attempts to remold the social system at a single stroke or in accordance with any a priori doctrine, with an optimistic view of the ability of rational men to find what is fair and reasonable in particular problems or cases.

Transferring this approach to international relations we find the following contrast. Hans Morgenthau, the arch realist, believes it possible to start with something called the national interest, which is known and definable in advance. To Morgenthau international politics is like a very special map on which the expert, by use of special glasses, can plot and read off the national interest; Acheson believes leaders are dealing always with an incomplete map and each problem requires that the statesman take pen in hand and draw in the reasonable connections to the national interest. The virtues of this approach are seen again and again in Acheson's style of dealing with allies like Britain and France. Instead of going to a conference with an a priori definition of the national interest, which was likely to divide the participants, Acheson went with the idea of solving a common problem, a course that had the advantage of orienting the participants toward areas of consensus rather than areas of conflict. When progress on NATO and E.D.C. became stymied by political and economic deadlocks in 1951, Acheson proposed the creation of a Temporary (NATO) Council Committee (presided over by Harriman, Plowden, and Monnet). The writ of this committee was so extensive that it practically rewrote the budgets of the member states. In this fashion NATO served as an instrument for overcoming the limitations of national sovereignty. In doing NATO business the United States could quite properly intervene in French internal affairs, and British and French attitudes toward Germany were adjusted to meet the common needs of NATO.[42]

Thanks to the reasonableness and tolerance of Acheson's style, old nationalistic bogies were allayed, France was persuaded to forego her claims against Germany, Germany was encouraged to link her destiny to the democratic West, and Britain was persuaded to accept the Coal and Steel Community. And through it all emerged little or none of the rancor that developed against his successor. By a curious irony Acheson was more of a hero in the eyes of the Europeans than he was in the minds of his own countrymen.

Acheson did not come to his test of truth by imposing the a priori assumption and tenets of *Realpolitik* upon reality. Rather he seems to have found in the verification and validation of each preceding act "clues and 'leadings'," as William James would say, to the next policy with which we feel all the while—such feeling being among our potentialities—that the original ideas remain in agreement. The connection

[42] Princeton Seminar.

and transitions come to us from point to point as "being progressive, harmonious, satisfactory."

This does not mean that Acheson's decisions were always right, but they had a certain reasonableness and proportion about them which they certainly would not have had, had they been derived from the a priori postulates of doctrinaire realism. They had about them the spirit of life and reason and hope, which engaged the response and will power of the sorely divided nations of Western Europe and beyond. In the midst of their suffering and anxiety Acheson neither preached to them nor did he scare them by insisting upon rigid moral "principles, categories, supposed necessities"; rather he encouraged in them a spirit of hope and confidence by "looking towards last things, fruits, consequences, facts." He acted in terms of problems and solutions, of real and immediate dangers, and of ways of overcoming them. By so doing he contributed to freeing the mind and will of Europeans.

The political value of such a pragmatically determined decision-making was immense. It bred in Europe a sense of purpose and confidence that Europeans had not felt for twenty years. It created movements in the European experience that were worthwhile because they led toward "other movements which it will be worthwhile to have been led to" such as European cooperation and federation. The breath of life was pumped into the spectral vision of an economically and politically federated Europe. The powerful appeal of communism and neutralism were countered by rekindling the vision of the role an independent and united Europe might once again play in world politics. These moves may have been made in reaction to moves taken on the initiative of the Communist world, but we now know that because of them Europe is a healthy, revitalized, and prosperous weight in the balance of world affairs.

By undertaking to solve their problems in terms that Europeans could understand rather than in terms of narrow national interest, Acheson established the moral and political ascendancy of America in Europe in a way that force and browbeating could never achieve. By the style of his actions Acheson became the guarantor if not the *auctor* of the European and North Atlantic communities. By resisting the course of expediency at home and of pseudo morality and cynicism abroad he was able to inspire confidence in the Europeans and others of the rightness of American action. By setting them the example, by answering "for the rightness of the action" and "for the certainty that it will yield good fruit to the man who undertakes it," Acheson became the inspiration for taking action, if not freely, at least in the knowledge that any other alternative was hopeless.

CHAPTER 14

POLITICAL NECESSITY AND MORAL PRINCIPLE IN THE THOUGHT OF FRIEDRICH MEINECKE

RICHARD W. STERLING

The publication of an English translation of Friedrich Meinecke's *Die Idee der Staatsraeson* [1] has stimulated a renewal of interest in the political ideas of Germany's most eminent twentieth-century historian. Particularly in the United States, newly emerged from isolation and suddenly finding itself at the center of world power and world conflict, thoughtful people have been seeking a more satisfying approach to the intellectual and moral dilemmas posed by the possession of great power and great responsibility. The old confidence in an inevitable progress and in an uncomplicated harmony between reason, power, and morality has vanished with the elimination of the geographic and strategic barriers that once insulated America from the harsher realities of world politics.

In such a situation, the reflections of a scholar who probed more deeply than any of his contemporaries into the ethical problems of foreign policy are peculiarly appropriate. Meinecke's sense of the tragic conflict between political necessity and moral principle can now find an understanding response in a country that has borne the terrible responsibility of making the crucial decisions in the long series of crises since 1945—Hiroshima, Korea, Hungary, Suez, Berlin, Cuba, and Vietnam. Each of these crises has harbored complex ethical as well as expediential challenges. All have demonstrated the ambiguity of both moral

RICHARD W. STERLING is professor of government at Dartmouth College and chairman of the Dartmouth program in international relations. He is the author of *Ethics in a World of Power: The Political Ideas of Friedrich Meinecke.*

This chapter is reprinted from the *Canadian Journal of Economics and Political Science,* XXVI, No. 2 (May, 1960), by permission of the publisher.

[1] *Machiavellism: The Doctrine of Raison d'État in Modern History* (New Haven, Conn., and London, 1957).

and political standards of conduct. It was precisely this ambiguity of standards to which Meinecke addressed his thought. His reflections have, if anything, more significance today than when they first found expression.

The central lesson of history for Meinecke was that mankind's cultural and political development displays an apparently inexhaustible diversity. Men and societies, as products and agents of diversity, are incapable of transcending their individualities to the point where they represent universal norms unalloyed by particular interests. Every attempt to do so must end in the self-contradiction of seeking to impose individually conditioned standards upon a world that will necessarily resist them. Hence Meinecke rejected all doctrines which implied that only one form of political organization could claim the sanction of reason and morality.

Moreover, in the ebb and flow of historical eras Meinecke found no suggestion that men were moving from diversity toward unity and the resolution of the ambiguities of morality and reason which diversity created. New loyalties replaced old, and larger communities superseded those of narrower scope, but only to yield once again to fragmentation and dispersion. Human subjectivity, irrationality, and self-concern were inevitable, indeed indispensable and often beneficial, components of any community of loyalties. But they also constituted the ferment which fated such communities to transience. Such a view of history could not be reconciled with the millenarianism implicit, for example, in the philosophy of a Karl Marx or a Woodrow Wilson. History was not a procession toward God in which each generation, possessed of a truer and more universal understanding of life, moved closer to the goal. Meinecke took his stand with Ranke on the proposition that every age was as near to God as any other.

These views of history required acceptance of the assumption that there is an ineradicable element of anarchy in political life. For domestic politics this meant that the problem of liberty and authority would never be finally resolved. The most one could expect was a succession of more or less successful adjustments to it. The state was the means to effect these adjustments. It was the indispensable restraint on anarchy. As such its security and continuity constituted a task of the first importance.

The implication which Meinecke drew for the international realm was consistent with his assumptions about human diversity. The state could successfully carry out its ordering functions where affinities deriving from language, religion, historical background, and propinquity helped it to counter men's heterogeneity. But it could not hope to embrace all of disparate mankind. Political organization was fated always to be geographically and culturally limited. Hence the world would continue to be the meeting place of a multitude of societies, chance and their own unique needs deciding at each moment whether there was to be cooperation or conflict.

It was in this great uncertain realm beyond the reach of the ordering state where the issue of survival came closest to the surface. For this reason Meinecke was moved to locate the chief threat to state security in the prospect of external violence. Within the limits of the organized society the use of force was only intermittent. But beyond these limits the threat of violence was constant, and the state's organization must be capable of meeting this threat.

These were the premises that led Meinecke to accept a doctrine radically at odds with Western thought in general and Anglo-American thought in particular. It was Ranke's doctrine that "foreign policy has primacy over domestic policy, that the internal constitution and development of the state are subordinate to the compulsions generated by the struggle for power and independence in the outside world. The state must build its internal organization in such a way that it will be in the best possible position to pursue its external interests." [2]

The idea of the primacy of foreign policy sheds a very different light on the nature of politics than does the Western concept of the constitutional state. The Western doctrine sees the key political issues taking place within the state. The problem is how to bend the state to the will of the individuals who comprise it. The Ranke doctrine, which also became the dominant German doctrine, saw the key political issues located outside the state. The problem was how to control the will of the people to assure the survival of the state in the external world. Foreign policy was not an incidental conditioner but the central determining factor in constitutional organization.

Whatever the merits or defects of this doctrine, it served to focus Meinecke's attention on the state as a coercive power. Indeed, all the concepts we have summarized here portray the world as a precarious environment and suggest that those who wish to survive will sometimes have to use harsh methods. The picture of the state demanding obedience from its citizens is far sterner than that of the citizens demanding freedom from the state. All these considerations pointed to a conflict between the needs of the state and the idea of morality based on individual freedom in a way that the dominant Western theory of the state could never do.

---

[2] *Vom geschichtlichen Sinn und vom Sinn der Geschichte* (4th ed.; Leipzig, 1942), p. 30.

A consideration of the needs of the state leads to the central theme of the relation between necessity and moral principle, for supreme among the state's needs is the necessity to survive. Meinecke used the term "necessity" as the imperative of state survival. He identified *raison d'état* itself, the idea around which so much of his political thought revolved, as the reflection of this necessity. *Raison d'état* is the formula which "tells the statesman what he must do to maintain the health and strength of the state." The meaning of *raison d'état,* Meinecke says in another place, is "determinism in political conduct." [3]

Ideally, then, conduct guided by *raison d'état* has no other criterion than the welfare of the state. Such an ideal runs directly counter to the concept of a universal moral law which claims for itself the function of ultimate yardstick for human conduct: acts must be judged finally by the generally accepted canons of good and evil and not according to their utility to the state. Here was the realm of principle where morality was the commanding consideration.

Necessity and principle were bound to clash. Their contending claims for supreme jurisdiction made antagonism a certainty even in cases where one might judge that the useful and the good coincided. Where there was no such coincidence, there the contest would be exposed in all its ramifications. Where circumstances did not permit moral political methods, Machiavelli said, the prince must learn how not to be good. His advice to the statesman confuted the injunction to avoid evil and do good. True, Machiavelli did not argue to the contrary. The statesman should not do evil all the time. He ought to do good where he can. On the other hand, and more important, an evil deed was not merely a regrettable aberration from the norm. It was not an aberration at all, but quite within the range of normality—to be resorted to whenever necessity required.

Machiavelli's doctrine was a radical usurpation of the position claimed by morality and natural law in Western society. It was, Meinecke observed, as if "the devil had invaded God's kingdom." [4] Yet this invasion was at once more subtle and less repugnant if one accepted Machiavelli's persuasive position that the state was a good in itself. As the bringer of that order indispensable to civilization, was not the state's preservation a purpose which commanded obedience and even veneration? Human freedom, in any meaningful sense of the term, also depended upon political order. Without it, the quality of social relations was bound to be deficient and unpromising.

All these services to cultural and moral values gave the state a moral

[3] *Staatsraeson,* pp. 1, 369.
[4] *Ibid.,* p. 49.

dignity of its own. Hence the conflict of political necessity and moral principle was not a clash of opposites but of approximates. The state's loss would not automatically be morality's gain; the world of morals would be the poorer for the lack of the state's ordering hand.

The relation between state survival and moral principle becomes still more ambiguous when its context is considered. The state is not an isolated entity but exists in a world of rivals. Should the state sacrifice its security needs to the commands of ethical behavior, the profit would go not so much to abstract morality as to a political rival. In this case the most that can be said is that the rival's claims to the status of a moral entity are as good or bad as those of the sacrificing state. The impossibility of achieving absolute justice, whether the statesman uses the standards of political necessity or moral principle, has the effect of making both standards relative. When faced with contradictory demands required by moral behavior and political survival, the statesman faces a choice not between moral and immoral action but between conflicting moral duties.

This was Meinecke's view in his first elaboration of the problem. "The laws of morality," he wrote, "of brotherly love, of sanctity of agreements, are eternal and inviolable. But the duty of the statesman to care for the welfare and safety of the state and people entrusted to him . . . is also sacred and inviolable. What happens when these two duties conflict with one another?" Meinecke reminded those who denied the possibility of such conflicts that "every authentic tragedy is a shattering demonstration that moral life cannot be regulated like clockwork and that even the purest strivings for good can be forced into the most painful choices. . . . In relations between states, moreover, clashes between private morality and state interest are plainly inevitable and as old as world history itself." [5]

How then was the statesman to decide between the two duties? In 1915 Meinecke's answer was that both "history and conscience teach . . . that in such cases the statesman can act only in accordance with the principle *salus populi suprema lex est*. This is exactly what Bismarck meant when he said that 'state egotism is the only healthy basis of a great state.' " [6] Such an answer was a telling illustration of the aggressiveness with which the "devil had invaded God's kingdom." The statesman's two absolutes of state responsibility and moral norm have become relativized only to permit the one to assert its permanent supremacy over the other. Here *salus populi* is not demanding mere equal

---

[5] "Kultur, Machtpolitik und Militarismus" in *Deutschland und der Weltkrieg*, Otto Hintze *et al.* (Leipzig and Berlin, 1915), p. 631.
[6] *Ibid.*

status to the moral law; it insists that morality subordinate itself to the needs of the state whenever the issue is drawn.

This is essentially the doctrine of Machiavelli which Meinecke was later to label both "great" and "demonic": "In politics state interest has precedence over morality. Morality is not denied; it is simply . . . relegated to the realm of secondary concerns." [7] Meinecke's own involvement with the doctrine testified to its demonic powers of attraction. There is ample evidence to suggest that his resolve to probe the nature of *raison d'état* was inspired in part by a sense of culpability in having failed on his first attempt to place any theoretically meaningful limits to state egotism.[8]

Whatever doubts and confusion attended Meinecke's post-war thought, he stood by the conviction that the establishment of such limits had become a task of utmost importance. He was too deeply shaken by the spectacle of the contending state egos in the First World War, each driven by its imperative of survival to cast away more and more of the moral restraints which also tended to restrict war's destructive powers. All the values which the state's existence was designed to protect—civilization, culture, and ordered liberty—were being wrecked in the struggle of the states to maintain themselves and destroy their enemies. In this perspective one could not derive much comfort from the doctrine that the existence of the state is a good in itself and that the presumed necessity of its continuation must override every other consideration.

This, then, was the background of Meinecke's study of *raison d'état*. All his investigations were directed toward an attempt to get the doctrine of necessity of state out into the open, to discover the extent of its validity as a concept. He wanted to know why it exerted such an obvious fascination for political thinkers and how to avoid entrapment by it. Thus he created a study that was in essence a dialogue between Machiavelli and all the generations that followed him. He documented the triumphs which Machiavelli celebrated in the camps of his critics—Bodin, Campanella, and the young Frederick. None could forego the Florentine's recipes, no matter how determined they were not to use them. But Meinecke also recorded the dangers which beset those who attempted a reconciliation with Machiavelli. Hegel, Fichte, Ranke, and Trietschke, all seminal influences in German thought generally and in Meinecke's own personal intellectual development, sought to effect a marriage between the expedient and the good. The result, as Meinecke's

[7] Introduction to *Machiavellis der Fuerst,* Vol. VIII: *Klassiker der Politik* (Berlin, 1923), p. 6.
[8] Cf. *Staatsraeson,* p. 27, and *Nach der Revolution* (Munich and Berlin, 1919), pp. 54–55.

own experience had indicated, was an ever stronger tendency for the expedient to suppress the good—to the point where expediency ruled alone.

The basic thesis of Meinecke's reappraisal was that both critics and admirers of Machiavelli failed to deal adequately with the challenge he confronted them with. Those who insisted that moral principle must always have primacy over the necessities of state could not be consistent. The complexities of subjectivity and diversity, of irrationality and self-concern which they shared with their environment were an insuperable obstacle. Narrowness of view and particularity of advantage continually betrayed their doctrines and their actions. As they attempted to disguise their inconsistencies they moved from expediency into hypocrisy and even beyond to the point where they themselves no longer realized when principle had departed from their conduct. At this point their appeals to principle fell on deaf ears among those whom their actions disadvantaged. The credibility of moral principle was undermined and with it the whole concept of a universal ethical standard superior to the interests of the individual state. Thus the opponents of Machiavelli and the doctrine of state necessity destroyed the very thing they had set out to champion.

It was in criticism of this process that those who sought to restore Machiavelli to respectability built their systems. After all, Machiavelli symbolized the protest against sham. He wanted to discuss the truth of politics and not what men imagined it to be. Let us concede that the state must sometimes violate the moral law, the argument ran, so that we will not deceive ourselves and embitter others by false preachments. But let us build into the state a moral value and a cultural creativity of such proportions that the egotism of its conduct may be justified. When it transgresses the laws of truth and justice in pursuit of its advantage, let it be done in the name of preserving that heritage of order and common enterprise without which none of men's spiritual and cultural values can flourish.

Here was the element of greatness in Machiavelli's doctrine. It challenged men to face the truth about politics and human nature. In their efforts to deal with life and society they could not avoid incurring guilt. "It seems," Meinecke wrote, "that the state must sin." [9] The recognition of this truth could serve as a spur to compensate for guilty actions in such a way that even sin could be productive of virtue. For the state this meant that it must have such virtue of its own that even a resort to the techniques of Machiavelli would not be without an element of moral grandeur.

[9] *Staatsraeson*, p. 15.

The building of such a state was a dazzling objective. It began with the confession that men were not gods but earthbound and sinful. It proposed to construct a society whose norms were honest enough to admit to this limitation. Its claim would be not to serve virtue in the abstract but in the only form which was socially meaningful—within the boundaries of the order-bringing state. Here the dignity and creative powers of men would be cultivated and given protection from the chaos of the surrounding world.

The state would not be diverted by the hopeless task of assuming similar responsibilities for humanity at large. It would resemble a great and free personality whose claim to exist in the world rested on its own moral and cultural achievements. When its existence was threatened it would not resort to cant but defend itself frankly on the proposition that it was dedicated to its own self-preservation. It would refuse to speak in terms of absolute right and wrong; in the light of its original self-limitation it could not assert with certainty that there were not contending rights. Its only certainty was its own interior worth and the need to sustain it.

If the necessities of conflict demanded the use of evil means, there was no cause for dismay among those who had already confessed that this was the way of the world. The ancient wisdom that men face only a choice of evils meant that evil must be used to outwit evil. Evil would be made to serve the good if its purpose was the virtuous state's salvation. At the end of this line of reasoning stood the admonition of Machiavelli: "Where the very safety of the fatherland is at stake, there should be no question of reflecting whether a thing is just or unjust, humane or cruel, praiseworthy or shameful. Setting aside every other consideration, one must take that course of action which will secure the country's life and liberty." [10]

Even here, where the consequences of the state's absolutization were revealed in all their nakedness, the element of humility in the original proposition could still be ascertained. After all, the state's decisions were being made by the men who were its rulers. Machiavelli's words were for them, and they were not a recipe for victory at any price—for the victory that would assure the rulers glory. The necessity of state embraced defeat as well as victory. If victory was beyond grasp, then its rulers must prepare the state for defeat, seeking to mitigate its losses and spare its vital parts. Here Machiavelli remarked, "It will always be difficult to induce the masses to accept decisions which appear to be cowardly and ruinous but which in fact bring safety and advantage." [11]

[10] *Discourses*, III, 41, quoted in *Staatsraeson*, pp. 55–56.
[11] *Discourses*, I, 53, quoted in *Staatsraeson*, p. 55.

Nonetheless, in the name of the state the rulers must accept their own loss of power and the humiliation which accompanies failure; they must be ready to save the fatherland even at the expense of their personal ignominy. "This is the summit of ethical pathos which conduct governed by state reason can achieve," Meinecke observed. Machiavelli's words "should have sounded in the ears of a great German statesman during the world war." [12]

It would be too much to say that Meinecke's own retreat from the doctrine of *salus populi* was rooted in his disappointment that there were no German leaders capable of following such an ethic. Indeed, the record of his previous positions and the tenor of his other wartime writings justify the contention that the idea of the state's knowing no law beyond its own survival would rest uneasily with him—that his avowal of the doctrine was a counsel of desperation and that the fact that he had given it unqualified articulation was itself the moving force which finally led him into his monumental endeavor to lay bare the meaning of *raison d'état*. It is true that he was an intellectual heir of the German tradition that built up the supremacy of the state's ego. He was touched personally and deeply by what he later called its demonic force. But he had long before developed positions of resistance to it. If Germany's crisis demonstrated that the men who ruled it could not meet the supreme ethical requirements of the doctrine of state necessity, one could draw some valid conclusions about their personal shortcomings. But in a more important sense it provided dramatic evidence that the doctrine itself was no solution to the dilemma of means and ends. Meinecke's assumptions about human diversity and the subjectivity and irrationality of human nature were given terrible confirmation by the very system that sought to allow for them.

If subjectivity and irrationality prevented the men who preached the supremacy of universal moral principles from seeing when principle had departed from their conduct, the same qualities prevented the state supremacists from seeing when virtue left the state. What was the basis for their claims that the state was virtuous? Was it that the state was truthful in admitting the egoistic nerve of its policies? But what had happened to truth when the rulers lied to hide the state's defeats in the name of maintaining morale? What chance did candor have when the destructiveness of world conflict made the people doubt whether preservation of the state's ego was sufficient justification for the carnage?

The resolve not to deal in terms of universal moral principles and absolute right and wrong collapsed before the necessity to gain allies and influence neutrals. One could not leave the enemy a monopoly claim to

[12] *Staatsraeson*, p. 55.

be fighting in the name of universal justice and of interests and standards that transcended the narrow ego of the individual state. Wartime associates must not be permitted to infer that their efforts in a common venture would benefit only one of the partners. As for the enemy, the greater the sacrifices demanded from the masses of civilians and soldiers, the greater the temptation to picture the enemy not merely as alien but unjust.

Finally, if the rulers claimed that the state provided the order that freedom and cultural creativity must have, what could sustain them when that order began to crumble under the pressures of war? As every nerve was strained in the struggle to survive, the freedom to dissent became narrower, every national energy was channeled into the war effort, and the complex conception of reality, upon which every thriving culture rests, was forced to give way to the black and white patterns of the propagandist.

All this experience must bring into question the whole concept of equating the state's ego with the *salus populi*. Were these not ambiguous concepts in themselves, coinciding or not as circumstances decreed? "The state's advantage is . . . always somehow related to advantages for the rulers," Meinecke wrote, and only too often "the state served not the general welfare but the welfare of the rulers." [13] True, this was a universal phenomenon of politics, not to be done away with by the mere alteration of a doctrine that elevated the necessity of state to the supreme commandment of life. But the destructive effects of this truth about politics were immeasurably magnified if people were trained to bow down and question not whenever the idea of *raison d'état* was invoked. Narrow interests, the product of man's inherent diversity, could find all too convenient a hiding place behind absolute ideas, whether of the virtuous state or of a universal code of morality and justice.

Necessity and principle—each when converted into an ultimate commandment distorted the real issues in man's political life. In this light the demonic element in the doctrine of *raison d'état* is clear enough. Its claim to the status of an absolute erects a creature between men and God whose demands of allegiance are God's own and which, if fulfilled, prevent men from seeing the true nature of the state and their duties transcending a being "higher than men but lower than God." But the demon of untruth is also present in the doctrine of the supremacy of moral principle in politics. The assertion that principle is always the guide in political decision is also a denial of truth, which deprives men of the capacity to understand the ambiguous meaning of their own actions and hence of the opportunity to purify them. The root of corrup-

[13] *Ibid.*, pp. 9, 429.

tion in both cases is the supposition that either can claim sole validity as a criterion for political conduct.

Thus Meinecke saw the two concepts as both antagonistic and complementary. Neither could be spared as a referent for political thought and action. Hence they joined a long list of conceptual polarities—nationalism and cosmopolitanism, power and morals, ideal and real, subjective and objective—upon which Meinecke built an ever more explicitly dualistic philosophy. Men were fated to be torn between the antipodes of these concepts, each of which had both positive and negative connotations. Only the apprehension of the human situation in these terms could discipline subjective, irrational, and diverse men to turn their limitations into cultural and moral assets. Only the recognition that the problems posed by these polarities are inherently insoluble could guard against the temptation to eradicate the ineradicable anarchy of human existence. Such a recognition also stands as a challenge to human beings to use this anarchy as freedom to build, to dissent from, and to change the transient, if necessary, modes of political order.

In regard to the specific problem of state necessity, Meinecke wrote that "monism, whether naive or consciously elaborated, whether idealistic or naturalistic, is not inevitably the foundation of a ruthless *raison d'état*. But it can become one; restraints can be sought only by means of some kind of dualistic approach. . . ." Thus the climax of his study of *raison d'état* gave the statesman a far more difficult task than Meinecke's earlier "monistic" recipe always to resolve conflicts between necessity and principle in favor of the *salus populi*. The statesman "must carry both God and the state in his heart to prevent the demon he cannot completely escape from overpowering him." [14]

This admonition imposes on the statesman a double obligation that no longer permits the automatic option for the norm of state necessity when it is in conflict with the norms of moral principle. The juxtaposition of the state with God emphasizes the claim and responsibility of the state to represent a moral content of its own, but it must strive always to find means of self-preservation in harmony with the transcendent moral obligations. Violations of these obligations are not ruled out, for the fact that good can sometimes come from bad is undeniable. But violations must be kept to a minimum for, "one must avoid any idealization of this fact. It is a demonstration not of reason's cunning but of reason's impotency." [15] Each violation is a confession of imperfection and incurs a guilt for which there can be atonement only by a renewed and more intense striving to abide by moral norms.

[14] *Ibid.,* pp. 536, 542.
[15] *Ibid.,* p. 537.

The pairing of the state and God in the statesman's heart has an obverse function. It warns him not to suppose that his conduct can be wholly without blemish. It reminds him that his relation to God can be only a mediate one, that his striving for good can never be truly universal in its significance and effects. It admonishes him that political order has, in fact, powerful claims and that he must be cautious in pressing against them his subjective concepts of what abstract morality requires.

Both aspects of the juxtaposition constitute a remonstrance to humility. Whether the statesman opts for state necessity or moral principle as the basis for decision, he must do so in the knowledge of his own fallibility. But here we are at the crucial distinction between Meinecke's one-time acceptance of the *salus populi* argument and the conclusions he reached in his study of *raison d'état*. The juxtaposition of state and God liberated the statesman from determinism in politics. It gave to his conscience the freedom not only to violate moral principles in the name of state survival but also to turn his back on the necessities of the state when he found its demands morally intolerable.

Meinecke did not spell out this radical consequence of the formula with which he capped his study of *raison d'état*. Indeed, the whole tenor of the book indicates an unwillingness to speculate on the possibility that the responsible statesman might be forced to make a choice in violation of the state's interests. What Meinecke had done, however, was to elevate the individual conscience to a seat of judgment over the contending claims of necessity and principle. Whatever Meinecke's subsequent deviations, his ultimate answer to the problem of political obligation was foreshadowed long before when in the early years of the century he wrote that "the inner freedom of the human being is the highest of all values." [16]

This inner freedom made it possible in the first instance for Meinecke as a private citizen to reject from the outset the *raison d'état* of the Nazi state. As the Hitler years brought ever more brutal violations of morality in the name of the state ego, Meinecke explicitly extended this inner freedom to responsible officials sworn to uphold the state. In his approval of the conspiracy against the Nazi regime,[17] he accepted the full consequences of his juxtaposition of God and the state. To the state whose necessities had become a moral enormity the only possible answer was treason.

This was, of course, a rejection of Machiavelli and all the subsequent doctrines that declared absolute the necessity of state. It also contra-

---

[16] *Das Zeitalter der deutschen Erhebung, 1795–1815* (4th ed.; Leipzig, 1950), p. 52.

[17] *Die deutsche Katastrophe* (Wiesbaden, 1946), pp. 143–50.

dicted the theory of the primacy of foreign policy in that it conceded the internal enemy could be as dangerous as any external foe.[18] Was it not also a rejection of the dualistic conclusions at which Meinecke had arrived in his study of *raison d'état?* Was not the devil clearly ejected from God's kingdom and the statesman presented with a hierarchy of values in which the necessity of state was clearly subordinate to moral principle?

In an ultimate sense one would have to answer in the affirmative and so accuse Meinecke of self-contradiction. But he would argue in return that it is not often that human fortune or misfortune provides the opportunity for such a clear-cut choice. Indeed, it must be the statesman's aim to avoid such moments of clarity, for they tend to come only when the state has become corrupt. He must strive to make the state virtuous and so justify its claims to survival. To the extent that he succeeds the counsel of Machiavelli will not be irrelevant. But his indispensable support in seeking to make the state a moral being is the knowledge that there are obligations that transcend the state. He must constantly endeavor to meet those obligations in order not to be forced by them to violate his political trust. The duty—and the tragedy—of a statesman, therefore, fates him to will a situation in which the dualism of necessity and principle constitutes a never ending challenge.

[18] *Ibid.,* p. 152.

CHAPTER 15

NATIONAL INTEREST AND MORAL THEORY: THE "DEBATE" AMONG CONTEMPORARY POLITICAL REALISTS

ROBERT C. GOOD

Debates on the national interest proceed from two perspectives.[1] One tends to be policy oriented; the other, ethically oriented. Though these two perspectives overlap in the blurred double vision of real choice in real situations, there is purpose in sorting them out.

The national interest as it bears on policy represents a rough guide to, and a restraint on, decision and action. It defines the limits of choice, beyond which responsible statesmanship must not trespass, because to do so would risk the security, perhaps the survival, of the nation. Exactly where this boundary line runs, and precisely what programs are to be pursued within its limits, are matters of constant debate among the many surveyors of the nation's interests. This is because "security" and "survival" (or "vital interest," or "our way of life," or "national welfare") are not fixed points on the political terrain; rather, their precise location, their size and importance and relation to one another, depend in great part on the lens settings in the instruments by which they are surveyed. Thus the Chamber of Commerce defines the boundary circumscribing legitimate choice differently from the Pentagon, the Pentagon defines it differently from the State Department, and the State Department differently from, say, the Atomic Energy Commission.

The second perspective, the national interest as a problem in political ethics, provides the subject for the present study. It is the problem of reconciling necessity and principle: the necessity is that of protecting the interests of the group for which one serves as trustee and the principle is that of loyalty to more inclusive values such as justice and equality for

---

[1] By permission of the publisher, this chapter is reprinted, with some changes and additions, from *Journal of Politics*, Vol. 22 (Nov., 1960), where it appeared under the title, "The National Interest and Political Realism: Niebuhr's 'Debate' with Morgenthau and Kennan."

all men. It is the problem of adjusting the moral claims laid upon one by his allegiance to the national community with the claims that derive from his loyalty to communities transcending the nation. It is the problem of dealing both realistically and creatively with self-interest, and nowhere is self-interest more stubbornly institutionalized, yet capable of greater concealment, than in the "national interest" of the sovereign state.

I. NATIONAL SELF-INTEREST AND THE NORMS BEYOND INTEREST

Few persons have analyzed this network of ethical-political problems with greater deftness than Reinhold Niebuhr—theologian, Christian moralist, irrepressible commentator on political life for two generations, and, according to many, America's most eminent political philosopher. It is not possible to separate Niebuhr's theology from his political philosophy because, for him, these are but two views of a single reality. Each helps to illumine the other. This union of political and theological insight is particularly apparent in Niebuhr's analysis of the moral problem of the national interest.

Niebuhr accepts national self-interest as a fact while rejecting it as a norm. He insists that the responsible view ". . . must know the power of self-interest in human society without giving it moral justification." [2] The contribution of the realist to politics, Niebuhr reminds us, is his awareness of the omnipresence of self-interest. When the United States decided to build the H-bomb, Niebuhr said that "no nation will fail to take even the most hazardous adventure into the future, if the alternative . . . means the risk of being subjugated." [3] On the occasion of the defeat of the European Defense Community, which would have required a greater sacrifice from France than from the other participants, Niebuhr suggested that this outcome should have been foreseen, in that "an explicit renunciation of national sovereignty . . . is probably beyond the moral competence of any nation." [4]

National self-interest is accounted for on the one hand by the nature of the human situation. The statesman, acting in his official capacity, is to be distinguished from the detached philosopher, Niebuhr says, not by the narrowness of his vision but by the breadth of his responsibility to the community he represents. Vital to this responsibility is the preservation of the interests of the countless persons he serves.

[2] Reinhold Niebuhr, *The Children of Light and the Children of Darkness* (New York, 1950), p. 41.
[3] Niebuhr, "Editorial Notes," *Christianity and Crisis*, X (Feb. 20, 1950), 10.
[4] Niebuhr, "European Integration," *Christianity and Society*, XIX (Autumn, 1954), 3.

But the claims of the nation that are partly justified are always partly pretentious. So impressive is the majesty of the national state that it assumes, in Hegel's phrase, "concrete universality." Through the instrumentalities of the nation, "human pride and self-assertion reach their ultimate form and seek to break all bounds of finiteness. The nation pretends to be God." [5] In its majesty, its power, and its seeming immortality, the nation makes plausible to its citizens the claim that its interests are not simply interests, but "unconditioned values," the defense of which is necessary to the preservation of all that is worth-while in human history.

So the legitimate pursuit of self-interest demanded by the political situation, as the statesman seeks to serve those whose interests he represents, is compounded with the illegitimate pursuit of self-interest growing out of the human situation. Anxious and insecure, men invest their collectives with universal meaning and prestige, receiving in return vicarious strength and pride.

Though national self-interest is an inescapable reality, it must not be accepted as normative. The contribution of the idealist to politics, Niebuhr maintains, is his awareness that man can see beyond self-interest. Self-love may be a universal *characteristic* of human existence. But love and not self-love is the *law* of human existence, since human fulfillment and brotherhood demand the sharing of self in the interest of one's neighbor.

The very behavior of nations proves their acknowledgment of a higher loyalty than that of self-interest. For the foreign policy which cannot be formulated without reference to self-interest is generally defended as consistent with norms beyond self-interest. It is claimed, for example, that such a policy serves mankind, universal values, or at the very least a civilization transcending that of the nation itself.[6] This claim is in part hypocritical, for nations always pretend greater devotion to more inclusive values than they actually achieve in practice. But the dangers of hypocrisy are no greater than the dangers of cynicism. "We may compare to our profit English vs. German politics," Niebuhr observes. "The Germans [under Hitler] said that they were not going to follow moral principle if it did not serve their own interest. The English appealed to moral purpose sometimes to the point of hypocrisy, yet it has given them something that Germany lacked." [7]

Niebuhr feels that unless the self-interest of nations is qualified by a larger loyalty (for example, to "the common civilization of the free

[5] Niebuhr, *Human Nature* (New York, 1949), p. 212.

[6] Niebuhr, *The Children of Light and the Children of Darkness,* p. 170, n. 4.

[7] Rockefeller Foundation, Conference on International Politics, May 7, 8, 1954, *Summary Report,* p. 10.

nations"), and qualified ultimately by the "spirit of justice," the parochial and competing interests of the nations will end either in overt
conflict or in the domination of the strongest. This "leavening influence
of a higher upon a lower loyalty" preserves the lesser loyalty from self-
defeat, for it points to those areas in which self-interest intertwines with
the interests of others.

> There are modern realists . . . who, in their reaction to ab-
> stract and vague forms of international idealism, counsel the
> nation to consult only its own interests. . . . But a consistent
> self-interest on the part of a nation will work against its interests
> because it will fail to do justice to the broader and longer inter-
> ests, which are involved with the interests of other nations. A
> narrow national loyalty on our part, for instance, will obscure
> our long range interests where they are involved with those of a
> whole alliance of free nations.[8]

Niebuhr identifies, then, two dangers: the danger of giving too little
attention to the fact of national self-interest and the danger of giving too
much. The idealist, recognizing that the law of love is the final norm for
man, fails to measure the persistence of self-love, and does not recognize
the hypocrisy that persistently taints the nation's claim to wider values.
The realist, understanding the power of collective self-interest, is not
sufficiently aware that if the cynicism of interest remains unchallenged by
a higher loyalty, interest will be defined so narrowly as to be self-
defeating.[9]

Between the sentimental illusion that nations can pursue moral cru-
sades without reference to interest and the cynicism that believes the
nation in practice has no obligations beyond interest, there is the possibility of limited "moral transcendence" or a "wise self interest" capable
of finding the point of concurrence between the interests of the self and
the general welfare.[10] Niebuhr has found the Marshall Plan to be a
prototype of such enlightened self-interest. Here, he wrote, ". . . prudent self-interest was united with concern for others in a fashion which
represents the most attainable virtue of nations." [11]

---

[8] Niebuhr, *Christian Realism and Political Problems* (New York, 1953), pp.
134–37.

[9] *Ibid.*, p. 146.

[10] Niebuhr, "The Hydrogen Bomb," *Christianity and Society*, XV (Spring,
1950), 5–7; and "Transatlantic Tension," *The Reporter*, V (Sept. 18, 1951), 14–16.

[11] Niebuhr, "Hybris," *Christianity and Society*, XVI (Spring, 1951), 4–6. See
also, by the same author, "America's Wealth and the World's Poverty," *Christianity and Society*, XII (Autumn, 1947), 3–4; and "Food for India—Self-Interest,
or Generosity?" *Messenger*, XVI (June 19, 1951), 7.

The concurrence of self-interest and the general welfare can be approximated only when interest is qualified by a loyalty and a sense of justice that are found beyond interest, and when the component of interest that still remains is acknowledged. Niebuhr summarizes his views as follows: "All political justice . . . is achieved by men and nations who have a margin of goodness or virtue beyond their self-interest. But they must not deny the interested motives which partly prompt their action. Otherwise their marginal virtue will turn to vice." [12]

II. THE PRIMACY OF THE NATIONAL INTEREST
IN MORGENTHAU AND KENNAN

It is interesting that the analysis of the national interest unites the self-acknowledged realists in a common front against the "illusions" of the idealist, while at the same time dividing them from one another. Hans J. Morgenthau and George F. Kennan, like Niebuhr, begin their analysis with a critique of political idealism. The idealist demands that states transcend all parochial interests. He is one of two types. The pretentious idealist does not see at all the hypocrisy in the nation's claims to transcendent values. Logically, this idealism results in fanaticism. The perfectionist idealist sees nothing but the hypocrisy in the nation's claim to universal principle. Logically, this latter type of idealism results in withdrawal Niebuhr has leveled his criticism at both varieties. Morgenthau and Kennan have chosen to focus their criticism on the hypocrisy of the pretentious idealist.

"The invocation of moral principles for the support of national policies," writes Morgenthau, ". . . is always and of necessity a pretense." His often repeated indictment of pretentious idealism contains two major points. First, the idealist becomes intoxicated with world-embracing principles that are too vague and general to provide guidance to policy ("defend and promote democracy," "freedom and the rights of man," etc.). Second, the idealist dresses parochial interests in the garb of universal moral principles and then presumes that the rest of the world, in refusing to grant his policy cosmic righteousness, is *ipso facto* less moral (or rational) than he.[13] This strains relations, worsens con-

---

[12] Niebuhr, "Hazards and Resources," *The Virginia Quarterly Review,* XXV (April, 1949), 204.

[13] Hans J. Morgenthau, "National Interest and Moral Principles in Foreign Policy: The Primacy of the National Interest," *American Scholar,* XVIII (Spring, 1949), 207, 211. See also his book, *In Defense of the National Interest* (New York, 1951), p. 35.

flicts of interest by investing them with moral content ("principles can, by their very nature, not be made the object of compromise"),[14] and results at the end in the moral crusade.

George Kennan finds this the crowning irony of the "legalistic-moralistic approach to international problems." The idealist is devoted to the elimination of war and violence, yet the rigidity and fanaticism he conjures up "makes violence more enduring, more terrible, and more destructive to political stability. . . . A war fought in the name of high moral principle finds no early end short of some form of total domination." [15]

Idealism is pretentious, continues Kennan, not only in its claim to incorporate universal values but in its presumed ability to know an inscrutable future and to wrench the developing pattern of history into designs of its own choosing. The idealist does not know that "the greatest law of human history is its unpredictability"; [16] he does not understand that life is an organic and not a mechanical process, the determinative forces of which may be channeled and deflected, but not abruptly turned off. Because he does not understand these limitations, the idealist gives himself to the colossal deceit of thinking that he can suddenly make international life over into his own image of the ideal society.[17]

Niebuhr concurs. "These are, of course," he has written in endorsing Kennan's critique, "precisely the perils to which all human idealism is subject. . . ." [18] The difference arises at the point of prescribing an antidote to this pretentious and illusory idealism. To this end, Kennan and Morgenthau have expounded their respective cases for the national interest. In doing so, they have raised the question that Niebuhr repeatedly returns to and to which Kennan and Morgenthau, in different ways, award less attention than it surely deserves—the proper relation of interest to norms transcending interest.

Let us have the modesty to admit, Kennan advises in a now famous statement, "that our own national interest is all that we are really capable of knowing and understanding." [19] He longs for an international community where this modesty might prevail, a "quieter and more comfortable community" in which conflicts of interest are recognized as just that, and not burdened with the freight of great moral principle. For then surely "it would be easier to clear away such conflicts as do

[14] Morgenthau, *In Defense of the National Interest*, p. 27.
[15] George F. Kennan, *American Diplomacy* (Chicago, 1951), pp. 100–01.
[16] Kennan, *The Realities of American Foreign Policy* (Princeton, N.J., 1954), pp. 92–93.
[17] Kennan, *American Diplomacy*, p. 69.
[18] Niebuhr, *The Irony of American History* (New York, 1952), p. 148.
[19] Kennan, *American Diplomacy*, pp. 102–03.

arise." [20] After all, asks Kennan, is it not perfectly true that questions of right and wrong in most international disputes are virtually unfathomable? On whose side resides justice in the conflict between Israel and the Arab states? Where is the right and the wrong in the dispute over Kashmir? [21] This is the error of the moralist-legalist approach, that it carries over "into the affairs of states the concepts of right and wrong [and] the assumption that state behavior is a fit subject for moral judgments." [22]

Kennan's alternative is to consult not principle, but interest. He would consult it modestly, without presuming that preferences dictated by one's own history and culture necessarily reflect the good of others. He would consult it soberly, with restraint of judgment and a readiness to adjust to the interests of others. He would have us "conduct ourselves at all times in such a way as to satisfy our own ideas of morality," with awareness that we do so out of no obligation to anyone but ourselves and without expectation that our view of morality will be valid for others.[23]

Morgenthau defends the supremacy of the national interest even more vigorously. He hoists his standard beside that raised by Hamilton in the days when the nation was young but its political sophistication was great. "An individual," wrote Hamilton, "may, on numerous occasions, meritoriously indulge the emotions of generosity and benevolence, not only without an eye to, but even at the expense of, his own interest. But a government can rarely, if at all, be justifiable in pursuing a similar course." Rather, insisted Hamilton, "self-preservation is the first duty of a nation." [24]

The ends of policy are determined, then, by interest. The capacity to achieve the ends of policy is determined by available power. Therefore, a realistic political analysis, says Morgenthau, turns upon the concept of interest defined in terms of power.[25]

With Kennan, Morgenthau refuses ". . . to identify the moral aspiration of a particular nation with the moral laws that govern the universe. . . . The light-hearted equation between a particular nationalism and the counsels of Providence is morally indefensible for it is the very sin of pride against which the Greek tragedians and the Biblical prophets warned rulers and ruled." [26]

[20] Kennan, *The Realities of American Foreign Policy,* p. 50.
[21] *Ibid.,* pp. 36–37.
[22] Kennan, *American Diplomacy,* p. 100.
[23] *Ibid.,* pp. 53–54, 102–03. See also Kennan, *The Realities of American Foreign Policy,* pp. 47–49.
[24] Morgenthau, *In Defense of the National Interest,* pp. 15–16.
[25] Morgenthau, *Politics Among Nations* (2nd ed.; New York, 1954), pp. 4–11.
[26] *Ibid.,* p. 10.

Moreover, continues Morgenthau, the national interest itself has moral dignity, because the national community is the only source of order and the only protector of minimal moral values in a world lacking order and moral consensus beyond the bounds of the national state.[27] So it is that both politics and morality demand for the nation "but one guiding star, one standard for thought, one rule for action: the national interest." [28]

To these views, Niebuhr has responded with a dialectical "yes" and "no." If it is true, as Morgenthau has suggested, that "the invocation of moral principles for the support of national policies . . . is always and of necessity a pretense," it is also true, Niebuhr insists, that "hyprocrisy is an inevitable by-product in the life of any nation which has some loyalty to moral principles. . . . The price of eliminating these hypocrisies entirely is to sink into consistent cynicism. . . ." [29] Surely it may be said that the nation represents a morally defensible entity; but it must also be said that the moral legitimacy of the nation is at best ambiguous, given the fact that the same power which assures order within the national community appears to guarantee disorder beyond it.[30] And if Kennan's admonition to modesty is valid, his solution is wrong—for egoism is not the proper cure for an abstract and pretentious idealism.[31]

Niebuhr acknowledges the inevitability of national self-interest and the futility of any policy that attempts to ignore or nullify it. But he is equally insistent that the national interest, pursued narrowly and rigidly, may be self-defeating. In Niebuhr's own words,

> Does not a nation concerned with its own interests define those interests so narrowly and so immediately . . . that the interests and securities which depend upon common devotion to principles of justice and upon established mutualities in a community of nations, are sacrificed? . . . It would be fatal for the security of the nation if some loyalties beyond its interests were not operative in its moral life to prevent the national interest from being conceived in too narrow and self-defeating terms.[32]

[27] Morgenthau, *In Defense of the National Interest,* pp. 38–39.
[28] *Ibid.,* p. 242.
[29] "The Moral Issue in International Relations" (unpublished paper prepared for the Rockefeller Foundation).
[30] Niebuhr, *Moral Man and Immoral Society* (New York, 1932), pp. 83–112.
[31] Niebuhr, *The Irony of American History,* p. 148.
[32] Niebuhr, "The Moral Issue in International Relations."

III. The Problem of the Gap between Interest and Norm

The polarity of Niebuhr's dialectic between interest and norm has been noted by Kenneth W. Thompson in a thoughtful critique of Niebuhr's position.[33] Niebuhr, Thompson points out, proceeds on two levels of analysis, and these tend to be contradictory. He defines first a realistic theory of state behavior, based on interest. And he defines, secondly, a normative theory which includes the concept of justice, based on standards which transcend interest. The problem arises of what relevance have norms that transcend interest to behavior that apparently is limited to interest? Since relations between states are not moral but political, would not Burke's concept of prudence be more useful in the accommodation of interests than Niebuhr's principles of justice?

Niebuhr does not deny the importance of prudence,[34] nor does he question that the discovery of a "concurrence" between parochial and general interest represents the highest achievement of statecraft. But for this accomplishment, he finds prudence an inadequate resource. "Any kind of prudence which estimates common problems from the perspective of a particular interest will define the interest too narrowly. It is necessary, therefore, to draw upon another moral and spiritual resource to widen the conception of interest. . . . The sense of justice must prevent prudence from becoming too prudential in defining interest." [35]

Niebuhr might have added that prudence, in addition to proving an inadequate resource, serves as a deficient guide. One supposes that by prudence is meant circumspection and caution, the opposite of rashness and indiscretion. Admittedly, prudence is an indispensable "procedural standard" if policy ends are to be consistent with policy means.[36] But

[33] Kenneth W. Thompson, "Beyond National Interest: A Critical Evaluation of Reinhold Niebuhr's Theory of International Politics," *The Review of Politics,* XVII (April, 1955), 167–88.

[34] In his study, *Moral Man and Immoral Society,* Niebuhr deplored the "imprudence" of nations in preferring short-run to long-run advantages (p. 267). This theme has been repeated frequently ever since.

[35] "Our Moral and Spiritual Resources for International Cooperation," *Social Action,* XXII (Feb., 1956), 18–19.

[36] In correspondence with the author, Niebuhr wrote: "Prudence is, I think, merely a procedural standard." Morgenthau edges close to this view when he defines prudence as the "consideration of the political consequences of seemingly moral action . . . the weighing of the consequences of alternative political actions" (*Politics Among Nations,* p. 9).

one wonders what prudence will be circumspect and cautious about? What restraint, what inducement to mutuality does prudence afford once a prudent analysis has revealed that one has the power to act unmutually and to get away with it? (Hitler thus was prudent when he invaded France in the spring of 1940, and imprudent when he invaded Russia in the summer of 1941.)

Nor is this the end of the problem. Upon closer inspection, it is clear that Thompson is not a lobbyist for the national interest pure and simple, even for an interest freed from the irresponsibilities of rashness and indiscretion. In the course of another review of Niebuhr's thought, he reveals that conflicting national interests ought to be "adjusted," "accommodated," or "made more compatible." [37] The point is that these normative judgments do not necessarily derive from prudence, though they represent norms which may be made compatible with interest.

In short, Thompson believes that the attempt to apply norms transcending interest to state behavior which is controlled by interest represents Niebuhr's "unsolved problem." Yet, Niebuhr's unsolved problem immediately becomes Thompson's when he introduces norms which presume to direct and judge interest from a perspective beyond interest. And if prudence should be thought of, as perhaps Burke thought of it, not as a procedural standard but as having moral content of its own, the problem remains.[38] The moral content of prudence, transcending interest, cannot be derived from interest.

All of this is well worth noting with care because what Thompson has done, Kennan has done also, and Morganthau too, though less consistently. As the idealist expects on the part of the state no less than transcendence over all parochial interests, the realist tends to expect no

---

[37] Thompson, "The Political Philosophy of Reinhold Niebuhr," in *Reinhold Niebuhr: His Religious, Social, and Political Thought,* ed. C. W. Kegley and R. W. Bretall (New York, 1956), p. 174.

[38] Thompson quotes Burke's famous line in which he speaks of prudence as "not only in the first rank of virtues political and moral, but . . . the director, the regulator, the standard of them all."

But, it must be recalled, Burke also had a standard of justice beyond prudence. There is the often quoted line from the speech on the conciliation with America: "The question with me is, not whether you have a right to render your people miserable, but whether it is not your interest to make them happy. It is not what a lawyer tells me I *may* do, but what humanity, reason and justice tell me I *ought* to do."

The role of prudence for Burke, as for Morgenthau and Thompson, may have been that of adjusting principle to circumstance. In this case, prudence must be thought of as more than a procedural standard, though as less than a moral norm in its own right. In the speech on the petition of the Unitarians, Burke says: "A statesman, never losing sight of principles, is to be guided by circumstances; and, judging contrary to the exigencies of the moment, he may ruin his country forever."

more than self-interest. To introduce universal norms for the purpose of directing, justifying or judging state behavior is, the realist argues, either a dangerous irrelevance or the occasion for masking interest behind ideology. Yet in denying the application of any criteria for directing or judging state behavior other than those derived from state necessity, the realist must end up the cynic. But Kennan and Morgenthau are anything but cynics. Indeed, their views of policy and international politics are replete with norms that serve to direct and judge interest. One difference between these realists and Niebuhr is that while Niebuhr openly acknowledges his transcendental norms, Kennan and Morgenthau tend to conceal them.

How can Kennan achieve "moral modesty"—a noble view for which he has been justly commended—unless he implicitly acknowledges a perspective from which an action is seen to be modest rather than pretentious? How can he know the difficulty of identifying the just and the unjust side in a dispute unless he has recourse to a concept of justice transcending all historical corruptions of justice? Kennan would have us "ease" the transitions and "temper the asperities" of international relationships; he wishes to "isolate and moderate" international conflicts; he seeks solutions "least unsettling to the stability of international life"; [39] he places before us "that tremendous task of learning, and of helping others to learn, how man can live in fruitful harmony." [40] These are none other than normative judgments. They derive, one would think, from a moral vision both higher and broader than that which is implied when Kennan professes to know "our own national interest" and that alone. For "our own national interest" itself must be brought under the tempering guidance and the hard judgment of these criteria.

Kennan has said repeatedly that it is inadmissible to introduce "morality as a general criterion for the determination of the behavior of states and above all as criterion for measuring and comparing the behavior of different states." [41] Yet in spite of this persistent denial, moral criteria occasionally poke through to show themselves clearly. In rebutting the Friend's tendency to equate too closely the inequities of American and Soviet power, Kennan wrote: "Both, as [the Friends] see it, are blind, heavy handed, onerous; there is nothing to choose between them. This is a vital point; for if modern totalitarianism is actually no more horrible than modern American democracy, the rationale of recent American foreign policy does indeed break down at many points. Ad-

---

[39] Kennan, *American Diplomacy*, pp. 96–98.

[40] Kennan, "Overdue Changes in Our Foreign Policy," *Harper's*, CCXIII (Aug., 1956), 33.

[41] Kennan, *The Realities of American Foreign Policy*, p. 49.

mittedly the differences between the one and the other are differences of degree. But are they unimportant?" [42]

These observations apply also to Morgenthau (though, as we shall see later, he does have a transcendental frame of reference). When he objects to the hypocrisy of America's presumed virtue he seems to do so from a vantage point beyond national interest. The charge of hypocrisy is a moral charge, not a political judgment. It is to protest that a man is not what he pretends to be, and more specifially is not as moral as he pretends to be. If the only standard for judging the behavior of states were national interest, one would not likely accuse the pretentious statesman of hyprocrisy, a term laden with moral censure. Rather, one would have to accept the wielding of moral claims, like the wielding of the sword, as justifiable when it was in the national interest to do so. And when it was not in the national interest to pretend all goodness and virtue, the pretense would have to be scored, not as moral hypocrisy, but as simple political stupidity.

Morgenthau's political realism is a function of his views concerning the omnipresence of the lust for power, the universal desire of the self to dominate the other. In international politics this is the "struggle for power . . . for national advantage." Operative principles must derive from this political reality. "All the successful statesmen of modern times . . . have made the national interest the ultimate standard of their politics." [43]

Curiously, Morgenthau's words, chosen perhaps for their cutting edge in a polemical contest with the idealists, do not fairly represent Morgenthau. Actually, as in Kennan, there is a restraining reference always present. When Morgenthau talks of diplomacy, he is not speaking of a procedure that may be placed in the service of any end or any system of values. Diplomacy itself becomes a kind of norm; it involves a certain kind of behavior, directed by certain motives toward certain goals. In his discussion of the diplomatic function, he says, "The objective of foreign policy is relative and conditional: to bend, not to break, the will of the other side as far as necessary in order to safeguard one's own vital interests without hurting those of the other side. The methods of foreign policy are relative and conditional: not to advance by destroying the obstacles in one's way, but to retreat before them, to circumvent them, to maneuver around them, to soften and dissolve them slowly by means of persuasion, negotiation and pressure." [44] One could spend from now

[42] Kennan, "Speak Truth to Power: A Reply by George Kennan," *Progressive,* XIX (Oct., 1955), 17.

[43] Morgenthau, *Scientific Man vs. Power Politics* (Chicago, 1946), pp. 192–93.

[44] Morgenthau, *Politics Among Nations,* p. 531.

till kingdom-come inspecting the national interest (which is presumed to offer a guide to conduct *not* based on moral principles) without discovering within its necessities operational norms such as these. If it is argued that the national interest demands a moderate and restrained diplomacy because only such diplomacy can create an ordered international society conducive to the values of democracy, one has not escaped "the invocation of moral principles" that Morgenthau and Kennan find so dangerous. Rather, one has simply invested the national interest with moral content.

This suggests an alternate way of looking at the matter, which Arnold Wolfers has called to our attention. Wolfers argues that we are never really dealing with interests *vs.* values, for these interests are themselves values. The practitioner of *Realpolitik* insists that the necessities of state leave no room for moral choice and that accordingly the statesman must be willing to act counter to his moral preferences. Wolfers observes, however, that "the 'necessities' in international politics, and for that matter in all spheres of life, do not push decisions and action beyond the realm of moral judgment; they rest on moral choices themselves. If a statesman decides that the dangers to the security of his country are so great as to make necessary a course of action that may lead to war, he has placed an exceedingly high value on an increment of national security." [45]

Questions pertaining to the definition and the importance of given national interests, according to this view, are always moral questions. They will be decided, of course, in the light of the statesman's interpretation of the objective circumstances, the means available, and the desired goals. Naturally it will make considerable difference if the statesman's frame of reference includes goals that transcend the nation or if his value system is rigidly circumscribed by the national community. But the point is that the definition of the national interest in each given situation "cannot be answered by reference to alleged amoral necessities inherent in international politics; [they] rest on value judgments." [46]

In practice, Morgenthau and Kennan would seem not only to accept this formulation, but to infuse the national interest with values more comprehensive than those deriving from a particular state. While constructed from the raw materials of self-interest, self-preservation, and power, Morgenthau's "national interest" incorporates in its design a notion of responsibility that by its nature must transcend pure self-interest. A "concomitant of policies based upon the national interest,"

[45] Arnold Wolfers, *Discord and Collaboration: Essays on International Politics* (Baltimore, Md., 1962), p. 58.
[46] *Ibid.*, p. 60.

he writes, is the "tolerance of other political systems and policies based on different moral principles." [47] And again, ". . . the national interest of a nation which is conscious not only of its own interests but also of that of other nations must be defined in terms compatible with the latter. In a multi-national world this is a requirement of political morality. . . ." [48]

What Morgenthau and Kennan only imply, Niebuhr makes explicit. There can be no health in the society of men unless the claims of self-interest are infused with a loyalty larger than interest, just as loyalty to larger principle must be chastened by a sober awareness of the force of self-interest. Niebuhr's candor is to be preferred, though as Kenneth Thompson has pointed out, the relationship between national interest and principles transcending the nation must remain at best problematic. The justifiable responsibilities of the statesman to his constituency, combined with the power of "collective self-concern," place the virtue of self-giving beyond the moral achievement of nations. Yet reference to such norms as justice and freedom, order and mutuality, ought to provide both a directive for and a judgment upon policy as the statesman searches for a concurrence between the nation's interest and the general welfare.

IV. Kennan's Relativism and Morgenthau's Transcendentalism

Though Morgenthau and Kennan have held the national interest to be a more reliable guide to intelligent policy than principle, neither one has entirely ignored this troublesome area beyond interest. Their views concerning the source and application of principle are strikingly divergent each from the other and both from Niebuhr.

It is not easy to assess George Kennan's position on the relation of principle to interest. His writings, it must be emphasized, possess a humility and a breadth characteristic of profound faith: a sense of the "weakness and imperfections," yet the potentialities for "breathtaking impulses of faith and creative imagination," in the human soul; [49] a note of awe before a providence of whose truths "we are the agents, not

---

[47] Morgenthau, "National Interest and Moral Principles in Foreign Policy: The Primacy of the National Interest," pp. 211–12.

[48] Morgenthau, "Another Great Debate," *The American Political Science Review*, XLIV (Dec., 1952), 977.

[49] Kennan, "Hope in an Age of Anxiety," *New Republic*, CXXVIII (July 1, 1953), 16.

the authors," [50] coupled with a deep feeling of historical responsibility, for "in the fabric of human events, one thing leads to another" and "every mistake is in a sense the determinant of all the mistakes of the future." [51]

Yet one suspects that Kennan has been so impressed with the pretense in every claim to the moral absolute that he has decided to occupy the less difficult and seemingly less dangerous position of moral relativity. Let us act with dignity out of obligation to no one but ourselves, he advises. Let us conduct ourselves according to those concepts "of a moral and ethical nature which we like to consider as being characteristic of the spirit of our civilization," but without the presumption that they are valid for others.[52] And again: "No people can be the judges of another's domestic institutions and requirements." [53]

Morgenthau makes the opposite error. As Kennan's formal ethic seems to be relativistic or immanental, Morgenthau's formal ethic is transcendental. (It is surprising, incidentally, that more attention has not been given to Morgenthau's views on morality and principle. The widely held assumption that he has simply updated Hobbes does him serious injustice.)

Morgenthau asserts that there are moral absolutes that set boundaries not to be trespassed under any circumstance in the pursuit of interest. "Moral rules do not permit certain policies to be considered at all from the point of view of expediency." Thus Clemenceau might complain that, from the point of view of French interests, there were twenty million Germans too many; or Stalin, from the point of view of Russian interests, that there were fifty thousand German officers too many. Churchill's retort to Stalin, that the infamy of mass executions would not be morally tolerable, was appropriate; there are absolute moral principles "which must be obeyed regardless of considerations of national advantage." [54]

Moreover, Morgenthau says, an awareness of the irremedial gap between "the moral ideal and the facts of political life" must be maintained lest one commit the sin of "the Fascist mind"—the indentification of "political and military success with moral superiority." [55] He asks for a "cosmic humility with regard to the moral evaluation of the actions of states." To know that states are subject to the moral law is one thing;

[50] Kennan, "Overdue Changes in Our Foreign Policy," p. 30.
[51] Kennan, American Diplomacy, p. 50.
[52] Kennan, The Realities of American Foreign Policy, pp. 213–14.
[53] Kennan, American Diplomacy, p. 53.
[54] Morgenthau, Politics Among Nations, pp. 213–14.
[55] Morgenthau, "The Escape from Power in the Western World," Conflicts of Power in Modern Culture, A Symposiun (New York, 1947), pp. 8–10.

to pretend to know what is morally required of states in a particular situation is quite another.[56]

The absolute principle thus prevents acts of gross immorality while at the same time identifying every political act as in fact political and therefore inconsistent with the moral law. Morgenthau knows well the vigorous judgment of the transcendental norm on every politically expedient act. This is one of the critical links between political necessity and principle in the formulation of a responsible political ethic, for it moderates the temptation to pretense and hypocrisy. The other link, equally necessary though paradoxically related to the first, is to understand that the norm is not only a judgment against, but the goal of, political life—a constant, relevant, directive force.

This theme is present in Morgenthau. "Both individual and state," he says, "must judge political action by universal moral principles, such as that of liberty." [57] But this theme is not consistently present. In relating interest to principle, Morgenthau, to say the least, is ambivalent.[58] Indeed, the net impact of his thought leads one to conclude that Morgenthau's concept of principle is so transcendental that it can play *only* a judgmental role in the life of political, sinful man, saving him from hypocrisy (by demonstrating to him that he is not God), but not necessarily saving him from cynicism (by failing to demonstrate that he is more than a beast).

Morgenthau sees two realms, the realm of the actual characterized by "the misery of politics," and the realm of the universal ethical norm. Between the two, he says, there must exist an "ineluctable tension." He knows that this tension is relaxed when one blithely identifies the political act with the requirements of the moral command. But the opposite danger is to stretch the distance separating the real from the norm so that the tension uniting the two snaps. If Morgenthau constantly balances on the brink of this error, it is because his ethic is only transcendental, which is another way of saying that his view of man is too pessimistic.

The "lust for power" in man, says Morgenthau, is a "ubiquitous empirical fact." To live in the realm of the universal ethical norm is to deny the "lust for power." But "there can be no renunciation of the ethical denial [that is, the lust for power] without renouncing the human nature of man." This view permeates much of his writing con-

---

[56] Morgenthau, "Another Great Debate," p. 984.

[57] Morgenthau, *Politics Among Nations*, p. 9.

[58] Contrast, for example, his frequent assertion that "politics is interest defined in terms of power" and a less quoted statement in which he says that "political action can be defined as an attempt to realize moral values through the medium of politics, that is, power" (Morgenthau, "Another Great Debate," p. 987).

cerning human nature. Note, for example, the following: "There can be no actual denial of the lust for power without denying the very conditions of human existence in this world." "There is no escape from the evil of power, regardless of what one does. Whenever we act with reference to our fellow men, we must sin." "The political act is inevitably evil." "It is . . . inevitable that . . . this corruption [the lust for power and selfishness] is inherent in the very nature of the political act." [59]

The unqualified character of these "musts" and "inevitables" is almost frightening. This is precisely Morgenthau's problem. He knows man is in a tragic situation. (Morgenthau is no happier in his political realism than Kennan is.) But his concept of tragedy is more Greek than Biblical. This is because the element of human will seems strangely absent. Man finds himself pinioned to the rock not so much because he has willed evil, but because this seems to be his fate. If human will were admitted, instead of being precluded by the assertion that human nature is sinful (the inevitability of sin, incidentally, is a contradiction in terms), then it would have to be acknowledged that to will evil implies the freedom to will the good. This would reunite one's view of man to the transcendental ethical norm and would re-establish the possibility of a fruitful tension between them.

But for all his protestations to its presence, that creative tension tends to be absent in Morgenthau's system. Divorced from the transcendent by the sinfulness of man, political life tends to develop its own operational rules. It is true that they derive ultimately from universal moral principles, such as justice and freedom, but by the time they have been reduced to terms capable of guiding political action, they have been so distorted by the institutions of sinful man that Morgenthau, in an extreme and again polemical statement, can talk of "moral principles derived from political reality." [60]

The political realist, Morgenthau summarizes, "is aware of the moral significance of political action" in that he refuses to identify his own acts with the pure requirements of principled action. He knows that "all nations stand under the judgment of God," but he also knows that God's

---

[59] Morgenthau, *Scientific Man vs. Power Politics*, pp. 196–202.

[60] Morgenthau, *In Defense of the National Interest*, pp. 33–34. It is in this sense that he says Hobbes was right; the state creates "morality" (pp. 34–35). Kenneth W. Thompson has stated this view even more vigorously. He has suggested that Niebuhr's "unsolved problem" of reconciling norm and interest may be resolved once one realizes that "moral principles . . . must be derived from political practice and not imposed upon it" ("The Political Philosophy of Reinhold Niebuhr," p. 174). While it is true that norms are filtered through, and so distorted by interest, this extreme view destroys the tension between self-interest and norm which is the virtue (as well as admittedly the problem) of Niebuhr's approach.

will is "inscrutable to the human mind." Morgenthau knows that the political actor must take the power of sin seriously. If he does not, he will be guilty of sentimentality and political folly. Morgenthau acknowledges the transcendent majesty of God. He knows that the political actor who presumes to perform fully God's will is guilty of hypocrisy and fanaticism. "It is exactly the concept of interest defined in terms of power," Morgenthau concludes, "that saves us from both . . . moral excess and . . . political folly," [61] though exactly why and how he does not say.

There is something almost Continental or Barthian in the orthodoxy with which Morgenthau presses his distinction between sinful men and a "wholly other" Divine Being, as perhaps there is something uniquely American in the humane relativism of Kennan. But the difference is not substantial. An absolute impossible of approximation creates the necessity of adopting a relative standard that is possible of approximation. So Morgenthau's final endorsement of a political standard based on the national interest is essentially no different from Kennan's.

Both Morgenthau and Kennan seek the abatement of pretentious idealism in international relations and the cultivation of restraint arising from tolerance. Kennan pursues this desirable result by demonstrating that all men are inevitably and irretrievably sinners in the eyes of a righteous God. Again, the difference is not substantial. Both positions ought to curb the crusading zeal and fanaticism of idealism. But there is no resource in either to prevent the development of a cynical awareness that one may expand at another's expense if one has the power to get away with it.

The restraint of genuine tolerance, Niebuhr suggests, arises from the Biblical paradox of having, yet not having, the truth—of knowing that there is a law of love applicable to man's life and an ideal of equal justice relevant to man's communities, but knowing too that "however we twist or turn, whatever instruments or pretentions we use, it is not possible to establish the claim that we have the truth," or that we have realized a relationship of love or the just society. "Our toleration of truths opposed to those which we confess is an expression of the spirit of forgiveness in the realm of culture. Like all forgiveness, it is possible only if we are not too sure of our own virtue. Loyalty to the truth requires confidence in the possibility of its attainment; toleration of others requires broken confidence in the finality of our own truth." [62]

[61] Morgenthau, *Politics Among Nations*, pp. 9–10.
[62] Niebuhr, *Human Destiny* (New York, 1949), p. 234.

V. Niebuhr's Dialectic

Niebuhr's response to the relativism of Kennan and to the transcendentalism of Morgenthau is complex, not simple. It consists of a dialectic rather than a set of fixed propositions. It is stereophonic rather than monaural. Kennan's relativism (that is, his "formal" ethic, not his practicing one) is a one-speaker system. It avoids the difficult problem of adjusting and synthesizing the bass tones of interest and the higher tones of principle. Kennan presumes that each nation's interest contains its own principles, applicable to itself but irrelevant and even mischievous if applied to others. Morgenthau's transcendentalism (again we refer to his "formal" ethic) is a faulty stereo system; the speakers have been so widely separated as to leave the treble of principle quite unintegrated with the predominating bass of interest.

Of course, an ethic that takes seriously both "love and self-love," unlike audio-electronics, cannot achieve a fully satisfactory integration of its several components. To maintain the proper balance demands constant attention. Thus, Niebuhr sees man in part free, and in part bound by necessity; as sinful, yet knowing himself to be a sinner; as capable of justice (which makes democracy possible) and inclined to injustice (which makes the balance of forces in democracy necessary); as "a lion who devours the lamb," but "a curious kind of lion who dreams of the day when the lion and the lamb will lie down together." [63] To overstress man's sin leads to cynicism; to overstress his capacity for mutuality leads to sentimentality. Each reality must balance the other.

Niebuhr understands the problem of government as that of maintaining order requisite to the harmony of the whole, but establishing a sufficient balance among the sources of power in society to prevent order from destroying the vitality of the parts, which is the prerequisite of justice. To overstress the principle of order leads to tyranny; to overstress the principle of justice leads to anarchy. Each must correct the excess in the other.

This dialectic Niebuhr applies to his understanding of man, of man's political life, and finally of man's pursuit of an ordered and just international life. We can define our responsibilities for best ordering the human community, he says, "if the individual is known in terms of both his capacity for love and self-love." [64]

[63] Niebuhr, "Christianity and Communism: Social Justice," *Spectator*, CLVII (Nov. 6, 1936), 802–03.
[64] Niebuhr, *The Self and the Dramas of History* (New York, 1955), p. 234.

Admittedly, when applied to the behavior of nations the dialectic is liable to buckle under the enormous stress. For in the nation, the persistence and the force of collective self-love are without parallel. In fact, Niebuhr frequently asks whether standards appropriate to individual morality can be applied to collective morality. He approves Hume's assertion that ". . . there is a system of morals calculated for princes, much more free than that which ought to govern private persons." [65] But as we have observed before, this is so, not because the individual is more moral, but because the statesman is more responsible—responsible, that is, to a constituency whose welfare must weigh heavily in the formation of policy. This is one of the main reasons why Niebuhr never tires of saying that "there can be no complete self-sacrifice or even 'generosity' in political or collective relations." [66] The environment of collective moral choice, therefore, differs in degree from the environment of individual choice. Individual morality may be judged by the willingness of the self to sacrifice self in the interest of the neighbor. Collective morality, however, has a dual mandate: to protect self-interest, but also to find the point of concurrence, and to establish reciprocity, between self-interest and a wider community of interests than that dictated by the parochial group alone.

This difference in environment cannot be ignored. Yet, at a deeper level, Niebuhr observes,

> . . . a valid moral outlook discerns the similarities in the conduct of individuals and communities. In both cases an action motivated solely by self-concern is immoral. In both cases the self-concern (or, in the case of the nation, sole concern for the national interest) is more powerful than the individual or the nation is inclined to admit. . . . It is possible for both individuals and groups to relate concern for the other with interest and concern for the self. There are endless varieties of creativity in community; for neither the individual nor the community can realize itself except in relation to, and encounter with, other individuals and groups. . . . It is interesting that a valid psychiatry has come to the same conclusions with respect to the individual as those at which a valid political science has arrived in regard to communities. This conclusion is that it is not possible permanently to suppress, by either internal or external pressure, the concern of the self for itself. The most loving parent combines

[65] As quoted in Niebuhr, *The Structure of Nations and Empires* (New York, 1959), p. 193.
[66] *Ibid.*, p. 212.

with "sacrifice" for the children a healthy pride in perpetuating himself or herself in the other generation. . . . A valid moral outlook for both individuals and for groups, therefore, sets no limits to the creative possibility of concern for others, and makes no claims that such creativity ever annuls the power of self-concern or removes the peril of pretension if the force of residual egotism is not acknowledged.[67]

Niebuhr is saying that there are not two separate realms, the moral and the political, nor two distinct ethics, individual and group. His great contribution is the unity and the wholeness of his view, which encompasses both politics and morality, both individual and collective ethics.

Arnold Wolfers (long Niebuhr's friend and admirer, and one whose "unique eminence" in political philosophy Niebuhr himself has extolled) endorses this view concisely in his landmark essay, "Statesmanship and Moral Choice." If, argues Wolfers, one rejects perfectionist ethics—controlled by what Max Weber has called "the natural law of absolute imperatives"—one will acknowledge the necessity to adjust one's moral choices to changing circumstances. When, for example, relations between states move toward enmity, the statesman places increasing value on measures designed to defeat the hostile claims levied by the opponent. Wolfers reminds us that the situation is no different in individual relationships; courts after all recognize self-defense and "unbearable provocation." The ethic of politics, Wolfers concludes, is a part of general ethics, not alien to it, for "there is no difference either in the method of evaluation or in the ethical standards, whether the case be one of political or private behavior." [68]

This view would hold that, though circumstances vary, no area of politics, even national self-interest, is ever exempt from claims and loyalties deriving from a community larger than the parochial community. To which Niebuhr characteristically adds that no reach for the morally ennobling act ever escapes the gravitational pull of self-interest. Carefully examined, the evidence is everywhere the same. Man—individual man and collective man, moral man and political man—acknowledges the worth and integrity of the neighbor, but manages persistently to prefer himself to the neighbor, while insisting that his self-interest serves best the interest of the neighbor as well.

Moral man will build a community which supports his own interests *and* those of his neighbors. As this happens, justice is approached. But if moral man knows himself intimately, knows himself from the perspec-

[67] *Ibid.*, pp. 30–31.
[68] Wolfers, *Discord and Collaboration*, p. 52.

tive of "the ultimate laws of God," he will also know himself as immoral man. He will acknowledge that the community of perfect justice cannot be achieved, and he will know that the very claim of achievement adds to the sin of self-preference the sin of hypocrisy to produce the antithesis of justice.

State behavior may exaggerate the selfishness and hypocrisy of individuals, and responsible statecraft surely must acknowledge the narrowed margin of choice when only those policies may be considered that do not sacrifice the welfare of the community for which the statesman serves as trustee. But there is no *raison d'état* by which to judge state behavior according to a universe of values alien to individual behavior. Niebuhr's Christian faith, in the final analysis, knows only one God, a God of judgment and forgiveness, and only one law, that of love. Each man, all men, and all nations are responsible to that God and bound by that law—and in the encounter discover again and again the pretense in every claim to having achieved a relationship of love or the just community.

Thus, Niebuhr echoes the prophetic voices of the Old Testament, which were raised first, not against individual Israelites, but against the nation Israel. "Ruling groups within a nation and hegemonic nations in a community of nations face the alternative of dying because they try too desperately to live, or of achieving new life by dying to self." [69] And again, "though on the whole nations are not expected to conform to a moral standard higher than that of a prudent self-interest, yet . . . nations are . . . subject, as are individuals, to an internal tension between the claims of the self and the larger claims [of love]." [70]

[69] Niebuhr, *Faith and History* (New York, 1949), p. 224.
[70] *Ibid.*, p. 97.

Index

INDEX

A

Acheson, Dean: and conception of government, 231–36; relationship with Truman, 232, 248–50; relations with Congress, 234–36, 239–40; conceptions of leadership, 237–42; and Far Eastern policy, 240–42; and China policy, 240–41; and Korean policy, 241, 249, 253; and intellect and innovation, 242–50; and European policy, 240, 245–48, 255, 256; and Truman Doctrine, 245–48 *passim;* and Marshall Plan, 245–48 *passim;* and MacArthur, 249–50; and style of international relations, 250–56; attitude toward cold war, 252; attitude toward Soviet Union, 252–53; compared to Holmes, 253–54; views compared with Morgenthau's, 255
Addi wa Bihi, 45
Adenauer, Konrad, 167
Adoula, Cyrille, 39; and Congo crisis, 153
Albania: and Soviet Union, 6
Alexander (King of Yugoslavia), 215, 223
Alliance for Progress, 120
Aloisi, Baron, 223
America. *See* United States
Anderson (Secretary of Defense), 175
Anti-colonialism: and United Nations, 77–79
Ascoli, Max, 175
Asian-African States: and United Nations voting strength, 70–72
Atlantic Alliance. *See* NATO
Attlee, Clement, 36
Austria, 211; and Austrian State Treaty, 162–63, 167, 168, 170
Ayub Khan, Mohammed, 35, 64

B

Balance of power: and India as buffer state, 57–59; and Franco-Soviet pact, ch. 12 *passim*
Baldwin, Hanson, 198; and Cuban crisis, 131–38 *passim*

Ball, George, 136–37
Bandaranaike: and Ceylonese foreign policy, 53
Bandung Conference (1955), 162; and India, 51–52
Baraduc, Pierre, 176
Bargeton, Paul, 217
Barthou, Louis: and Franco-Soviet pact, 219–23 and ch. 12 *passim*
Bay of Pigs incident, 128
Beck, Joseph, Col., 210, 220
Belgium: and Congo crisis, 141ff and ch. 9 *passim;* alliance with France, 209–10
Belgrade Conference (1961): and India, 61
Benedict, Ruth, 97
Berlin: and Soviet policy, 5
Bhutan, 53
Bialer, Seweryn, 163
Bipolarity: and India, 51, 58–59, 64
Bismarck: on the state, 261
Bohlen, Charles, 172
Bosch, Juan, 118
Bourguiba, Habib, 35
Brandeis, Justice, 243; influence on Acheson, 232–33
Brecher, Michael, 54, 60
Bretton Woods agreements, 232, 234
Briand, Aristide, 224
Britain: "special relationship" with United States, 34; and Congo crisis, 143 and ch. 9 *passim;* and 1955 Geneva Conference, 161 and ch. 10 *passim;* and interwar diplomacy, ch. 12 *passim*
Bulganin: and 1955 Geneva Conference, 163*n,* 172–76 and ch. 10 *passim*
Bundy, McGeorge: and United States-European relations, 27
Burma, 194; relations with India and China, 52
Byrnes, James: as Secretary of State, 230

C

Cairo Conference on Problems of Economic Development (1962), 81